The University of North Carolina Press   Chapel Hill and London

Gretchen Lemke-Santangelo . . . .

.... Abiding Courage

African American

Migrant Women

and the East Bay

Community

Gretchen Lemke-Santangelo
is assistant professor of
history and director of
women's studies at Saint
Mary's College in Moraga,
California.

Library of Congress
Cataloging-in-Publication Data
Lemke-Santangelo, Gretchen.
Abiding courage : African American migrant
women and the East Bay community / by
Gretchen Lemke-Santangelo.
p. cm.   Includes bibliographical references and
index.
ISBN 0-8078-2256-6 (cloth: alk. paper).
ISBN 0-8078-4563-9 (pbk.   )
1. Afro-American women—California—San
Francisco Bay Area—Social conditions.
2. Afro-Americans—California—San Francisco
Bay Area—Migrations—History—20th century.
3. Rural-urban migration—California—San
Francisco Bay Area—History—20th century.
4. San Francisco Bay Area (Calif.)—Social
conditions.   I. Title.
F868.S156L45   1996   95-23508
979.4'600496073—dc20   CIP

For my mother and father

Contents . . . .

A section of photographs begins on page 97.

Tables . . . .

Acknowledgments . . . .

It gives me pleasure to acknowledge that this project was a collective endeavor. I owe a great debt to William Chafe, who encouraged me to take creative risks and provided invaluable criticism and editorial assistance. I am also grateful for the suggestions that I received from Raymond Gavins, Kristen Neuschel, Julius Scott, and C. Eric Lincoln. As ideas for this study emerged and coalesced, my friends at Duke University and the University of California, Berkeley, provided unflagging support and helpful insights. Kirsten Fischer, Martha Jane Brazy, Nancy Quam Wickham, and Greg Hise, who all read drafts of the manuscript, greatly enlarged my interpretive framework and analyses. Charles Wollenberg, a California historian, also provided encouragement and helpful insights. After I submitted the manuscript to the University of North Carolina Press, Barbara Hanrahan and Christi Stanforth shepherded the manuscript through the revision and publication process with great kindness, tact, efficiency, and attention to detail. The readers selected to review the manuscript, including Paul Spickard, offered insightful, concise, and often brilliant suggestions that significantly enhanced the quality of the finished work and greatly expedited the revision process.

I am most deeply indebted to the women whose stories form the center of this study. Their trust, generosity, and encouragement made this project possible and multiplied the personal rewards I derived from the research process. I only hope that this work does justice to the extraordinary drama of their lives. From the beginning of this project, I have relied on the kindness and warmth of friends. I particularly want to thank Anna Marie Daniels, Margaret Marie, Jim Boland, and Doug Strong. I owe the most to Anthony Santangelo. His laughter, tenderness, affirmation, social vision, and curiosity sustained and enlivened this endeavor. I am ever grateful for his love.

The African American Museum and Library at Oakland; the Regional Oral History Office at the University of California, Berkeley; the Bancroft Library; and Drew Johnson at the Oakland Museum provided gracious and professional research assistance. I am also grateful for the financial support provided by an American Dissertation Fellowship from the American Association of University Women; an Andrew W. Mellon Graduate Fellowship in the Humanities, awarded by the Graduate School of Duke University; the Anne Firor Scott Research Award, granted by the Duke University history department; and the Faculty Development Fund at Saint Mary's College of California.

Abiding Courage . . . .

Introduction . . . . . .

On October 20, 1943, Theresa Waller stood in the colored waiting room in the Houston, Texas, train station. Dressed in her Sunday best, this tall, dignified twenty-four-year-old felt an odd mixture of fear, expectation, excitement, and uncertainty. Her strong will and poise—traits that marked her as a person who "wanted to go somewhere and be someone"—had propelled her to this embarkation point. In a few moments there would be no turning back. A young woman who "wanted to do something good and big but couldn't name it" was about to leave everything that she had known as a child for the promise of a new life in the San Francisco East Bay Area.

In Houston, Theresa had worked as a domestic servant; each morning she left her home in the predominantly black Fifth Ward for the rich white neighborhoods in the heights. As she worked at jobs that "didn't amount to much," she endured the dangers and humiliations of segregation. Struggling to describe her experience, Theresa remarked, "You just don't know what it was like. They [white people] would try to make you feel like you weren't human." Facing a future limited by Jim Crow, she began to dream about leaving the South. And when a kind white employer described California, Theresa's dream assumed a more concrete form.

Early in 1943, Theresa met a man who worked on the Houston waterfront. Through a network of fellow workers, he learned of plentiful, high-paying jobs in the East Bay Area. Their relationship flourished on shared dreams, and soon they married. Within weeks he moved to the East Bay, found housing and a job, and sent for his wife. Theresa, about to embark on a journey that would reunite her with her husband and profoundly change her world, felt small and alone on that October day in the Houston train station. But as her personal journey unfolded, it would bear striking resemblance to the journeys made by countless other women during the World War II years.[1]

Between 1940 and 1945, thousands of African Americans migrated from the South to the East Bay Area in search of social and economic mobility associated with the region's expanding defense industry and reputation for greater racial tolerance. Prior to World War II, the black population in the East Bay was small and highly insular. But the wartime economic boom, fueled by federal investment in shipbuilding, changed this whole demographic landscape. African Americans from the South who heard about defense jobs from labor recruiters, from railroad workers, at employment bureaus, from newspapers and, most important, by word of mouth joined thousands of white workers in a westward exodus. As a consequence, the East Bay's black population grew significantly—by up to fivefold in many communities across the bay from San Francisco. In Richmond, for example, the African American population grew from 270 in 1940 to 10,000 in 1945. Similarly, Oakland's black population grew from 8,462 to over 37,000 during the same period. Of the African Americans who joined the migration to the East Bay, most came from Texas, Louisiana, Mississippi, Arkansas, and Oklahoma, and roughly half were women.[2]

This study examines the migration and community-building efforts of African American women who moved from the South to the East Bay during World War II. Drawing on fifty oral interviews with former migrants, it details who these women were, how they experienced the migration, and how they used their southern cultural traditions to keep their families together and establish new communities in the East Bay. The study emphasizes migrant women's activism, describing how they built community-supporting institutions that contributed to social and political change in the East Bay cities of Oakland, Berkeley, and Richmond—cities that underwent major demographic changes as migrants were drawn to the region's defense industries.

Migration has long been a feature of the African American experience. Since Reconstruction, African Americans have been highly mobile, moving from farm to farm, from the rural South to southern towns and cities, and from southern cities to northern and western metropolitan areas. For migrants, these journeys have served as imagined or actual passages to something better. As such, they provide examples of African American agency and resistance, and they offer insight into how new communities are established and maintained. Historians, who have long recognized the incredible drama and poignancy of these mass population movements, have produced a rich and varied migration literature.

A number of excellent studies document black migration during the first two decades of the twentieth century and describe the impact of male migrants on the economic, political, and social institutions within receiving communities.[3] However, migration during World War II, and the particular experience and contributions of black women, have received little attention. By placing women like Theresa at the center of analysis, this study generates new perspectives on where and how social change takes place and how community is established and maintained.[4]

Similarly, the literature on women and World War II discusses labor force participation, employment discrimination, and shifting gender roles, but it only partially reconstructs how African American women experienced the war. In defense centers across the nation, most black women were workers and migrants. As they made the transition from field and domestic work to jobs in an industrial economy, they struggled to keep their families together, establish new households, and create community-sustaining networks and institutions. Though white women too negotiated the double burden of wage labor and housework, African American women shouldered substantially more. Filling defense jobs and caring for their families, they also performed many of the tasks associated with relocation and community-building: finding schools and housing; locating markets, churches, and medical services; establishing new institutions; building reciprocal relationships with other migrants; and maintaining ties to those back home. Moreover, black migrant women facilitated chain migration by encouraging friends and family to join them and by providing newcomers with food, shelter, and emotional support until they found their own jobs and housing. Though white migrant women faced some of these same challenges, they did not have to contend with racial discrimination—a burden that forced black migrant women to create new institutions and multiplied their housing and employment difficulties.[5]

Indirectly, this work contributes to an increasingly lively debate on the origins of postwar urban poverty. Nicholas Lemann, whose work *The Promised Land: The Great Black Migration and How It Changed America* revived the "culture of poverty" thesis, argues that the contemporary black "underclass" shares an "ethic of dependency" fostered by the southern sharecropping system and transplanted to urban centers by migrants from the South. The women whose lives are told in these pages tell a different story. Whether raised on farms or in the urban South, all came from poor or working-class families that shared a common regard for economic autonomy, hard work, education, worship, family ties, charity, and independent self-help institutions. When they left the South, motivated by self-determination rather than dependency, women drew on these values to establish new communities and resist the prejudice and discrimination that greeted them.

Following the war, the economic vitality of East Bay migrant communities was severely undermined by poorly planned redevelopment projects, capital flight, and continuing residential segregation and employment discrimination. In the absence of sustained societal commitment to providing jobs and housing for black communities, working-class migrants like Theresa Waller fought to stabilize their neighborhoods in the hard economic times of the postwar era. Their helping ethic, desire for economic independence, and commitment to institution-building—all pieces of a southern cultural legacy that allowed their forebears to resist the economic and social costs of Jim Crow—were turned to helping their communities resist chronic unemployment and its accompanying dislocations.

Before, during, and after the war, migrant women's lives reveal an extraordinary level of self-determination. Indeed, their efforts to provide for their families and neighbors support historian Jacqueline Jones's contention that "embedded in the historical record of ordinary families . . . is a powerful refutation of the culture of poverty or culture of dependency thesis." The experience and contributions of women like Theresa Waller thus challenge generalizations about inner-city communities—generalizations that obscure both the residents' diversity and agency and the historical processes that led to urban poverty.[6]

Finally, this work details change and continuity within a specific geographical area: the San Francisco East Bay region. However, many of the same changes took place elsewhere, with similar consequences. Los Angeles, Long Beach, San Francisco, Portland, and Seattle also experienced wartime growth and simultaneous cultural, political, and economic transformation. The East Bay thus provides a lens through which to view interracial conflict, civil rights activism, class formation, and urban change in various parts of the country during and after the war.

In the opening chapters, the book proceeds chronologically, describing women's childhood years in the Jim Crow South; their young adulthood; and their decision to migrate to the East Bay. Most of the women in my sample came from deeply religious, two-parent, working-class families. These findings are consistent with several wartime studies that have characterized migrants as predominantly urban, relatively well-educated, and highly skilled members of an expanding black southern working class.[7]

Church and family formed the center of migrant women's girlhoods. There they learned how to create and sustain the reciprocal relationships that were vital to community and individual survival. This ethic of care—rooted in an awareness that survival was linked to the well-being of relatives and neighbors—coexisted with a fierce desire for economic independence from white people. Migrant women recalled how their parents counseled them to "own your own," and they often went on to reflect that it was all-black institutions that insulated them from the hardships and humiliations of Jim Crow.

This generation, schooled to be independent, came of age just as the wartime boom was transforming the East Bay into a virtual Canaan for both skilled and unskilled workers. Not surprisingly, most of the women in my sample were neither bitterly poor nor middle-class. Unlike their poorer neighbors, they had the resources to leave. And unlike the middle class, they had little if any economic stake in their communities of origin. Had working-class migrant women remained in the South, few could have expected more than a domestic service job paying two dollars or less a week. And since many had recently married and started families, the personal desire for a better life was now charged with the added responsibility of parenthood.

Once women made the decision to migrate—a decision usually made jointly with other family members—they viewed the migration as a rite of passage, a major life transition that they frequently described in biblical terms. However, many women made the journey alone or with small children. For this group, excitement was often overshadowed by fatigue, loneliness, and fear of the unknown. Nevertheless, women played a central role in the migration process, often remaining behind to sell property while male family members searched for work and housing in the East Bay. Women then packed belongings, made travel arrangements, and safely conveyed children across the country on crowded, poorly equipped Jim Crow cars. Women also maintained contact with friends and family who had already moved west. These contacts allowed migrants to make informed decisions about what to pack and what to leave behind and helped insure that newcomers would receive temporary shelter and assistance finding employment when they arrived.

Following this discussion of migration, the book examines women's efforts to create homes for their families in the East Bay, their wage labor and workplace resistance during and after the war, and their commitment to institution-building, cultural preservation, and social change. As young wives and mothers, women performed most of the orientation tasks associated with a major move: creating comfortable living quarters in an impossibly tight and discriminatory housing market; locating essential services; building friendships with other migrants; and maintaining ties to those back home. Finding housing was particularly daunting; initially, most migrant families doubled up with friends, relatives, or new acquaintances in crowded, older housing in existing black neighborhoods. Lacking privacy and adequate cooking and laundry facilities, women struggled with routine chores as they attempted to transform substandard housing into reasonably comfortable accommodations.

Fortunately, most migrants eventually moved from these temporary quarters into one of several war housing projects. Although war housing was poorly constructed and maintained, migrant women expressed satisfaction with indoor plumbing, space heat, hot and cold running water, modern cooking facilities, and greater degree of privacy that it offered. Above all, government housing was woman-centered, spatially conducive to the formation of helping networks. The projects, in addition to housing large numbers of newcomers, contained common yards and laundry facilities that women defined as shared space. In these common areas women assisted each other with such tasks as finding markets, churches, and social services. There women watched children, made friends while doing laundry, and exchanged garden produce and recipes.

Greater residential stability also supported the growth of migrant communities and institutions. While living in war housing, women facilitated chain migration by encouraging friends and relatives to come west and by providing temporary shelter to newcomers. They also began to establish new churches and mutual aid organizations that addressed migrants' needs. This process of institution-building, which continued after women moved from war projects into more permanent housing, contributed to the stability of new communities and the formation of a common identity.

On their arrival in the East Bay, most migrant women entered the wartime labor force at the lowest level of the occupational ladder, filling jobs that were circumscribed by both race and gender. But however bad these jobs were, women relished the fact that "we were at least getting paid to put up with it. In the South it had been nothing but hard work and bad treatment. Here I was making more in a day than I made back home in a month."[8] After the war, migrant women were the first fired. Some found relatively secure, high-paying jobs with the federal government, the single largest employer of East Bay black residents during the postwar years. Most, however, were forced into the low-paying institutional service sector as cooks, custodians, and nurse's aides, a variation of the domestic service jobs many had held in the South.

Because they filled the lowest-paying jobs in the labor force both during and after the war, migrant women created an alternate source of status and identity as homemakers, church women, and community workers. By defining their labor on behalf of family and community as "real work," migrant women resisted categorization as menial or marginal laborers. At the same time, however, much of their community work directly challenged employment discrimination and complemented their workplace resistance; this suggests that their labor force participation was, in fact, an important source of identity and self-esteem.

After securing employment, migrant women created the exchange relationships and institutions that sustained migrant communities. In the racially hostile climate of the East Bay, where established white and black residents regarded migrants as unassimilable guest workers, migrant women made homes for their families, helped other migrants find jobs and housing, founded community-supporting institutions, and organized other newcomers to demand better schools, housing, jobs, and recreational facilities. Women's organizing skills and leadership abilities were part of a black southern cultural inheritance passed from mother to daughter. Rather than being ashamed of where they came from, migrant women used their traditional values and resources to establish permanent communities and counter the destructive impact of racial discrimination on their friends and family. Viewed as undesirable outsiders, newcomers found a sense of solidarity with other migrants and drew on their southernness as the currency of group identity and cohesiveness.

This discussion of migrant women's political and institution-building activities often moves between the war years and the present. In contrast to the linear way in which they described their childhood, migration, housing, and employment, these women characterized their activism in more fluid terms, with less attention to fixed boundaries of time and place. This revealing habit may suggest that activism was an organic, continuous aspect of their lives, one that blurred the division between public and private spheres and transcended both youthful idealism and mature ambition. But continuity and fluidity create difficulties for the historian: when to end the story, and whether to make distinctions or impose structures that are irrelevant to informants. These questions, which are still unresolved, create an opening for dialogue between reader and writer.

Finally, the reader should also be aware of my theoretical choices. Male migrants, when they appear in the following pages, fill supporting roles as spouses, siblings, children, and parents, much as women have in previous migration studies. This work, then, is intended as a corrective to scholarship that privileges or universalizes male experience. However, it is a playful corrective rather than a vindictive one. Although the work emphasizes women's experience, it in no way suggests that men were insignificant participants in the migration and community-building process or that men and women had vastly different expectations and experiences. It simply adopts an alternate orientation to the subject and invites the reader to decide whether gender significantly shaped the drama of wartime migration.

Feminist theory not only informed this study's orientation but also shaped its methodological framework. From the beginning of this project I was deeply committed to a participatory model that allowed women to tell their own stories using their own narrative structures. I was also concerned about the potential power imbalance between respondent and interviewer, and I looked for ways to shift control to the respondent. As the interview process began, many of these concerns fell by the wayside. These were strong individuals who had two or three times my life experience. Moreover, they voluntarily agreed to participate in this study and knew that it depended on their willingness to divulge their life stories. Ultimately, the interviews were fluid exchanges where power and control shifted between informant and respondent. To deny migrant women's power in the research process—power stemming from their status as elders and as owners of valuable information—is to adopt a patronizing stance, one that uncritically accepts and perhaps reinforces assumed hierarchies.[9]

In the end, I presented the women's stories much as they were recorded. Not surprisingly, the women represented themselves and their communities as self-determining, existing in opposition to and in spite of white control, but also as independent, true, and whole. They did not feel "tragically colored" or stripped of their agency, despite their long and painful association with white racism. Nearing the end of the project, I began to care less about the accuracy of the women's memories, whether they were flawlessly recalling "what really happened." What mattered more was how they used the past to create their own counternarrative, one by which the women claimed the truth of their experience despite the efforts of outsiders to portray them as victims or failures.

Oral history is notably unreliable. As a product of memory it is easily warped by trauma, forgetfulness, and the all-too-human temptation to selectively recall or embroider past events. But these "problems" also provide a different way of examining history, one that shifts the focus from "what really happened" to how people use the past to produce individual or collective meaning and identity. Just as memory shapes identity, identity also shapes the meaning we draw from the past. Migrant women, for example, drew on Old Testament metaphor to tell their life stories, reaching into their southern religious heritage to construct narratives that clearly resemble morality plays. This device was both an unexpected marker of their collective identity and evidence that their shared history generated a common perceptual orientation toward the past. The limits of oral history thus produced surprising interpretive possibilities.

This study was based on fifty oral interviews—ranging from two to five hours in length—and supporting documentation from more conventional sources. All of the interviews were used to compile aggregate statistics such as place of birth, date of birth, parent's occupation, age at migration, and frequency of return visits home. Roughly half of the interviews— those that were most richly detailed and personally revealing—are presented as migration narratives. Finally, care was taken to select narratives that revealed differences as well as similarities in the women's experiences.

I met most of my informants at East Bay senior centers and churches. After introducing myself and describing my project, I asked if anyone wished to be interviewed. Some interviews were conducted on the spot, and others in women's homes at a later date. All of my informants can be characterized as successful migrants. They were proud of their lives and willing to share their stories. They had worked hard at blue-collar or service-sector jobs, raised families, and managed to save for modest but comfortable retirements. None had given up on the East Bay and returned to the South, although most retained strong connections to friends and family back home. A majority of black migrants did, in fact, remain in the East Bay, and many who left returned to the South to start businesses or buy land with wartime savings.[10] Nevertheless, my sample does not include those who, broken and bruised, returned home or slipped into poverty and anonymity in East Bay inner cities. As we delve into the world of Theresa Waller and her cohort, the existence of those less fortunate migrants should be held in mind and used to temper any unintentional generalizations about the migrant experience.

Chapter One . . . . . .

. . . . . . **It Was Just Like Living in Two Worlds**

Growing Up in

the Jim Crow South,

1910–1940

Elmgrove, Longleaf, Tupelo, Laurel, Pelican, Utility, Canton, Cordova. To the unknowing, these place-names conjure up images of small towns settled on yellow, dusty crossroads or spread out along sun-hardened streets. Farms come to mind. So do hot, humid summers. The very names coax up the mercury and warn off those who cannot patiently bear heat. But paired with childhood, these names suggest comfort, and they sound like places where children were loved and safe. Here, in the region of the imagination, the young trundle through cool, raw-scented grass among a twilight assembly of fireflies and cicadas, as parents and neighbors sit easily together on their wide and solid front porches.

The black women who grew up in these towns between 1900 and 1940, and who left during the World War II years—we will call them "migrant women"—recall their childhoods with a terrible sweetness. Terrible because each of these places was home to Jim Crow, and sweet because much of life took place outside of humiliating assertions of white supremacy. In each town, parents, neighbors, clergy, and teachers pieced their varied skills and talents into a continually evolving, transgenerational quilt that sheltered the young from racial hatred, provided the basis for personal and collective identity, and engendered a deeply satisfying sense of security and belonging.

But Jim Crow could not be completely avoided. Its forms differed from place to place, but its purpose never varied: to institutionalize the inferior status of African Americans and protect white supremacy. Implemented by the politically and economically powerful, but eagerly embraced by whites of all classes, segregation controlled potentially explosive competition between white and black workers, masked class tensions among whites, perpetuated an illusion of white privilege as a disincentive to interracial unity, and maintained a supply of cheap black labor.[1]

Patterns of Segregation

Jim Crow laws were most explicit where status was uncertain or in constant flux, such as the rapidly industrializing cities of the New South. Rural areas, which often lacked formal systems of separation, had elaborate behavioral codes enforced by tradition. Thus, legal statutes were not the only reliable measure of white racism; in many places, separation and black subordination were so entrenched in the white view of the world that written laws were unnecessary.[2] Whether segregation's rules were of urban or rural origin, they were reinforced with racial violence. Pauli Murray, a nonmigrant lawyer and activist, recalled how these rules had to be learned and negotiated if one was to survive: "learning about race did not for the most part come in terrifying shocks although there were those too—especially news of lynchings, which, frequently unreported in the newspapers[,] traveled by word of mouth. More often race was the atmosphere one breathed from day to day, the pervasive irritant, the chronic allergy, the vague apprehension which made one uncomfortable and jumpy. We knew the race problem was like a deadly snake coiled and ready to strike, and that one avoided its dangers only by never-ending watchfulness."[3]

The metaphorical snake lived in every town and city in which migrant women came of age. Born during the "Age of Jim Crow," this generation grew up with the violence and humiliation that accompanied the proliferation and elaboration of racial barriers. During a twenty-year period, between 1900 and 1920, southern whites drafted laws mandating separate parks, hospitals, schools, drinking fountains, restrooms, exits, entrances, telephone booths, and even courtroom Bibles. Other laws specified racial separation in public facilities such as libraries, buses, trains, waiting rooms, and workplaces.

Racial violence, which escalated following Reconstruction, continued into the first decades of the 1900s as the chosen method of enforcing the new Jim Crow laws. Between 1882 and 1927—a period that spanned migrant women's childhoods as well as the adult lives of their parents and grandparents—white mobs lynched over 3,500 black citizens. Far from being softened by the progression of the twentieth century, white supremacy now reached its most refined and elaborate stage. Migrant women, most of whom were raised in Mississippi, Texas, Louisiana, Arkansas, and Oklahoma, shared their early years with an equally youthful Jim Crow, the monstrous product of white fear and greed that clouded young black lives with fear and humiliation.[4]

Within the towns and cities of the South, whites drew boundaries around their neighborhoods. Only servants or people with business who conducted themselves purposefully and deferentially were able to cross over safely. Even then, tension and fear were constant companions, and most black citizens simply avoided the gulf that separated white from black and schooled their children in the risks of transgression. Theresa Waller, who worked in a white section of Houston before coming to California in the early 1940s, was repeatedly hit and pushed by white youths as she walked from her employer's house to the nearest bus stop. Only after her white employer spoke with the youths and established Theresa's connection to a white family in the community could Theresa pass unmolested.[5]

Spatial boundaries enforced hierarchy as well as physical separation. Black residents, who paid taxes like other citizens, coped with vastly inferior services; their neighborhoods were short on street lighting; paving; police and fire protection; sewage, gas, and electrical connections; recreational facilities; and schools. The larger cities, like Houston, usually contained one or more black sections located in or near the older, urban core. These neighborhoods were more self-sufficient, supporting several churches, benevolent associations, markets, restaurants, clubs, recreation facilities, clothing stores, professional offices, schools, barbershops, and beauty parlors. Many families could thus minimize their contact with the white world. Pauli Murray remembered that her "meager contact with white people was paradoxical, since the two races lived close together," but she proceeded to explain that her family "preferred never to cross the gulf that separated us from white people unless we could do so without losing our dignity and pride."[6]

In smaller towns, like Laurel, Mississippi, black neighborhoods stood on the edge of white areas and were more dependent on outside businesses for goods and services. Here, as in large cities, a simple shopping trip could easily turn into a series of humiliating encounters. To get downtown, one either walked or used segregated public transportation, because automobiles were a luxury few could afford. In stores, black customers endured the rude familiarity and poor service meted out by white shop owners and clerks. Some restaurants and cafes served black patrons on a take-out basis or in the kitchen; others refused them service altogether. "Negro" or "colored" restrooms, if they existed, were dirty and poorly maintained. Finally, whites retained exclusive use of most swimming pools, skating rinks, bowling alleys, and parks, and they relegated black spectators to less desirable sections of movie theaters and ballparks.

Medical care was separate and unequal. Few white hospitals and physicians served black patients except in the case of extreme emergency, and even then, care was far from certain. Family histories invariably include stories of loved ones who died because the "Negro" hospital was too far away and the white hospital refused care. Equally common are stories that recount humiliating encounters with white doctors and dentists. Maya Angelou, whose work I Know Why the Caged Bird Sings describes her childhood in Stamps, Arkansas, and her family's migration to California in the 1940s, recalled a trip to a white dentist who refused to treat her, even though her grandmother had loaned the dentist money. Her grandmother said, "I wouldn't press on you like this for myself but I can't take No. Not for my grandbaby. When you come to borrow my money you didn't have to beg. You asked me, and I lent it." The dentist responded, "Annie, my policy is I'd rather stick my hand in a dog's mouth than in a nigger's."[7]

White school administrators, making no pretense of equality, systematically undercut the aspirations and efforts of black parents, children, and teachers. Throughout the South, school districts diverted funds to white pupils, while neglecting the needs of black students. Disparities were even greater on a county-by-county basis: cotton counties had the lowest expenditures per black pupil. Black schools in these areas also operated on a shorter year than white schools, because white plantation owners set the school terms to coincide with their desire for cheap black labor to cultivate and harvest cotton; clearly, the white South did not view black child labor as a problem. Henrietta McAlister, who taught in rural Mississippi while a student teacher at Jackson College, hesitated to call what she did "teaching." "It was an affront. We gave what we had, but it wasn't enough and they [white school administrators] really didn't care."[8]

During the same period, black teachers and school personnel were grossly underpaid. As late as the mid-1930s, for example, Mississippi's white teachers, supervisors, and principals earned almost three times more than their black counterparts. This calculated misallocation of funds—per teacher and per pupil—led to inferior facilities as well as fewer schools. In many areas, parents created their own classrooms in churches, lodges, and homes, while their tax dollars were diverted to white schools.

As if these obstacles were not sufficient to dampen aspirations, school administrators made it difficult for black students to get to school; white students rode buses, while black children walked. In Arkansas, black students constituted 27 percent of total school enrollment but received only 2 percent of total transportation funds.[9]

In the late 1930s, when most migrant women were of high school age, 87 counties in a sample of thirteen states with segregated school systems had no black high schools. An additional 115 counties provided black high schools, but none of these schools offered four-year programs. Instead, teachers struggled to fit high school curricula into two years or, if necessary, into the normal curricula of the seventh, eighth, and ninth grades. Parents also sacrificed, sending their children to board with friends and family who lived near good schools, or moving the entire family to a better district when a son or daughter reached high school age.[10]

Willa Henry, raised on a farm near Elmgrove, Texas, lived with relatives in Jacksonville so that she could attend an accredited high school. The couple who took her in, the owners of a small pharmacy, supported her through high school and lovingly called her "daughter." Later, when she attended Prairie View College, her paternal grandfather and aunts, all of whom graduated from college, helped her financially. Gracie Potter, born in Pelican, Louisiana, boarded less comfortably with a minister in Mansfield while she attended high school. Regarded as a renter rather than a family member, she had to wash her own clothes and buy and cook her own meals.[11]

Most families did not have the resources to send children away. Lacey Gray, whose family owned a farm in Longleaf, Louisiana, walked two and a half miles to school and two and a half miles home. All seven grades met in a single drafty hall where grownups held evening and weekend meetings. In this less than ideal environment, three instructors managed to teach more in seven grades than Lacey's own daughters later learned in twelve. The nearest black high school was miles away, in Baton Rouge, much farther than her parents could afford to send her, and the distance to the nearby white high school—just one mile—was equally unbridgeable. But even assuming that one had the resources and fortitude to finish school, few good jobs awaited black high school graduates—or even black college graduates.[12]

In southern industries, employers assigned black workers to the least desirable, lowest-paying occupations or tasks and to separate shifts, rooms, or sections of the shop floor. Black workers were also required to use separate washrooms, water fountains, and entrances. Class-based occupational differentiation occurred only within the black community, where a small middle class and elite worked as teachers, doctors, lawyers, nurses, accountants, and storekeepers and in other clerical and professional positions.[13]

The shifting economic interests of white employers and workers continually redefined which jobs were "white" and which were "black." In the early years of the twentieth century, black-operated barbershops, beauty salons, and caterers, which had once served white customers, lost their business to white entrepreneurs. During the same period, whites took over the skilled trades and trade unions, such as bricklaying, plastering, and carpentry, which had once been the province of black workers. Occupational choices narrowed even more during the Great Depression, as black-owned businesses collapsed and white workers took over "Negro" jobs.[14]

By 1930, black workers filled the most dangerous, lowest-paying, and least secure jobs within a dwindling number of occupational categories. Industries with the greatest concentration of black, male employees included turpentine farms and distilleries, fertilizer factories, saw and planing mills, lumber camps, tobacco factories, charcoal and coke works, mines, sugar refineries, cotton gins, cottonseed presses, and brickyards.[15]

Because of chronically low wages and lack of job security, a family's financial security often required two wage earners. Many black women contributed to family income by taking in boarders, but over 40 percent worked for wages—mostly in domestic service, laundry, and unskilled factory work. During the Great Depression, black women made as little as $1.50 a week in private households and $3.75 per week in factories. At the same time, their labor force participation declined from 42 percent to 38 percent as their jobs were eliminated or turned over to whites.[16]

Theresa Waller, raised in Houston, Texas, during the depression, recalled that her entire family had to work in order to make ends meet. Her father put in long hours at a cottonseed compress, while her mother cleaned homes and worked in a poorly ventilated, unheated warehouse sorting salvageable cotton out of damaged bales. After finishing high school, Theresa went to work caring for children and cleaning houses. Her brothers shined shoes or sorted cotton. Theresa's parents had already made sacrifices to keep her in high school, and she wanted to go on to college as some of her middle-class friends had done. Bright and "strong-willed," she "worried" her mother about school for months before accepting the family's financial limitations.[17]

As late as 1940, the majority of black southerners labored in the region's fields, growing and harvesting crops by the same methods used nearly a century earlier. Mechanization, which was not widely adopted until after World War II, did not represent a major threat to the livelihood of this generation. Rather, institutionalized debt peonage, the boll weevil, and New Deal farm policies that gave landowners an incentive to evict tenant farmers kept men and women on the edge of what is humanly tolerable. Of all farm families, fewer than a third owned their own land. Indeed, black farm ownership steadily declined during migrant women's childhood years.[18]

Those who owned their land frequently worked for wages or ran side businesses to offset fluctuating crop values, discriminatory credit policies, and the increasing costs of seed, fertilizer, and equipment. They also had to contend with white hostility toward black ownership. In at least one state—Mississippi—black farmers were denied agricultural extension services, singled out by night riders, frequently denied credit to buy land, and sold overworked, infertile farms. These owners, however, could make their own decisions about what to produce, and they usually mixed cash crops with large subsistence gardens for home consumption. They could also obtain better prices for their harvests by selling directly to buyers.[19] Lacey Gray's family, for example, farmed eighty acres of corn, vegetables, cotton, cane, and fodder; raised chickens, cows, horses, and hogs; and owned their own gristmill and smokehouse. They would trade half of their cane crop to a mill in exchange for syrup, and they bought flour and lard. Aside from this, they were nearly self-sufficient. "We never had to do without. When the depression came, we didn't know anything about it because we grew our own."[20]

The majority of black farmers sharecropped or rented. If the farmer avoided debt, renting could afford greater autonomy in decisions about what and when to plant and how to allocate the labor of family members. But debt, which was institutionalized through the crop lien and sharecropping systems, was an essential part of southern agriculture. Merchants and landowners profited through high interest rates, inflated prices for goods, and the fraudulent manipulation of tenants' accounts; consequently, poor farmers endured a system of peonage. The life of the chronically indebted contained serious hardship and frequent hunger. In 1930 the average annual income of a black sharecropper stood at $295, compared with $417 for his or her white counterpart.[21]

During the depression, conditions for tenants went from bad to worse. Because New Deal agricultural reforms offered them compensation for plowing crops under or holding land out of production, landowners evicted thousands of tenant families. Between 1930 and 1940 the number of sharecropping farms declined by 234,987. Displaced black tenants either moved to other farms or, increasingly, migrated into southern cities, where they joined the ranks of the unemployed or marginally employed.[22]

On farms and in cities, white southerners expected black citizens to move when asked, respond to disrespectful forms of address, step off the sidewalk, answer intrusive questions, and unfailingly conduct themselves with exaggerated respect in the presence of whites of all ages. Any miscommunication, failure to anticipate the moods of white people, or inaccurate reading of a particular situation extracted a heavy penalty. To Pauli Murray and most other black citizens, this "intricate racial code" made for a "straightjacket existence, which became more oppressive as I grew older. Each of us had to deal with it as best we could. Some were ultimately destroyed, some led crippled lives, some endured, and some fled the South."[23]

Efforts to remove the straightjacket—even efforts that were sanctioned by law—were severely hampered by white-on-black violence and legislation. By 1910 all southern states had adopted laws that disfranchised the majority of black citizens. These statutes, which coincided with the adoption of Jim Crow laws, "marked the termination of any flexibility in race relations that previously existed, and completed the degradation of the Negro into a separate and unequal position within southern life."[24]

Although the white primary, poll tax, and literacy tests would endure into the 1940s and beyond, black southerners protested disfranchisement from the beginning. As a consequence, most black citizens knew how the political process was supposed to work. Indeed, migrant women who had never voted in the South registered shortly after their arrival in California, joined or established political and civil rights organizations, and took the lead in voter registration drives. Nor were black southerners ignorant of national political events and debates. Though black periodicals were often intercepted by white postal officials, the Chicago Defender, the Atlanta Independent, and other large-circulation black newspapers sometimes reached small southern towns with news of Marcus Garvey, Pan-African affairs, the Harlem Renaissance, Ida B. Wells's antilynching campaign, the debates between W. E. B. Du Bois and Booker T. Washington, and the social and political activities of club women. Many rural families not only had kin in southern cities but also maintained direct links to the North through relatives who had migrated there.

In larger cities and towns, black residents frequently established NAACP chapters; there were varying degrees of opposition from white residents, who viewed the organization as radical and incendiary. Willa Suddeth, whose working-class uncle worked on voter registration with the NAACP in Bossier City, Louisiana, prior to World War II, was told by local whites that "horses would be swimming in blood before black people voted" there. But despite such threats, these local chapters used legal support from the national office to challenge voting restrictions, school segregation, the lack of laws punishing racial violence, and the exclusion of black citizens from juries. At the same time, civic leagues, political clubs, and women's charitable organizations successfully pressed for better social and public services in many communities.[25]

A small number of black citizens—impoverished sharecroppers and members of the growing urban proletariat—joined the Unemployed Councils and the Sharecroppers' Union, both sponsored by the Communist Party, or the Christian-socialist Southern Tenant Farmers' Union. As Ned Cobb testified in *All God's Dangers*, membership in these organizations carried considerable personal risk but imparted a sense of self-worth and entitlement. Moreover, by attributing racism to capital's desire to divide the working class, the radical left provided a persuasive explanation and proscription for white supremacy. Though they sometimes underestimated the tenacity of racism, these organizations provided significant opportunities for black leadership and helped forge coalitions and institutions that continued to struggle for black civil rights well beyond the 1930s.[26]

Black resistance is a variable concept, filtered through the limitations and opportunities of any given moment, as well as through class, gender, and age; and most black southerners found that putting food on the table, educating children, making a home, caring for the old and sick, and maintaining a spiritual life was protest enough. When the map of white supremacy is viewed in its entirety, simple acts of living clearly amounted to acts of resistance for the majority of the African Americans belonging to this generation.

In the black world, boundaries between public and private spheres were blurred by fluid conceptions of kinship and the economic exigencies of living with Jim Crow. The home, which served as hospital, school, recreation center, boardinghouse, and workshop, was both public and private. There, esteemed friends became "family," cousins were "sisters," grandmothers were "mothers," and neighbors assumed parental authority and responsibilities. In these small, tightly woven communities, teachers, clergy, and other public figures were known and held accountable by numerous threads of real and fictive kinship.

Women's lives regularly crossed public and private boundaries. Black women worked outside the home much more frequently than white women, though their selection of jobs was proscribed by race and gender. They also filled a variety of "public" roles within their homes, taking in laundry and boarders, or providing the sort of medical care that white people normally received in hospitals. Finally, women took an active role in the most public of African American institutions—the black church. Like the home, the black church was the site of social, political, economic, and spiritual life: a place where core values were both expressed privately and communally and passed to successive generations.[27]

These black institutions were centers of daily resistance, life-affirming sanctuaries where one became a valued part of the social fabric rather than a marginal being. In the black world, whites were the outsiders, viewed as morally and physically inferior. And they knew it. Having created the boundaries that separated them from black people, whites faced the disturbing realization that they too were seen as outcasts—a realization that undermined their assertions of supremacy. Indeed, white people were even more thoroughly excluded from the black world than blacks were from the white world; black people worked for whites in the most intimate of settings and daily witnessed actions that contradicted white claims of superiority.

For all their separateness, white and black worlds were inextricably entwined in an uneasy relationship, one in which the black community, although defined by whites as marginal, claimed its own center; one in which whites could alternately feel powerful and diminished; and one where the daily resistance of ordinary black citizens existed alongside the everyday rhythms of life, which occurred not in reaction to white supremacy but in the context of human needs and desires. In spite of Jim Crow, and with extraordinary creativity and flexibility, black citizens crafted the world that migrant women would recall with sweetness.

Definitions of marginality and resistance thus depend on one's position in relation to ever-shifting boundaries of race, class, and gender. One reason whites tend to know so little of the black world is that they define and analyze institutions and power relations from their particular social position, labeling black communities as marginal and powerless. White-formulated notions of class, gender, and public/private spheres, like definitions of resistance and marginality, are also position-related concepts that describe as well as inscribe a particular set of power relations. When applied to black communities, they fail miserably, because they measure human experience by deviation from or correspondence to a privileged standard, suppress important differences, and sacrifice descriptive richness for theoretical consistency.

Regional Variations in Jim Crow

Most black migrants to the East Bay Area came from Texas, Louisiana, Mississippi, Arkansas, and Oklahoma. In these places, Jim Crow assumed different forms, with varying degrees of harshness. Of these five states, Mississippi held the fewest opportunities for African Americans. Beginning in the 1880s, state and local governments passed laws prohibiting intermarriage and mandating segregation in education, hospitals, asylums, jails, trains, streetcars, taxis, and waiting rooms. Segregation of hotels, restaurants, theaters, water fountains, parks, and restrooms was often informal, regulated by custom rather than law. Moreover, African Americans were completely excluded from many facilities such as libraries, pools, and service establishments. Finally, segregation was accompanied by disfranchisement. As early as 1890 the state instituted poll taxes, residency requirements, literacy tests, and reapportionment plans that effectively disfranchised black voters.[28]

Discrimination in public education, by which whites sought to keep black Mississippians politically and economically disadvantaged, complemented white control over state and local politics. Of the five states considered here, Mississippi had the highest black adult illiteracy rate: in 1930 it stood at 30 percent. Between 1935 and 1936, per pupil expenditures for school facilities averaged $147 for white students and $11 for black students. By 1940, over one-third of the state's counties had no black secondary schools, and those that existed elsewhere were usually built by black parents with private funds. Until 1940, Alcorn A&M was the only state-funded four-year college in Mississippi. Other colleges, like Rust and Tougaloo, were privately funded and forced to adopt a racially conservative posture to survive racial hostility.[29]

Black Mississippians, who constituted 50 percent of the state's population in 1930, were predominantly rural. Indeed, in 1930, 76 percent of all black Mississippians lived on farms—a higher proportion than in Texas, Louisiana, Arkansas, and Oklahoma. Of all black farms in the state in 1930, only 12 percent were operated by owners, while 56 percent were farmed by sharecroppers. Compared with the other four states, Mississippi had the lowest rate of black farm ownership, the highest rate of farm tenancy, and the lowest average value of black-owned farms.[30]

Black farm ownership was kept at a minimum through declining soil fertility, high interest rates, falling cotton prices, boll weevil infestation, and white hostility. Whites either refused to sell land to black farmers or sold them land that was no longer productive. Blacks who managed to acquire farms frequently became the target of white violence. Thus, a majority of black farmers either rented land or labored as sharecroppers on white-owned farms and plantations. Ever mindful of their dependence on cheap, docile labor, white planters supported legislation that limited black mobility and independence. Vagrancy laws, contract enforcement statutes, and antienticement regulations bound African Americans to the land, particularly during periods of labor shortage. Many white planters also resorted to forced labor: they leased convicts, paid fines in exchange for a term of service, held black workers in involuntary servitude, and bought and sold indebted tenants.[31]

In Mississippi's towns and cities, like Jackson and Vicksburg, most African Americans filled domestic service and manual labor occupations. Of all five states, Mississippi had the lowest percentage of black male workers in skilled and semiskilled occupations in 1930. Instead, men filled dangerous and physically exhausting jobs as unskilled laborers in turpentine and lumber camps, highway maintenance and construction firms, trash collection and street-cleaning operations, iron and steel mills, and building trades and the transportation sector. By 1930, only 3 percent of black male workers were employed as skilled craftsmen, and white competition and hostility increasingly limited them to serving black customers only.

In Mississippi, black women comprised 74 percent of the total female labor force in 1930. Of this number, 70 percent worked in agriculture, and another 27 percent worked in domestic service. In the latter occupation, women earned roughly the same wages in 1940 that they had in 1865. Even with two wage earners, most families struggled to make ends meet. In 1939, 77 percent of all black families wholly dependent on wage and salary income earned $499 or less, which placed them at a lower income level than those in the other four states.[32]

Not surprisingly, few black Mississippians could afford decent housing. In 1930, 56 percent of all black nonfarm families occupied dwellings valued under $1,000, compared with only 6 percent of white homeowning families. Of the majority who rented, 61 percent paid ten dollars or less per month, compared with only 12 percent of white families. Here again, Mississippi's standard of living trailed behind that of the other four states.[33]

Although Mississippi had a smaller black professional class than Texas, Louisiana, Arkansas, and Oklahoma, it led the nation in the development of black enterprise between 1890 and World War I. In towns and cities, black Mississippians limited their contact with hostile whites by patronizing their own businesses, doctors, lawyers, pharmacists, banks, and insurance companies. Mound Bayou, an all-black town founded in 1887, stood as an additional reminder of African American racial solidarity and determination to escape white control.[34]

However, in both rural and urban areas, black Mississippians were forced to move with caution. Reading a northern newspaper, acquiring a small amount of property, and failing to abide by local and idiosyncratic codes of deference could bring harsh and swift reprisal. Throughout the state, social, political, and economic hierarchies were maintained by an all-white justice system and the threat of racial violence. Between 1889 and 1945, for example, Mississippi led the nation in the number of lynchings and the sheer sadism and public acceptance of mob violence. And for each lynching there were countless other acts of violence: barn and crop burnings, whippings, rapes, verbal threats, economic reprisals, forced confessions, and false imprisonment.[35]

Black resistance, which was muted but not fully contained by white violence, took several forms: black entrepreneurship; preservation of families; the establishment of independent schools, churches, lodges, and mutual aid associations; personal acts of defiance, like carelessness, dissemblance, and theft; and migration. Black Mississippians had a long history of "protesting with their feet." In 1879, for example, thousands of blacks left Mississippi for Kansas as whites solidified their control following Reconstruction. A second migration, promoted by the Chicago Defender and fueled by wartime labor shortages in the North, carried an additional 100,000 migrants out of the state between 1915 and 1920. World War II, which provided economic opportunities in places like the East Bay, ushered in a third period of mass migration. Finally, many black Mississippians found refuge in the state's urban areas before leaving the state altogether. Between 1890 and 1940, for example, the urban black population increased from 5 percent to 17 percent—a significant jump in a largely rural state.[36]

Louisiana, like Mississippi, disfranchised its black citizens and instituted segregation following Reconstruction. Similarly, its schools were separate and unequal, and this situation contributed to a black adult illiteracy rate that equaled Mississippi's. There were, however, significant differences between the two states. Of the five states under consideration here, Louisiana had the second largest black population—37 percent of the total in 1930. But unlike black Mississippians, black Louisianans were much more likely to be urban. In 1930, 33 percent of the state's black residents lived in urban areas, while 48 percent were classified as rural/farm residents.[37]

In cities like Shreveport and, to a greater extent, New Orleans, black residents enjoyed a degree of occupational mobility that rivaled that of the four other states. In 1930, almost 7 percent of gainfully employed black males worked in skilled and semiskilled occupations. In New Orleans, 28 percent of the city's carpenters and joiners were black, as were 62 percent of all coopers, 65 percent of all masons, 22 percent of all painters, and 75 percent of all longshoremen. Black workers in this city also had a long history of labor activism, having formed several unions and benevolent associations in the years following Reconstruction.[38]

Black women had fewer employment options. Louisiana was second only to Mississippi in the percentage of African American women in the female labor force. Constituting 58 percent of all female workers, black women labored primarily in agriculture and domestic service. However, in cities like New Orleans, women also worked in independent hand trades and in hotels, restaurants, and boardinghouses.[39]

Because Louisiana had a higher percentage of male workers in skilled trades, black wage earners and salary earners had higher average incomes there than in Texas, Mississippi, Arkansas, and Oklahoma. Urban black homeowners and renters also enjoyed better housing with a substantially higher value than in the other four states. Such benefits varied from city to city, however. New Orleans, which had a much larger black population, provided more opportunities for skilled black workers and housed a larger number of independent black businesses, schools, churches, and cultural organizations; these services allowed residents to minimize their contact with whites. In 1930, New Orleans had a black population of 129,632 and a black professional class of 1,775. Between 1869 and 1930, three private black universities—Leland, New Orleans, and Straight—trained the majority of the city's teachers, doctors, and lawyers and added significantly to the cultural and intellectual richness of New Orleans.[40]

Shreveport, a much smaller city, provided fewer opportunities for skilled workers and black professionals. Following Reconstruction, skilled tradesmen who had once catered to black and white clients were forced to limit their business to the African American community. In 1901, for example, a Shreveport union voted down a motion to organize black carpenters. By 1921, the same union was taking action against builders who employed black tradesmen. Residential segregation was also more pronounced in Shreveport than in New Orleans. By World War I, St. Paul's Bottom, located west of downtown Shreveport in the city's low section, was almost entirely black. There, white landlords doubled the density of housing, cramming as many as twenty-four houses into a single block. Housing in the Bottom was poorly constructed. In 1925, the average cost of a new black dwelling was $875, while the average cost for new white housing was $4,567.[41]

Yet even in Shreveport, urban life had its benefits. Along a three-block section of Texas Avenue on the outskirts of downtown, a self-supporting black business community evolved. There, in 1920, Melvin L. Collins began to publish the *Shreveport Sun*, a black weekly newspaper. By 1925, the avenue housed four fraternal orders; black doctors, undertakers, drugstores, barbershops, cafes, pool halls, and insurance companies; and the legal practice of Charles Roberson, who was listed by *Who's Who in Colored Louisiana* as the best black lawyer in the state.[42]

Farm ownership rates and land values were only slightly higher in Louisiana than in Mississippi. Still, fewer of Louisiana's black farmers were engaged in sharecropping. In 1930, 56 percent of all black farms in Mississippi were operated by sharecroppers. In Louisiana the figure stood at 44 percent, pointing to a slightly higher rate of cash tenancy among Louisiana's farmers. The most significant difference between Mississippi and Louisiana, however, was in the ratio of urban to rural residents. For predominantly rural black Mississippians, church and home were the only institutions that buffered white control and hostility. In Louisiana, where the urban black population was larger, options for economic advancement, self-help, and racial solidarity were greater. These differences suggest that the two populations may have left the South for different reasons during World War II: black Mississippians for opportunities that were virtually nonexistent in their home state, and Louisiana's black residents—particularly those from New Orleans—to build on their relative advantage.[43]

Early in the century, Texas attracted black migrants from states like Mississippi and Louisiana with the promise of cheap land and more fluid race relations. Texas placed fewer voting restrictions on African Americans than the other two states did. However, by instituting the all-white primary for state and local elections, white Texans severely limited African

American political participation. Segregation accompanied disfranchisement, as it had in the other two states. Texas mandated racial separation in railroad cars and stations in 1891 and separate schools for black and white children in 1876. Although black schools received more funding than those in Mississippi, state expenditures per pupil revealed unsettling inequalities. In 1924, for example, Houston's black schools received only 7 percent of the district's total appropriations for buildings and equipment, although black residents comprised 25 percent of the city's population. Overcrowding was a persistent problem. In 1923, Houston Colored High School had an enrollment of over one thousand pupils, but only five hundred seats. Nevertheless, the state's adult illiteracy rates were appreciably lower—17 percent in 1930, compared to 30 percent in Mississippi and 29 percent in Louisiana.[44]

In 1930, 48 percent of all black Texans lived on farms, a percentage equal to that in Louisiana. However, the dream of landownership was much more attainable in the Lone Star State: in 1930, 24 percent of black farms were operated by owners—nearly twice as many as in Mississippi (12 percent) and Louisiana (14 percent). Black-owned farms in Texas were also more valuable; in average worth, they were second only to those in Oklahoma. Sharecropping, however, was almost equally prevalent in Texas as in Louisiana. By 1930, 42 percent of all black farms in the state were operated by sharecroppers. This percentage would increase during the 1930s as the Great Depression eroded the fragile measure of economic independence held by black farm owners at the beginning of the decade.[45]

Texas, like Louisiana, had a large black urban population—one that increased as the depression displaced the state's rural population. Black Texans who moved to cities like Houston found fewer opportunities in skilled and semiskilled trades than Louisiana's black urbanites had. They did, however, find slightly better professional opportunities. Thus, wage earners and salary earners in Texas and Louisiana had roughly comparable incomes, earning more on average than those in Mississippi, Arkansas, and Oklahoma.[46]

Among African Americans, Houston, more than any other city in the South, gained a reputation for racial harmony and economic opportunity. Jesse O. Thompson of the National Urban League reported in 1929, for example, that "the relationship existing between the races in Houston is much more cordial than is found in many places in the South." But according to historian James SoRelle, "Heavenly Houston" had a dark underside. Racial harmony, when it did prevail, depended on a high degree of racial separation and on blacks' deference toward whites.[47]

City ordinances segregated streetcars (1903), hotels, housing, theaters, restaurants (1907), and parks (1922). Until 1907, black residents had no library, and when one was finally established, it received just over 4 percent of the city's library budget. City hospitals maintained segregated wards, with few beds for black patients and no black doctors or nurses. On the brighter side, large numbers of black residents owned their own homes: 20 percent in 1910 and 31 percent in 1930. But as late as 1940, 23 percent of Houston's black households lacked running water, compared with just over 5 percent of white homes. Moreover, black neighborhoods were overcrowded and frequently lacked streetlights, sidewalks, or pavement. Finally, residential segregation concentrated the black population into the Third, Fourth, and Fifth Wards.[48]

Occupational segregation and discrimination also plagued black Houstonians. In 1880, 84 percent of all black workers were employed as domestic servants or in unskilled and semiskilled occupations. Only 1 percent were classified as professionals and 9 percent as skilled workers. By 1940, the number of black professionals had increased to almost 5 percent, but just under 90 percent still held menial, unskilled positions. Houston did, however, have a large number of segregated trade unions for skilled black workers, despite the fact that few filled jobs in that category. In 1914, for example, the Houston ship channel opened, and black and white longshoremen established segregated unions that split waterfront jobs equally.[49]

Police brutality and mob violence enforced codes of deference and racial separation in Houston and elsewhere in Texas. Women who later moved to the East Bay were children in 1921 when Houston Klan members castrated J. L. Cockrell, a local dentist, for allegedly associating with white women. They might also have recalled Robert Powell, who was lynched by a white mob in 1928, or C. F. Richardson, the editor of a Houston black newspaper, who received death threats and had his office vandalized after he printed editorials criticizing the city's record on race relations.[50]

What little heaven existed in Houston was found in the bustling Third, Fourth, and Fifth Wards. By 1930, the city's black population stood at 63,337. It was primarily concentrated in these three districts and provided the basis for independent businesses and institutions. In the Fourth Ward, businesses clustered along West Dallas Street; in the Third, along

Dowling; and in the Fifth, along Lyons. There black Houstonians could find all of the goods and services needed to sustain their families. Indeed, by 1929 Houston had the thirteenth largest black population in the nation but ranked tenth in black entrepreneurship, with per capita sales exceeding those of black businesses in New Orleans, Atlanta, and New York.[51]

By the late 1920s, black Houston supported twenty-two doctors, fourteen dentists, four lawyers, and seven registered pharmacists. It also boasted 116 churches, numerous lodges, and its own park, hospital, YWCA, YMCA, playhouse, and press. By 1930, four black newspapers kept residents informed of local and national events. A teacher's college, three senior high schools, one junior high school, and seven elementary schools educated the young. Ninety black postal carriers delivered mail. Most significant, Houston supported a militant black leadership. In 1912, residents established the Houston NAACP, which by the 1920s was challenging the all-white primary and disparities in school appropriations and teachers' salaries. NAACP pressure during the 1920s and 1930s resulted in school improvements and the establishment of Houston Colored Junior College in 1925. The white primary was finally defeated in 1944 when the Supreme Court ruled that it was unconstitutional. By the mid-1930s, the newly established Negro Chamber of Commerce was promoting racial solidarity through its "buy black" campaign. In contrast, Mississippi's few black urbanites, and even Shreveport's black residents, faced greater personal risk when openly promoting civil rights or race-conscious consumerism. Of all the cities in Mississippi and Louisiana, only New Orleans approximated Houston in the size and activism of its black community; this statistic may indicate the strength and safety in numbers.[52]

Oklahoma, like Texas, simultaneously dampened and fostered black ambition. Beginning with Oklahoma's admission to statehood in 1907, whites moved to disfranchise the state's black population. The state adopted a grandfather clause in 1910. The Supreme Court struck this clause down in 1913, but in 1916 the state replaced it with another restrictive registration law. The first state legislature also prohibited interracial marriage and sanctioned segregated schools and public transportation. Later the legislature mandated segregated phone booths and bathhouses. On a local level, most Oklahoma cities passed residential segregation laws. When the Supreme Court invalidated such ordinances in 1916, most municipalities either ignored the ruling or revised existing laws to meet the court's objections.[53]

Education was separate and unequal. In 1930, per pupil expenditures stood at $62 for each black child and $115 for each white student. During the same year, black residents, who comprised just over 7 percent of the state's total population, received only 5 percent of state expenditures for educational facilities. But although schools were unequally funded, they were better than those in the other four states. As a consequence, Oklahoma's black adult illiteracy rate in 1930 was a mere 12 percent.[54]

Of the four states considered here, Oklahoma held the greatest opportunities for black farm ownership. Slightly over 36 percent of all black farms were operated by owners in 1930, while only 20 percent were farmed by sharecroppers. Moreover, black-owned farms were larger and more valuable than those in Texas, Mississippi, Louisiana, and Arkansas. However, farm ownership declined sharply with the depression. By 1940, for example, black farmers owned only 66 percent of the farms that they had held a decade earlier, and those that they retained had declined in both acreage and value. As a result of economic dislocation, more than 37,000 African American farmers left the land between 1930 and 1940, swelling the state's urban population. In 1920, only one-third of the state's black population was classified as urban, but by 1940 this figure had increased to 47 percent. This pattern of dispossession and urbanization was repeated in Texas and Arkansas, providing an incentive for migration out of the South as World War II created new opportunities in the East Bay Area.[55]

In Oklahoma's urban areas, few black men found opportunities in skilled or semiskilled trades. Their employment in this sector trailed behind that in Texas and Louisiana but exceeded that in Arkansas and Mississippi. Not surprisingly, wage and salary income mirrored occupational status, with Oklahoma's black wage earners and salaried workers earning less than their counterparts in Texas and Louisiana but more than those in the other two states. Oklahoma did, however, provide the greatest opportunities for black professionals. In 1930, just over 3 percent of all black male workers and just over 7 percent of all black women in the labor force were categorized as professionals. Aside from having slightly more professional opportunities, women still confronted limits to occupational mobility. Although only 12 percent of black women workers were engaged in agriculture in 1930—the lowest percentage in all five states—77 percent worked in domestic service. In Tulsa, for example, 81 percent of the black female labor force worked in domestic or personal service.[56]

Although they represented only a small percentage of the state's total population, black residents—both urban and rural—still became targets of white violence and hostility. As early as 1901, violent whites drove African Americans out of the little town of Sapulpa. And by the early 1920s the Klan was active in almost every county in the state. In Tulsa alone, the Klan was responsible for over sixty whippings in 1922 and between forty and forty-five in 1923. The worst instance of mob violence occurred in 1921, when Tulsa whites burned and looted thirty-five blocks of "Little Africa," including Tulsa's major black business district. An elderly black couple was shot while praying. A. C. Johnson, a respected black surgeon, was shot and killed after whites promised to protect him. Official casualties, mostly black, were listed at thirty-six, but this figure probably underestimates the actual number of deaths. Migrant women from Oklahoma also remembered Henry Argo's murder. In 1930, nineteen-year-old Argo was arrested and imprisoned in Grady County for allegedly raping a white woman. An angry white mob converged on the jail with sledgehammers, poles, and other heavy objects; they eventually shot Argo through a hole they had battered into his cell.[57]

Black residents found some solidarity in numbers in urban areas like Tulsa, Oklahoma City, and Guthrie. There, in highly segregated enclaves, they established thriving black businesses and institutions. In 1913, African Americans established the state's first NAACP chapter in Oklahoma City, and a decade later, ten other chapters had been organized throughout the state. Activists in these organizations worked to defeat the state's restrictive suffrage law, which was finally struck down in 1940. Thereafter, they focused their efforts on challenging educational discrimination. As in Texas, the black press was closely aligned with the NAACP. In 1915, Roscoe Dungee founded the Black Dispatch in Oklahoma City; he earned the title "Little Caesar of Civil Rights" over the next several decades. Thus, periodic episodes of white mob violence coexisted with high levels of black activism and self-sufficiency, suggesting that in places like Texas and Oklahoma, white supremacy was less constant and monolithic. In Mississippi and Louisiana, where boundaries of race and class were firmly rooted and vigilantly patrolled, open challenges to the white power structure were immediately suppressed.[58]

During Reconstruction, Arkansas drew large numbers of African Americans from Louisiana and Mississippi with the promise of economic mobility and greater racial equality. There, "black men voted, schools were built, and an Arkansas civil rights law guaranteed equality in public places." Along the delta, white planters paid $15 to $25 a month, nearly twice the wages offered in neighboring states. But by the late nineteenth and early twentieth centuries, this promise evaporated. Planters shifted from wage labor to sharecropping; and in addition to institutionalizing this system of debt peonage, they also devised various forms of forced labor, including the convict lease system. In 1891, the legislature disfranchised African Americans by instituting a poll tax and secret ballot. This move was followed, in 1906, by the adoption of the white primary. The Separate Coach Law of 1891 mandated racial separation in railroad cars, and a second law in 1903 enforced streetcar segregation. School segregation came even earlier, in an 1873 civil rights law that mandated "equal and like accommodations" in public education. Finally, local governments enacted laws separating whites and blacks in public accommodations.[59]

Mob and police violence reinforced Arkansas's new racial hierarchy. Between 1889 and 1918, whites lynched 182 African Americans, including five women. In 1919, when destitute black sharecroppers in Phillips County formed a union, a white mob aided by the U.S. army killed and arrested its members. During the trials that followed, all-white juries sentenced twelve union members to death and sent sixty-seven to prison for one- to twenty-one-year terms. Local black leaders, working secretly with the national NAACP, eventually obtained the release of the defendants, including those who had been sentenced to death.[60]

In regard to land tenure, Arkansas came to resemble Mississippi and Louisiana. During the early twentieth century, large numbers of Arkansas's black citizens did acquire land; by 1910, 23 percent of black farmers were landowners. But by 1930, only 14 percent of all black farms were operated by owners, while 57 percent were operated by sharecroppers. Since 68 percent of the state's black population lived on farms—a rural tendency second only to that in Mississippi—high rates of tenancy take on added salience. By 1930, 70 percent of the state's black male workers and 50 percent of women workers were engaged in agricultural occupations.[61]

Dispossession accelerated with the Great Depression, prompting many to migrate to urban areas or out of the state. By 1930, 5,000 had left for Memphis, 10,000 for St. Louis, 12,000 for Chicago, and countless others to Pine Bluff, Little Rock, and other Arkansas cities. In the state's urban areas, few men found jobs in skilled or semiskilled trades. Indeed, in 1930 Arkansas ranked only slightly higher than Mississippi both in the percent of black male workers employed in this category and in wage and salary income. Women, like those in the other four states, worked in agriculture or domestic occupations. In Little Rock, for example, 74 percent of all employed black women worked in domestic or personal service.[62]

A small black professional class provided essential goods and services to black residents in cities like Little Rock, Pine Bluff, and Helena. Pine Bluff, for example, supported sixteen black groceries, seven restaurants, five saloons, four blacksmiths, and two dry-goods merchants by 1903. In Little Rock, black club women raised funds to support various charities, including the M. W. Gibbs Home for Elderly Women, and men established several fraternal orders and business-owners associations.[63]

More than any other institution, the church reflected a commitment to self-help and racial solidarity. Between 1880 and 1920, African Americans organized 607 churches in the state. Women, who dominated the membership, raised money to pay ministers and to fund church construction, programs, and charities. Churches also ran schools, partially compensating for the inferior quality of public education. By 1916, thirty black private schools operated within Arkansas, several of which trained teachers. Partly as a result of these efforts, black adult illiteracy in the state stood at 21 percent in 1930, only slightly higher than that of Texas, and 8 to 9 percent lower than that of Mississippi and Louisiana.[64]

In short, Mississippi had the worst record in terms of racial violence and blacks' standard of living. Its largely rural population lacked access to landownership and to the urban centers that provided refuge to African Americans from the other four states. For black Mississippians, migration had long been a major form of resistance to white supremacy. Arkansas and rural Louisiana, like Mississippi, held few opportunities for aspiring black landowners, but urban Louisiana—particularly New Orleans—contained a relatively large, skilled black working class with a long history of labor militancy and unionization.

In New Orleans and, to a smaller degree, Houston, black male wage earners and salary earners enjoyed relatively high levels of occupational mobility. In both places, black longshoremen and stevedores secured a high percentage of waterfront jobs, suggesting that World War II employment in the East Bay shipyards and docks may have held particular attractions for these workers as well as those in skilled and semiskilled positions. Indeed, Charles S. Johnson's survey of wartime migrants found that the majority came to the East Bay Area from Louisiana and Texas.[65]

Both Texas and Oklahoma supported large numbers of black farm owners, but their small margin of independence eroded with the depression, leading to increased urbanization. This category of workers may have viewed migration as a way to save family farms or salvage the economic autonomy that they had enjoyed in the recent past. In all five states, women worked almost exclusively in domestic service or agriculture. Limited to these occupations regardless of education or skill level, they had little reason to remain behind when employment opportunities opened up elsewhere. Indeed, in cities like Jackson, Tulsa, Little Rock,

Houston, and New Orleans, black women outnumbered men by several hundred to several thousand; these numbers indicate that the women wanted to improve their economic position, even if only slightly, by abandoning rural agricultural labor for urban domestic service.[66]

Residents of all five states lived with segregation and racial violence. However, modes of resistance varied, and Texas and Oklahoma provided blacks with the greatest opportunities for direct challenges to the racial status quo through organizations like the NAACP. In Mississippi, rural Louisiana, and Arkansas, African Americans circumvented white economic and social control by maintaining independent churches, schools, businesses and, in some cases, whole towns. A common theme, however, was commitment to racial solidarity and self-help. In the Age of Jim Crow, African Americans in all five states created separate worlds that insulated them from the hardships and humiliations of white supremacy. All African Americans inherited a cultural tradition of resistance to enforced dependency—a tradition revealed in efforts to preserve families, assist neighbors, acquire land, and create independent institutions. A final connecting theme was that of migration. Leaving one plantation for another, moving from farms to cities, abandoning exploitative jobs, or migrating from the South to the North or West were common, historically rooted forms of resistance. Faith McAllister, a migrant woman from Louisiana, recalled that "mother didn't stay in one place very long. She was always trying to better herself. The whole family was like that. They were all hard workers and always tried to better themselves."[67]

The Black World

While all African Americans experienced the sting of Jim Crow and incorporated various modes of resistance into their daily lives, black communities were not without internal, class-related divisions. These divisions not only produced class tensions but also influenced occupational choices, gender relations, forms of individual and collective resistance, modes of worship and recreation, and styles of leadership. Most migrants, including the women in my sample, came from working-class backgrounds. The stories that follow, drawn from oral histories of former migrants, thus reveal common characteristics of southern black working-class life in the years before World War II. They also provide insight into the values and skills that migrants acquired from their elders and used to create new communities out West.[68]

The majority of the women in my sample were born between 1900 and

Table 1. Percent and Number of Births of Migrants between 1900 and 1933

1900–1911	19%	9
1912–1923	66%	31
1924–1933	15%	7
Total	100%	47

Table 2. Migrants' Childhood Residence, by Place

City	38%	19
Town	34%	17
Farm	28%	14
Total	100%	50

1933; the highest concentration of births occurred between 1912 and 1924 (see Table 1). Most (72 percent) were raised in cities and towns (see Table 2). Among the fathers of this nonrural group, 28 percent worked as skilled craftsmen and 14 percent as professionals, semiprofessionals, or clerical workers. However, the majority (58 percent) worked in domestic and service occupations or as unskilled or semiskilled laborers and factory operatives (see Table 3).

Despite relatively high proportions of skilled craftsmen and professionals among male family heads, these families were far from economically secure. A higher-than-average percentage of nonfarm mothers (80 percent) worked for wages as domestics, laundresses, seamstresses, and caterers. The remaining 20 percent were described by their daughters as housewives (see Table 4).

Only 28 percent of migrant women in my sample—a much smaller percentage than in the southern black population as a whole—spent the major portion of their childhoods on farms. Of this number, roughly half belonged to families that owned their own farms, and a third belonged to those that rented. Nearly 60 percent of male farm heads worked seasonally for wages to augment their farm income, while most women worked full-time on the farm tending large kitchen gardens and small livestock; caring for children; and canning, sewing, cooking, and cleaning. Women and girls performed heavy farm work only when male hands were short and the family could not afford to hire extra labor (see Table 5).

Most migrant women in my sample (81 percent) were raised in two-parent families consisting of biological parents, married relatives, or a biological parent and step-parent. The remainder were raised by a single

Professional worker or business owner	8%	3
Craftsman, artisan, or skilled tradesman	28%	10
Service worker (nondomestic)	19%	7
Clerical worker	6%	2
Unskilled or semiskilled laborer, factory operative	39%	14
Total	100%	36

Table 3. Percent and Number of Migrant Fathers' Nonfarm Occupations

Schoolteacher	6%	2
Unskilled or semiskilled laborer, factory operative	6%	2
Laundress	6%	2
Domestic servant	37%	13
Cateress	14%	5
Seamstress	11%	4
Housewife	20%	7
Total	100%	35

Table 4. Percent and Number of Migrant Mothers' Nonfarm Occupations

mother (13 percent) or a single female relative (6 percent). These figures conform to the 1930 census, which indicates that 81 percent of all black families were headed by two parents and 19 percent were female-headed. The figures for white families were 88 percent and 12 percent, respectively; higher levels of widowhood and absent husbands among black families account for nearly all of the 7 percent difference. Indeed, black female heads were less likely to be single (as opposed to widowed or married with an absent husband) than were white female heads. Racial discrimination forced black men to take jobs that lowered their life expectancies and took them far from home for extended periods of time. This, rather than the abstract notion of a black "matriarchy" or family "disorganization," produced the slightly higher levels of single-parent households among black families.[69]

In summary, the majority of migrant women in my sample came either from families that either owned or rented farms or from town- or city-

Table 5. Percent and Number of Migrant Fathers' Farm Occupations

Farm owner	50%	7
Farm renter	36%	5
Farm laborer (sharecropper or migrant farm worker)	14%	2
Total	100%	14

Table 6. Percent and Number of Family Types among Migrants

Two-parent (biological mother and father)	66%	31
Two-parent extended	15%	7
Single-parent (biological mother)	13%	6
Single female relative (aunt or grandmother)	6%	3
Total	100%	47

dwelling families that lived comfortably off the income of two wage-earning parents. In both farm and nonfarm settings, two-parent families were the norm. Urban and rural nonfarm families outnumbered farm families, and even those with farms commonly relied on nonfarm wage work to supplement income. Nonfarm families also claimed a greater-than-average number of skilled craftsmen and professionals among male family heads. Migrant women who came from these homes enjoyed relatively high levels of education and geographic stability and tended to marry men with higher-than-average skill levels. These findings contradict studies that have portrayed migrants as disoriented peasants who lacked the resources and skills to survive in an urban environment.[70]

Migrant women describe their parents' relationships as complementary and egalitarian. Unlike black middle-class women, whose roles more closely approximated those of white middle-class women, working-class women made essential and highly visible contributions to family income. Unlike the very poor, they enjoyed more formal education, were tied to families that had the resources to offer protection in the event of domestic violence, and married men whose status as "breadwinner" was not continually undermined by harsh economic conditions.[71]

Most working-class mothers, as their daughters recall, formed partnerships with respectful, loving men who needed and valued their wives' expertise. Migrant women's descriptions of their early family lives provide

Professional worker or business owner	7%	3
Musician	7%	3
Skilled craftsman, artisan, skilled tradesman	16%	7
Service worker (nondomestic)	16%	7
Clerical worker	5%	2
Unskilled or semiskilled laborer, factory operative	33%	14
Farm owner and renter	7%	3
Sharecropper or migrant farm laborer	9%	4
Total	100%	43

Table 7. Migrant Husbands' Premigration Occupations

evidence of shared parental authority, where both parents commanded respect, enforced discipline, contributed to family income, and taught spiritual and moral values. Such marriages were solid and enduring, strengthened by shared accomplishments, spiritual values, and economic necessity.

Most migrant women were born in their mother's or grandmother's homes, with a midwife there to assist their delivery. An expectant mother often returned to her mother's home and stayed until a month or more after giving birth. Ethel Phillips, who had moved to a small Louisiana town after she married, returned to her parents' farm to have each of her children. Her mother, a midwife, delivered each child and saw to it that Ethel rested for a month following the births. It was customary to keep both mother and child inside and out of daylight for a month and to wrap the new mother's stomach with cloth to help her abdominal muscles retract.[72]

Ethel Tillman's first child was born at home, and her next three at the house of a midwife, who kept both mother and child for ten days after the birth.[73] Sara Brooks described the process this way: "And then when you having a baby in the country you had to stay in a dark room a whole month 'cause no light could come in there on the baby. Then when that baby was a month old, you took it outdoors. You take that baby and wrap it up and you go all the way around the house with that baby, and then you bring the baby back in the house. It's free to go then anywhere."[74]

For rural migrant women, home usually consisted of a wood frame structure with a metal roof and a broad porch. Depending on their resources, a young couple started out with as few as two rooms: one for cooking, eating, and socializing, and the other for sleeping. As the family grew, more rooms were added. Sara Brooks's father started with a two-room cabin and ended up with a large house that contained a kitchen, dining room, company room, and three bedrooms. Few families, however, had indoor plumbing or electricity. City people also added on as their resources grew. Lucille Moss, who was raised by her aunt and uncle in New Orleans, has early memories of a two-room house that her uncle gradually enlarged. He received help from neighbors, whose labor was sustained by her aunt's cooking and her uncle's promise to return the favor.[75]

Children were quickly integrated into the economic, social, and spiritual life of the home; at an early age they learned the virtues of hard work, charity, obedience, and family loyalty. Most migrant women describe deep attachments to their parents, despite memories of the harsh punishments used to extract obedience, and despite a near-absence of physical affection in the parent-child relationship. While secure in the knowledge that they were loved, members of this generation were linked to their elders by reciprocal obligation rather than emotion. "My parents sacrificed so much for us" is a common theme in the oral histories. In contrast, bonds between siblings were more overtly affectionate and playful. And since older children took much of the responsibility for child care, bonds between siblings were frequently as strong as those between parents and children.

In both nuclear and extended families, the home was a center of social activity. Lucille Moss remembers that her childhood home was always full of friends and family. Her aunt's clients, who came to buy her handmade wedding gowns and shrouds, also filled the home with their comings and goings. Ethel Tillman remembers Sunday dinners that rotated among two aunts and her mother. Louisa Hall, whose father's sister and brother lived with her family on the same farm but in their own homes, was just as close to her aunt as to her own mother.[76]

When they were not working for wages, family members were involved in all aspects of farming, livestock raising, food preserving, cooking, cleaning, home repair, furniture making, gardening, quilting, mending, sewing, baking, washing, and numerous small business ventures, such as dressmaking, catering, millinery, and home laundry. Survival depended on the industry of each family member and on making the most of every resource and opportunity.

Children as young as four and five helped clean the house and yard and gather wood chips for the fire. By age twelve, and sometimes earlier, girls assumed adult workloads. Ethel Phillips, who was small for her age, stood on a wooden crate to cook meals on the woodstove for her entire family. Afterward, she supervised chores and minded her younger siblings. By age twelve she had also learned how to make her own clothes, preserve food, quilt, and perform all types of farm work. Henrietta Bolden grew up helping her mother do day work, and by junior high she had her own evening job washing dishes for a white woman. At fifteen, after completing the last grade of school offered to black children in her town, she went out to work full-time at a dollar and a half a week. During her time off, she "never sat down with idle hands. Always was mending, piecing a quilt, or crocheting." Other migrant women laughingly recall times when they tried to get out of household chores by feigning sickness or doing a careless job. These transgressions of the work ethic brought harsh punishment and provoked uncomfortable levels of guilt, because their labor was essential to the family's well-being.[77]

Working-class families, who lived uncomfortably close to poverty, were as devoted to community service as the black middle class and the elite, but without condescension or a preoccupation with racial uplift. For this group, charity was a matter of economic survival, not a means of social control.[78] Louise Steele, raised by a grandmother who ran a home laundry, helped with ironing after school and accompanied her grandmother on visits to sick neighbors and relatives. As soon as school was out for the summer, Louise spent each day "waiting on" her grandmother's infirm niece—a job she learned to regard as a Christian duty.[79]

Louisa Hall, who at age eleven was chopping and hoeing in the fields, going to school, and helping with housework, was already learning lessons about the virtues of hard work, frugality, and sharing. "Father said, 'Always think about your needs, not your wants, because if you get everything you want, you won't have anything for your needs.' " To this end, her family stretched every resource, wasted nothing, and turned over any surplus to less fortunate neighbors. She and her siblings wore clothes stitched from sugar and flour sacks; when these garments were outgrown, they were passed on to other children. And each week her mother "tithed" a few dozen eggs for poorer people in their community. Louisa learned that if she did not have anything to share, she could share her time. "I learned all of that growing up, and that stayed with me throughout the years." Having given in this manner, she could accept similar gifts in times of need without feeling like an object of pity or embarrassment. Thus, charity was more than a Christian duty. It was also essential to individual and collective survival. Using a biblical passage to stress the importance of placing one's faith in a Christian community, Louisa put it this way: "Peter walked on the water, and when he began to think of himself, he started to sink." Such work in the service of the family or broader community gave young women a sense of independence and competency that partially offset the pain and humiliation of racism.[80]

Interdependence and reciprocity, fostered in the home and community, coexisted with a fierce desire for economic independence from white people. Willa Suddeth, raised on a family-owned farm outside Shreveport, Louisiana, still recalls the conviction in her father's voice as he repeatedly told her to "own your own." She went on to reflect that "we had our own churches, stores, schools, land. Grandfather and his brother went to great lengths to buy their own land, and it's still in the family."[81]

Independence from white people and interdependence within the black community were sustained by familial and social networks. Both women and men used these connections to find employment and generate income. Women, however, prided themselves on their ability to create, sustain, and extend relationships beyond the workplace. By watching their mothers, migrant women learned to create the networks that were indispensable to personal well-being, feeding and clothing families, finding help with children, obtaining medical advice, solving problems with spouses and children, adjudicating neighborhood conflicts, and maintaining churches, schools, and charitable institutions.[82]

Lessons on how to build these relationships began in the home, through the give-and-take between female relatives and family friends. During the winter months, Willa Suddeth's mother hosted quilting parties where she and her friends made quilts for poorer families while discussing everything from canning to voter registration. Willa recalls how she learned to value and cultivate female friendships by observing these women.[83]

Carmelia Chauvin and Cornelia Duvernay, twins raised with five other siblings in New Orleans, had a mother who brought neighbors together with her cooking. She would make stuffed crabs, fried fish and chicken, gumbo, and potato salad, and serve them to friends in their backyard for a small fee. Those who could not pay, however, were never turned away. The twins, who decorated the yard with Chinese paper lanterns and served food, remember how these social events also helped their family survive the depression.[84] Similarly, Ethel Tillman's great-aunt used her knowledge of folk healing to create mutual-aid relationships with neighbors, providing essential medical services in exchange for chickens, eggs, vegetables, and other barter.[85]

The home was also where migrant women learned how to negotiate the white world. Lucille Moss grew up knowing "that white people treated black people wrong and that we were as good as anyone else." Her uncle would sit her on the front porch and tell her to be careful of white folks, because "while you're sleeping, they're reading. And when they come to you, they have thought over how to use you. And the best thing is, don't lie to them. Whatever comes, tell them the truth about it." However, if someone could come to harm if you told the truth, her uncle said it was best to feign ignorance. This was not the same as lying. Indeed, he considered it another form of the truth—one that was grounded in relational rather than legalistic ethics. He went on to tell Lucille, "Never hold a conversation with a white person if it's someone to harm. It's better to say 'I don't know.' There are some white people who will try to make you tell, but you just continue on saying 'I don't know, I don't know.' And that way you'll be a whole person, a grown woman or a grown man telling the truth."[86]

Others learned about white people by overhearing adult conversations or by direct experience mediated by a more experienced relative. Theresa Waller, who was raised in Houston's largely black Fifth Ward, remembers listening to grownups talk about segregation and racial violence long before she had direct experience with either. She distinctly recalled one conversation between her mother and some neighbor ladies during which her mother expressed fear for her male children, "because naturally menfolk have a real hard time in very segregated areas." The twins, Carmelia and Cornelia, do not remember learning about segregation directly; it was something they absorbed on shopping trips down to Canal Street with their mother or on bus rides with their siblings. Few women remember abrupt shocks—painful testimony to the care adults took in introducing children to the rules. Humiliation and anger, however, were inevitable and lasting products of the learning process. Theresa Waller put it this way: "You just don't know what it is. They would try and make you feel like you weren't human. They'd say, 'Get out of my way,' and you would have to get off the sidewalk—even for children in certain areas. And if you didn't, they would knock you off."[87]

For many migrant women, this pain and humiliation reached almost unbearable levels during adolescence, a time when their adult responsibilities brought them into closer contact with the white world and away from the safety of their families. At the same time, a growing sense of sexual danger accompanied their physical maturation. For reasons that remained unclear, men were to be avoided.

Most migrant women, and their mothers before them, knew very little about sexual intimacy and reproduction until they married and became pregnant. Young women were closely watched by female relatives and were warned, in cryptic terms, not to bring shame on the family. Lucille Moss remembered her aunt telling her, "Any boy touch you, you just let me know. You don't do that. You can be flying if you want, but if you come here and you can't see your big toe, you'll get it. Outdoors you'll go. And don't you think I'll make a boy marry you. Outdoors you'll go. When you lie down in bed with a man, those things happen."

Lucille understood little of what her aunt told her, but was frightened enough to decide that she "didn't want no man" touching her. After a three-year courtship, she married a jazz musician whom she had met at a church picnic. He was forty-one, and fortunately "so soft and kind and gentle." After she became pregnant, she finally learned what her aunt meant about not being able to see her big toe. Similarly, Sara Brooks never kissed a man until the night her suitor asked for her hand in marriage, and she had no idea what to expect on her wedding night. That first sexual encounter turned out to be "the worst experience I ever seen in my life. Now that's the truth!"[88]

There were exceptions, however. Lovie McIntosh had a baby by a minister's son who lived up the street from her family, but she refused to marry him because she did not want anyone to feel sorry for her. Instead, she went on to business school while her mother and grandmother helped with the baby. Just as she finished, she met and married a man whom she felt confident would make a good husband. Lovie's mother had similarly refused to marry Lovie's father. He was going away to college, and she did not want to leave her family. They both married other people, but Lovie remained close to her biological father; she lived with him and her stepmother for most of her childhood.[89]

At twenty—the average age at first marriage—many young women were still content to be with their families and had to be pushed out of the house. Theresa Waller, who at twenty was "like a five-year-old girl [when it came to] the facts of life," felt pressured into "a marriage which should not have happened." Ethel Phillips, who married at nineteen after a year-long courtship, moved onto her new husband's farm, which was an hour's distance from her parents. She cried and moaned for several days;

			Table 8. Religious Affiliation of Migrants
Baptist	56%	28	
C.M.E.	14%	7	
A.M.E.	10%	5	
Catholic	12%	6	
Church of God in Christ	4%	2	
No affiliation	4%	2	
Total	100%	50	

in response, her husband told her not to waste her time, because she was there to stay. For many migrant women, the difficult transition to marriage and motherhood would coincide with World War II and their migration to California—a convergence of major life events that made the migration experience all the more powerful.[90]

From infancy, migrant women were integrated into the life of the black church, their second home. This experience was shared by most African Americans. However, churches that served the working class and the poor were more central to the spiritual, cultural, and economic well-being of their congregants. In addition to generating funds to help the needy, churches functioned as extended families—arenas for the exchange of resources. Moreover, working-class churches embraced a distinct style of worship, placing less emphasis on "correct" and "restrained" conduct and more on the liberating experience of the service.[91]

Without exception, all of the women in my sample felt that the church was central to the formation of their characters and values, and they attended services at least once a week throughout their childhoods. The church not only filled the community's spiritual and charitable needs but also provided numerous opportunities for female leadership, although the forms such leadership took were less individualistic and hierarchical than those granted to men. And given that the women in my sample were predominantly Baptist and Methodist and adhered to strict prohibitions against dancing, gambling, drinking, and other forms of entertainment, church provided the major social outlet for young and old alike (see Table 8). Even among Catholics, home and church were the primary centers of social life. Louise Steele's grandmother spoke for other women of her generation when she told Louise that young ladies did not participate in social events outside of church.

Being a good Christian was a central concern of working-class individuals, and it required active membership in a Christian community. Indeed, many women recall their conversion experience—which was necessary for church membership and usually coincided with adolescence—as the most powerful moment of their lives. For example, following months of emotional introspection, Ethel Phillips "accepted Jesus" as her "personal savior" and left the mourner's bench to join the ranks of the "saved." Her membership was celebrated by total immersion in a lake with a large group of fellow converts.[92]

To remain a member in good standing, one had to attend church regularly. At a minimum, this meant weekly attendance at a church service lasting from Sunday morning to Sunday evening. However, most families that lived reasonably close to church also attended weekday services, prayer meetings, Bible study, and one or more board meetings. Lacey Gray's family donated the land on which their church was built, so getting there was simply a matter of walking across a pasture. Her father, the head deacon, bought the grape juice for communion. Her mother, a stewardess, baked the communion bread and washed and ironed the white cloth bands that the men and women wore when they took the Lord's Supper.[93] Lucille Moss similarly remembers the church as a big part of her youth. She attended mass every day at school and also on Sunday. And "if I didn't go to church, I didn't do anything. No jump-rope, no playing records. Could only sit." School, she said, only taught her how to read and write, but church and her aunt and uncle taught her right from wrong.[94] Similarly, Louise Steele remembers attending Baptist services that lasted "for hours and hours." Children sat with the adults, she recalled, and were spanked if they wiggled.[95]

In churches, migrant women learned a particular style of leadership—one that valued individual strength in the context of collective action and group harmony. for example, Louisa Hall remembers how women who worked behind the scenes, never calling attention to their contributions or "placing themselves above others," gained the respect and admiration of other church members.[96] In the same manner, Olive Blue watched her mother and other church women quietly raise money, bring in new members, care for sick parishioners, and pool skills and resources for the benefit of all. These church women, she recalls, "knew everyone and were always linking people together."[97]

School was the final part of the triad that formed the foundation of migrant women's childhoods. Working-class parents made great sacrifices to educate their children—particularly daughters, whose labor did not

			Table 9. Formal Education among Migrants
Grades 1–6	6.5%	3	
Grades 7–11 (no high school degree)	22.0%	10	
High school degree	41.0%	19	
Business school	6.5%	3	
Some college (no degree)	11.0%	5	
College degree	13.0%	6	
Total	100.0%	46	

command as much as sons', and who were seen as more vulnerable to sexual exploitation in the few jobs open to black women. Parents thus tried to keep their daughters in school as long as possible, often building their own schoolhouses and drawing on the resources of numerous relatives to do so.[98] In my sample, 94 percent completed seventh grade, and 72 percent finished high school.

The most frequent explanation for not completing all twelve grades was that there were no black high schools close to home. Indeed, of those who graduated, 16 percent boarded out with other families for those four years.[99] Nearly 25 percent of my sample attended some college, typically at all-black teachers' training schools, such as Prairie View in Texas. Of that number, 13 percent received degrees and went on to teach. Teaching, one of the only occupations open to educated black women, paid very little but kept young, unmarried daughters in their own communities, where they were safe from white men and would never have to serve a white woman.

Since many working-class mothers worked in white people's homes, it was a point of pride to protect their daughters from the same fate. Willa Suddeth, whose family moved to Denver before coming to California, once wanted to earn money baby-sitting for a white family. Her parents told her that she would never under any circumstances lift a hand for a white person as long as she was in their care. Faith McAllister, raised by a single mother who worked as a domestic, never helped out because "mother wanted something better for me." After finishing three years of high school, she married and went to work as a waitress in a black eating establishment.[100]

Henrietta McAlister, raised by an industrious widowed mother who worked for white families, finished high school and teachers' college in Jackson, Mississippi. In Jackson, "mother had a friend who kept an eye on me and saw to it that I toed the line. It was almost like being home." When Henrietta finished, she returned to her hometown to teach, accepting a prestigious but low-paying position. But such attainment meant little to white people. One afternoon, while walking home from downtown, Henrietta was stopped by her mother's employer. The woman asked Henrietta if she made good coconut pies, because she wanted to show up a friend who was coming for dinner and always bragged about her cook's pies. Henrietta responded, "No, Mrs. Cooper," but then used a simple "yes" and "no" to some following questions. The woman asked Henrietta where she had picked up that "Yankee talk" and let Henrietta know that "I wasn't to yes and no her."[101]

Most women did end up working for employers such as Mrs. Cooper. And even those who escaped domestic service—like Henrietta McAlister— were discouraged by the lack of alternatives that provided a living wage and decent working conditions. Such limited options were particularly unpleasant for relatively well educated working-class women, whose dreams had been neither completely dampened by harsh economic realities, like those faced by sharecropping and migrant farm families, nor fulfilled by the means available to relatively affluent parents. Daughters of the working class, poised on the edge of adulthood with relatively high expectations, eagerly sought the opportunities generated by the war-driven economy of the early 1940s.

In short, migrant women's stories reveal a history of resistance to economic marginalization and dependency. The drive for self-determination and the skills required to achieve independence were passed from one generation to the next. Learning from their mothers and other female relatives, migrant women mastered a series of tasks that were essential to family and community survival.

In his recent book The Promised Land, Nicholas Lemann revived the "culture of poverty" thesis, arguing that sharecropping fostered an "ethic of dependency" among poor, black southerners. This ethic of dependency— characterized by substance abuse, out-of-wedlock pregnancy, a predatory mentality, and the lack of a work ethic—supposedly came North with southern migrants and ultimately contributed to the formation of an urban "underclass."[102]

While few of the women in my sample were sharecroppers, most had neighbors and family members who were. Indeed, a majority of migrant women were only a generation or two removed from sharecropping.

Thus, the values they acquired from their elders—family loyalty, frugality, self-sufficiency, cooperation, reciprocity, and respect for education—came directly from sharecropping roots. Their parents and grandparents, demonstrating a characteristic desire for independence, scraped and saved for their own farms or moved to towns and cities in search of wage-based employment. In turn, migrant women would leave the South in search of greater opportunities out West. Instead of transplanting an ethic of dependency, they would arrive with a hopeful determination to create better lives for themselves and their families.

Chapter Two . . . . . .

. . . . To Make the Two Worlds One

Migration from
the South to the
San Francisco
East Bay Area

Young adulthood, if we return
to the safe, small towns of our imagination, brings to mind images of
healthy, well-loved adolescents eagerly advancing toward promising futures. But this image, like the one of small-town childhood that opened
Chapter 1, tells us little about how young black women experienced the
transition to adulthood, revealing instead a white, economically privileged, and mostly male view of the world. Generations of African American women tell us as much, describing their transitions as a coming to
terms with limits. Maya Angelou's experience at her high school graduation illustrates one such passage. A white school administrator gave the
commencement address, praising the black graduates for their athletic
abilities. For Angelou the message was clear: "The White kids were going
to have a chance to become Galileos and Madame Curies and Edisons and
Gauguins, and our boys (the girls weren't even in on it) would try to be
Jesse Owenses and Joe Louises." She and her classmates, painfully deflated
during what should have been a celebration of their accomplishments,
learned that "We were maids and farmers, handymen and washerwomen,
and anything higher that we aspired to was farcical and presumptuous."[1]

However, the migrant women whose story is told in these pages reached
young adulthood during an extraordinary time. By 1940, almost two
thousand miles from Laurel, Pelican, and Tupelo, war industrialists with
huge defense contracts were transforming California into a virtual Canaan

for both skilled and unskilled workers. As wartime labor demands grew, gender and racial barriers to industrial employment fell, providing unprecedented economic opportunities for black and female workers. Migrant women, who were confronting futures limited by Jim Crow, seized this rare historical advantage—one that promised to demolish the limits imposed on the lives of their mothers and grandmothers. They would learn, however, that the promise was imperfect: it raised new, equally painful barriers in place of the old. These barriers will be discussed in following chapters. Why and how women migrated to California—their dreams and expectations—are the subjects of this chapter.

The West's economic boom, a primary source of migrant women's expectations for a better life, was fueled by World War II defense spending. Between 1941 and 1945 the federal government invested over $70 billion in California aircraft, shipbuilding, food processing, clothing manufacturing, and other war-related industries. The San Francisco Bay Area, which received nearly $5 billion in government shipbuilding contracts, rapidly became the nation's largest shipbuilding center. The East Bay, home to twelve ship-repair and -building industries, was the locus of Bay Area expansion, employing the majority of the area's shipyard workers during the course of the war.[2]

Richmond's Kaiser company, the largest shipbuilding operation in the country, employed over 90,634 people at its peak. Its employees, motivated by patriotism and relatively high wages, produced over 727 cargo ships by the war's end; one Liberty ship was assembled in a record-breaking four-day period. Kaiser's pioneering application of mass-production technology to shipbuilding allowed it to substitute unskilled labor for skilled workers. These innovations, along with extraordinary levels of worker productivity, slashed production costs and time. Because they coincided with with acute labor shortages, such changes also had positive implications for women and other workers who had traditionally been excluded from relatively high-paying blue-collar jobs.[3]

The Kaiser yards, along with numerous supporting service and defense industries, transformed Richmond into a boomtown within a two-year period. A quiet town of 23,642 in 1940, Richmond housed 100,000 by 1943. The chamber of commerce, which described Richmond as the "city that grew from an old Mexican rancho" into a self-advertised "arsenal of democracy," praised Henry Kaiser as "America's miracle man"—a "forward looking [citizen] of the highest type who guided [the city] constantly toward the star of destiny." This star, whose brightness was sustained by an ever-expanding number of workers, drew African Americans from the South, increasing Richmond's black population from 270 in 1940 to 10,000 in 1945.[4]

Vallejo, just north of Richmond, housed Mare Island Naval Shipyard, another major shipbuilding center of the East Bay. However, unlike the Richmond yards, Mare Island served as an assembly and launching point for ships that were fabricated at the Rocky Mountain Arsenal in Denver, Colorado, and moved by railroad to the East Bay.[5] Still, Mare Island's labor demands were prodigious, increasing from 5,000 in 1940 to 45,000 in 1942. As a consequence, Vallejo's tiny population, which before the war was only slightly larger than Richmond's, increased to 100,000 by 1943. Its black population, which stood at 438 in 1940, increased tenfold during the war years.[6]

Oakland was the third star in the East Bay's shipbuilding crescent; the city contained Moore Dry Dock Company Shipyard, a naval supply center, a major port of embarkation, an army base, an airport, and several food processing plants that were vital to the war effort because of Allied reliance upon American food supplies.[7] Moreover, Oakland was the East Bay's largest city and the nearest urban center to major naval installations at Treasure Island and Alameda. Even as Richmond, Berkeley, and Vallejo grew, Oakland absorbed the majority of newcomers—black and white—and served as an important commercial and entertainment center for the entire East Bay. By 1944, Oakland's population stood at 345,345, up 47,182 from 1940. During the same period, the city's black population grew from 8,462 to 21,770.[8]

While this economic boom produced attractive opportunities for migrant women, it was not the only factor contributing to their decision to leave home. The South, too, experienced war-related economic growth concentrated in the defense centers of Mobile, Alabama; Pascagoula, Mississippi; Brunswick, Georgia; Beaumont-Orange, Texas; Norfolk, Virginia; Knoxville, Tennessee; Charleston, South Carolina; and Key West, Florida. However, African Americans were largely excluded from skilled, relatively high-paying jobs within defense industries. For example, the Gulf Shipbuilding Corporation, in Mobile, Alabama, had a total labor force of 10,505 by September 1942, but there were only twenty African Americans on its payroll. Although Gulf eventually hired more black workers, few if any held skilled positions. Similarly, an ordnance plant between Shreveport and Minden, Louisiana, employed about five thousand mostly female workers by 1942, reserving only four hundred unskilled jobs for African Americans.[9]

Finally, increased population growth in the South's defense centers heightened competition over city services and exposed the inefficiencies of segregation. Whites who were already afraid that blacks were being infected with democratic ideals adopted a violent offensive against real and imagined black competition. For example, when the Alabama Dry-dock Company upgraded twelve black workers to skilled positions in late spring of 1943, white employees—male and female—brutally attacked their black co-workers. The riot ended when U.S. army troops were called in to restore order, but many black workers were too frightened to return to the job. Others returned to work only after the company built separate shipways that isolated black workers from whites. One worker, who left Alabama for the East Bay following the riot, commented,

> I was working as a laborer in the shipyard in Mobile, Alabama, Ship-building and Dry [Dock] Company. I had worked there only a short time, then they had this riot there and a lot of colored workers got beat up and I was afraid to go back in the yard. The white men rode around in cars at night and threw rocks in our houses. I never had a thought about coming out here before, but the day after the riot, I said to my wife, "We can't stay here any more; we have got to get out of here." We didn't know where we would go. Some of the other Negroes said they were going to the West Coast, so we decided that we would go there too. . . . I didn't even wait for my check.[10]

The war highlighted racial tensions everywhere, but particularly in the South. For migrant women, as for most black southerners, the war exposed the contradictions between what America claimed to be and what it actually was. Jim Crow's strictures and a future limited to domestic service or, at best, teaching in an underfunded, segregated school appeared all the more odious during a so-called war for democracy. And while many whites did become more tolerant, most did not, as a result, racial violence increased sharply. Few migrant women expected a complete absence of racial discrimination out West, but most did anticipate fewer of the divisions that separated white and black worlds in the South.

Not all migrant women viewed California as a permanent refuge from Jim Crow. Some came to make money so that they could return to the South and buy property or start a business. Their goal was economic independence, a traditional means of buffering Jim Crow's impact without undergoing a dramatic separation with the past. But whether permanent or temporary, migration was a means to the same end—a way to heal the more painful divisions between white and black worlds.[11]

However, the confines of Jim Crow and the economic boom in California only partially explain why this particular group of women migrated when they did. One equally important factor was that they had reached a stage in their life cycles where they felt the limits of Jim Crow very keenly. In combination with their working-class economic resources and their consciousness of the historical and religious significance of migration, this factor gave additional weight to their decision to leave. By 1940, the average age of migrant women in my sample was twenty-three. Over half of all women were between sixteen and twenty-five years of age, a period of major life transition: most were finishing school, leaving home for the first time, holding down a first full-time job, marrying, or giving birth to a first child. These life events simultaneously heightened and dampened aspirations, sharpening the dissonance between white and black worlds.[12]

Lacey Gray married in 1937 at age twenty-one and had her first child in 1939. Her husband worked twelve hours a day at a planing mill, and she took washing and ironing into their two-room, company-owned house. Even with two wage earners, the family barely made ends meet, so Lacey moved back with her parents while her husband took on a better-paying job in a distant southern city. This type of familial separation, which stemmed directly from discriminatory employment practices and was quite common among working-class blacks, forced many wage earners to spend months away from their families. Even farm families typically sent one or more male members in search of seasonal nonfarm employment to supplement family income. But even these jobs paid inferior wages and made it necessary for workers to maintain two households during periods of separation. These prolonged separations were particularly painful for young, recently married couples and for new parents. Thus, for Lacey and her family, migration to California promised family reunification as well as freedom from Jim Crow.[13]

As a young single woman entering the workforce for the first time, Theresa Waller was similarly dissatisfied with the limits imposed by Jim Crow. Theresa was bright and ambitious and had wanted to go on to college after graduating from high school. Instead, she went to work as a domestic servant to help support her parents and siblings. For Theresa and many young women like her, California represented the opportunity to escape domestic service and the chronic economic hardship that no amount of hard work and thriftiness could erase. Later Theresa summed up her feelings with simple eloquence: "I wanted to get away from home and have an aim in life. Wanted to do something good and big, but couldn't name it." Just as the war started, Theresa married a man with matching ambition, and she moved west within months of the marriage.[14]

Migrant women like Lacey and Theresa were able to leave the South because of their demographic and economic position. As working-class women, they aspired to more than they could hope to attain in their hometowns. But unlike poorer women, they and their families had the resources to leave. Both male and female migrants had more years of formal education and were more highly skilled and more likely to own property than were poorer black southerners. But unlike black professionals or business owners, members of the working class had fewer reasons to remain. They had achieved a tenuous economic security at great cost, and they viewed migration as a better investment than remaining behind.[15] Moreover, migrants were young. Family farms, many of which are still owned by migrant women and their siblings, remained in the care of older relatives and younger siblings. Migrants frequently sent money home, adding to, rather than diminishing, the family trust. In time many older relatives followed, but the initial migration was primarily a youthful one.[16]

The decision to migrate also had a communal, socioreligious component. Migrant women shared a cultural experience organized around themes of collective destiny, flight from bondage, and liberation. They grew up hearing Old Testament references to Exodus and deliverance, standard themes in black religious oratory and sacred music. Family histories, passed by elders to each new generation, tied these biblical references to individual and collective acts of liberation; migrant women all recount stories of ancestors or folk heroes who refused to stay within the physical, spiritual, or intellectual boundaries of slavery or Jim Crowism. Flight or migration thus had spiritual, communal, and liberation components that were unique to black history and culture. By virtue of this tradition, migrant women had cultural permission to migrate.[17]

Woven in and around these larger economic, social, demographic, and religious forces shaping women's decisions to migrate were varied, highly individual reasons for leaving. Personal transitions—a death in the family, a farm foreclosure, sickness, divorce, or loss of property in a flood or other natural disaster—were equally central to the migratory drama. If we pause to reflect on our own reasons for leaving or staying in a certain place, we recognize that our comings and goings occur within a larger social, economic, and political context. But they are also shaped by our own individual needs and desires, which commingle with these larger forces.

The most dramatic and tragic personal story, and one that also illuminates strands of the cultural and spiritual meaning of black migration, belongs to Louisa Hall. As a young married woman living in the South, she watched everything she and her husband had worked for wash away in a flood. She and other townspeople found refuge at a hilltop church, living there for over two weeks with nothing more than the clothes they were wearing. Her house was underwater for a month.

Although she had never learned to swim and had always been afraid of water, she volunteered to go by boat to salvage the life savings of an elderly couple who had lived on the upper floor of one of the still-flooded homes. They accepted her offer, and after she stepped into the upstairs window, Louisa miraculously found the old coat whose lining held the money. This deed became a life-orienting symbol of transcendence, a moral compass directing her to serve others in her own time of need.

After the flood, which coincided with the wartime economic boom in California, she and her husband moved to the West to start new lives and forget their losses. However, the flood and their subsequent migration— events of enormous personal significance made all the more powerful by the symbolic centrality of suffering and redemption to the black experience—continued to shape their lives for years to come.[18]

Olive Blue's story similarly illustrates the confluence of external forces and personal events in the decision to migrate. Olive gave birth to her first child in New Orleans just before her beloved father died. Her husband, who had been drafted, was at Pearl Harbor when it was bombed; fortunately, he survived, but he was not home to comfort his young wife, now a mother for the first time. For Olive, migration to California, where an aunt offered support, promised both a good job and relief from painful memories.[19]

Migration, then, had different meanings for individual women. The desire to escape the strictures of Jim Crow, to improve one's economic position, to make the two worlds one, were major themes in women's stories but were articulated in highly personal terms; such themes were interwoven with the love of one's children, the desire to preserve the family unit, the haunting recognition that there must be more to life, and the flight from suffering and loss.

Having established why this particular group of women became migrants, I can now discuss how they found out about the opportunities in the Bay Area, decided to leave, and prepared for the journey. Most black migrants, including the women in my sample, came to the Bay Area between 1942 and 1945, and 1945 was the peak year of black migration. Compared with white migrants, who began to arrive in early 1941 and whose numbers peaked in 1943, black migrants were relative latecomers.

This lag in black migration—a product of discriminatory union membership policies and industry recruitment and hiring practices—ended only when labor shortages and growing African American protest forced unions, industry, and the federal government to make concessions to black workers.[20]

By 1942, as Bay Area defense industries were beginning to hire large numbers of black and female workers, black southerners had become increasingly disenchanted with the slow pace of change in their region. Ignoring federal directives against employment discrimination, the South's defense industries continued to reserve the best jobs for white workers. At the same time that black disenchantment was rising, recruiters from Bay Area industries, such as Kaiser, were going to the South to find workers. By late 1940, for example, Kaiser began to send recruiters out of the state, offering to front train fare to the Richmond shipyards. During the course of the war, 37,852 workers took advantage of this offer, and another 60,000 paid their own way after receiving job referrals from Kaiser recruiters. These and other labor agents no doubt contributed to the first wave of black migration to the Bay Area. However, there is some evidence that recruiters selectively discouraged black workers, telling them that no housing was available in East Bay defense centers. Indeed, in 1943 the War Manpower Commission reported that almost three-fourths of black migrants to the Bay Area had had no direct contact with recruiters.[21]

The majority of migrants, including most of the women in my sample, heard about the Bay Area's opportunities through friends and relatives who came before them. After the first wave of migration in late 1941 and early 1942, the migrant population snowballed: each new group of migrants attracted numerous friends and relatives through positive reports about Bay Area jobs and working conditions. For many, migration became a community concern, encompassing large numbers of migrants from the same churches, neighborhoods, and towns. Lacey Gray, who endured the painful separation from her husband while he worked away from home, heard about high-paying jobs in the Richmond shipyards from a sister who had moved there in 1942. This sister's husband in turn heard about California from an aunt and uncle who had moved to the East Bay in 1941.[22] Louisa Hall, who lost everything in the flood of 1943, learned about California from a minister whom she had met several years earlier. He and his wife were traveling evangelists from Texas who used to stay with Louisa's family on their way through Huntington, Arkansas. The minister later moved to California to work in the shipyards, and when he heard about the flood, he wrote to Louisa and urged her to come west.[23]

Others heard about the Bay Area where they worked. Theresa Waller, who married a man who matched her ambition "to do something good and big," learned about California from a white employer who used to live there. This employer, "who treated me so nice and talked to me like I was a person," told Theresa that there was much less discrimination out West. When Theresa's husband, a Houston waterfront worker, heard from co-workers about labor shortages on the Bay Area's docks and about the antidiscrimination stance of Harry Bridges's International Longshoremen's and Warehousemen's Union (ILWU), he and Theresa decided to make the move.[24] Similarly, Ethel Tillman's husband, who found defense work in southern Mississippi and Florida, heard about better-paying jobs from his network of co-workers.[25]

In addition to spreading word of opportunity, friends and relatives provided concrete offers of support: a place to stay, help finding a job, friendship, and warmth. Myrtle Eaton, who moved to Richmond in late 1943 with her new husband, heard about California from a friend who had come earlier in the war. This friend, a woman named Priscilla, convinced Myrtle and her husband to come and offered them a temporary place to stay. "Without Priscilla we wouldn't have known just which way to go or the ways and means to get a place to live. Priscilla was one of the main ones that caused us to manage to stop in Richmond and remain here."[26]

Ethel Phillips, who had found work in a Minden, Louisiana, defense plant, heard from a couple who had moved to Oakland early in the war that Bay Area jobs were paying higher wages. Equally attractive was their offer of a place to stay and assistance finding employment. Thus, women were central to the information and support networks that generated and sustained the migration. As workers, homemakers, and church women, their networks were more extensive than men's. They were often the first to hear of opportunities out West because of the connections they fostered and maintained. Moreover, those who had already moved, like Priscilla, were frequently the first to extend hospitality. On a more basic level, it was women who made a home into something worth extending to friends and relatives.[27]

Word of better opportunity out West sent soon-to-be-migrant women to a major crossroads in their lives: should they leave home for a less certain, but more promising future? Most of the women in my sample answered this question in a familial context as wives, mothers, and daughters rather than as individuals. The question was rarely one of "whether I should leave"; instead, it was usually "whether *we* should leave." We should now explore the context in which women asked this life-altering question.

Most of the women in my sample were married. Indeed, this particular migration consisted primarily of stable, married couples rather than single men and women. Charles Johnson, who surveyed those who migrated to the Bay Area during the war years, found that 53 percent of migrant households consisted of married couples with children; 33.6 percent of married, childless couples; 6.7 percent of single women with children; and 5.4 percent of single adults without children. In comparison, nonmigrant black households in the Bay Area were more likely to be headed by a single mother (8.9 percent) or contain only one person (13 percent). Migrant families were also more likely to include extended family members, with 548 collateral relatives per thousand household heads, as opposed to 413 per thousand nonmigrant heads. Thus migrant women were likely to arrive in the Bay Area as part of married couple and/or extended family. As such, their decision to leave was made in a familial rather than individual context.[28]

Most married women negotiated the decision to leave on equal terms with their husbands. Some, however, took the initiative in favor of the migration, aggressively pushing their more cautious partners into making the move. Conversely, some women felt coerced by their husbands and agreed to migrate against their own wishes. In the latter case, women frequently felt forced to choose between husbands and family. If a marriage was new, or trust had been broken between spouses, this choice was particularly painful.

Ethel Tillman and her husband agreed to take the risk so that their children would receive a good education. An aunt agreed to move with them, offering to care for the children so both Ethel and her husband could work to save money for a home. Ethel's husband also agreed to move earlier in order to find housing, employment, and a church. Their decision to move was thus based upon careful, joint planning for their family's future. It was reached by mutual agreement—a process that was probably smoother because Ethel and her husband had grown up together.[29]

Estelle Peoples, fed up with the discrimination and lack of opportunity in Marion, Arkansas, heard about California's better weather and economic climate from cousins who had moved out earlier. Her husband, who worked as a vent picker at a rubber company, wanted to stay, but Estelle insisted. "I sent him out here a couple of months before I came. . . . I said, 'You go first and see how you like it, because my people are going to be nice to you.' Then I came two months later, because I wanted to get my bills and things paid up."[30]

Lovie McIntosh, who married a man sixteen years her senior because "I'd rather be an old man's doll than a young man's slave," was forced to follow him to California shortly after the wedding. Her new husband, a lumberman, decided to leave Arkansas after seeing a job notice for the shipyards in the local employment office. He came out to Richmond in late 1941, found work in the shipyards, and begged Lovie to join him. He patiently supported two households for the next six months until she made up her mind. "My grandmother told me he was my husband, he is taking care of you, and you need to be with him. And at the time it sounded real cool coming from her, like she didn't care. So I thought about it and agreed to sell our things and come to California. Had to get rid of our dog, and deal with a lot of stuff. It was hard leaving friends and roots—all I knew. It was really hard, but I came."[31]

Other women made the decision on impulse, with mixed results. In the spring of 1945, Gracie Potter came home to Pelican, Louisiana, for a weekend break from teachers' college. A male acquaintance who had moved to Oakland to work in the shipyards returned that same weekend for his father's funeral. They fell in love, and after he returned to Oakland, he sent her a train ticket. Her mother threatened to disinherit her; she left anyway, but during the four-day train trip she realized that she had made a mistake.[32]

Although the migration of African Americans from the South to the San Francisco East Bay Area was primarily a migration of married couples, young, single women made up the next largest category of migrants. This is a most unusual exception to other migrant populations—within the United States and from outside—which have historically been mostly male. Indeed, in this migration to the East Bay, women outnumbered men by almost two to one among fifteen- to twenty-four-year-olds.[33]

The relatively large numbers of single women in this migration can be traced to several factors. First, many single men who might have migrated under normal circumstances were drafted instead. In other words, there may have been more men in the migrant pool if it had been peacetime. Second, this was a war that produced unprecedented employment opportunities for all women—married and single. Shipyards, food processing industries, naval supply centers and laundries, military postal offices, and all of the service industries associated with the massive influx of civilian workers and enlisted personnel increased women's range of job options and provided vastly superior wages and benefits. Moreover, wartime propaganda, although directed at white women, promoted these jobs as patriotic, exciting, and compatible with societal notions of femininity. This propaganda effort, the relatively good wages and benefits of war jobs, and the traditional acceptance of female wage labor among the working class attracted large numbers of single women to the Bay Area.[34]

Finally, most single women migrated with friends or family members or had relatives and friends waiting in the East Bay Area with assurances of support. Thus, to say that single women migrated in large numbers is somewhat misleading. They may have been unmarried, but they were far from unattached. Rather, they were part of extensive support networks that they benefited from and helped maintain. Frankie Patton, a single schoolteacher from Guthrie, Oklahoma, moved to the East Bay in 1942 to join her brother, a younger sister named Laura, and Laura's husband. In 1943 another single sister in their family moved to the East Bay, and their parents followed in 1947. Willa Henry was also part of a family migration. In 1942, during her second year at Prairie View, Texas, her father and two uncles moved to the East Bay and found work in the shipyards. Once they were settled, they sent for Willa's two brothers and a male first cousin, who were subsequently drafted. In the early summer, an uncle returned to Texas intending to move his wife out West with him. Willa, who was home for the summer, decided to move with them, work two months in the shipyards, and return to college in the fall. When she arrived, she lived with an aunt and uncle and found work through her father, who enrolled her in a welding course at the shipyard. After the training course, she went to work as a welder and made "more money than I ever earned in my life. One of the fellows asked me if I had ever made that much money in a day, and I said, 'No, I have never made that much in a month.'" The money was so good that Willa never returned to college. In 1943 her mother and sisters came to the East Bay, and a couple of years later they were joined by the mother's oldest sister.[35]

Often, migration became a means of preserving one's place in the family unit. If the majority of family members left the South, single women who remained behind were particularly vulnerable. Cornelia Duvernay, a mother of two young children, was abandoned by her husband shortly after her own mother and sisters had moved from New Orleans to the East Bay. Isolated from her own kin and forced to live on handouts from her in-laws, Cornelia decided to join her mother and sisters. Her twin, Carmelia, met her at the station looking considerably plumper than she had the last time they had seen each other. Cornelia remembers saying, " 'If I look like that by being out here, I'm going back to New Orleans.' But before long, with my mother's cooking, I looked like that too." Having regained a secure place within her own family, she later laughed at the triviality of that concern.[36]

Other working-class women who were temporarily single because their husbands had been drafted also decided to migrate with other family members or friends rather than wait out the war alone and pass up the opportunity to make some money. Ethel Phillips, for example, met her husband while she was working at a defense plant in Minden, Louisiana. He was drafted shortly after they married, and Ethel, who had a long history of independent action, decided to move to Oakland with a woman friend. Once there, they stayed with a couple from Minden who had moved out earlier in the war. Ethel's husband was never able to join her, for he was killed overseas.[37]

Ethel's migration showed exceptional independence; most migrant women made the decision to leave within a familial context. Although women constituted a large percentage of the migrant pool and shared initiative in the decision to leave, the actual journey reflected a protective attitude toward women as well as their embeddedness in the family unit. In most cases, women moved west only after male relatives—fathers, brothers, uncles, and husbands—secured employment, housing, and in some instances the savings needed to send for others. Even in cases where a couple came out together, both for the first time, they were usually preceded by a male relative or close male friend. Marlene Lewis's brother-in-law left Arkansas for Oakland early in the war. He then sent for his wife—Marlene's sister, Ruth, who transformed an older, dilapidated house into a habitable dwelling. In 1941, Marlene's brother moved to Oakland and sent for his wife. They moved into the downstairs half of Ruth's house. In 1942, Marlene and her husband drove across country and moved in with Ruth; the four of them shared the upstairs until Marlene and her husband found their own apartment six months later.[38]

Although many couples moved together, particularly newlyweds or those without children, most moved in two stages: husbands and fathers first, mothers and children last. While men were away, women took sole responsibility for maintaining a household, settling family finances, selling property, deciding what to take and what to leave behind, packing belongings, and making travel arrangements for remaining family members. Women's role in this first stage of migration required formidable organizational skills, particularly in light of their ongoing responsibilities as caregivers. Thus, to conclude that men took primary initiative or responsibility for this phase of the migration process ignores the less visible, but equally demanding contribution of those who temporarily remained behind.

Cornelia James, who was eight when her family migrated to Richmond, remembers that her mother was the last to leave. Her father, a traveling evangelist and construction worker, went west first; he found a job in the shipyards and rented a home. Cornelia came next, along with her oldest brother, his wife, and their children. A second and third brother followed. "Then," James recalled, "about eighteen months later, my mother and baby brother came out, because she had to sell all of the livestock and household things." Estelle Peoples took sole responsibility for advance planning, sending her reluctant husband out first and staying behind for two months to settle their bills. Her cousins, who had migrated to Oakland earlier, agreed to house her husband and help him find a job until she could come out and find a permanent place to live.[39] Thus, women such as Cornelia and Estelle had the dual responsibility of dismantling one home and preparing to establish another.

Ethel Tillman's story illustrates the rigorous nature of this role. Her husband, who had been doing defense work in southern Mississippi and Florida, moved to the East Bay in 1942 after hearing about jobs at the Mare Island shipyards in Vallejo. Ethel remained behind with their ten children to pack and make travel arrangements. To Ethel, maintaining a sense of family history was central to the task of creating a new home. She could trace her lineage back to 1843 and was raised on stories passed down through the generations—stories that taught her lessons about family loyalty, spiritual faith, and self-worth. She decided it was far more important to preserve the material remnants or visual reminders of this past than to transport more mundane household articles. Three heirlooms were particularly important to her and had to come west: a serving platter and cast-iron washpot that belonged to a great-great-grandmother who was born in Africa and lived her life in slavery, and a smokehouse lock that had belonged to the German immigrant who married and manumitted this African woman's daughter and thus became Ethel's great-grandfather.

Ethel, who was an accomplished homemaker, had a large store of fruit that she had canned throughout the spring and summer months. She decided that this, too, had to come west because it represented a considerable investment of her own labor and promised to deliver an immediate reminder of home. She also packed bedding, metal utensils, and cast-iron cookware. A network of friends who had already made the move had informed her that pots and pans were in short supply because of wartime demand for metals. Clearly, women's connections, maintained across thousands of miles, not only provided newcomers with assurances of support but also supplied valuable information about what to bring to ease a family's transition.

After her husband found housing and a job, Ethel loaded her belongings and children onto a westbound train. A friend who worked for the railroad checked her baggage, bypassing the white agents who were charging black passengers higher shipping fees than whites. He also packed the fruit— "illegally, because you weren't supposed to ship fruit to California." The four-day train trip was difficult, but Ethel, "like Abraham," had little doubt that she had "reached a fork in the road and chosen the right path."[40]

For some women, the waiting and planning stage of the migration process was particularly difficult. The following letter, written by a woman whose husband had preceded her, reflects the uncertainty and anxiety that many wives and mothers undoubtedly felt when they remained behind.

Dear Wilfred,

Yes I can come for April 15. I had planned to leave here on April 1st, so since you say the 15th will be a lot better for me I'll stop work on the 31st of this month and I can have time to rest a few days because that's such a long trip. Just you be sure to have enough money here. The sooner, the better, because now that I have given up my job, I'd be left with no job and no money. I am giving you this chance, so don't let us down. I am going to mail Sonny's toys to you next week. We have not been paid yet, but when I get my check I am going to take Sonny to the dentist and buy a trunk. And that will give me another check so I can pay some more on my hospital and doctor bill. Thanks for the money. I'll save it so I can soon have enough to come out there.

Answer soon. As ever, Anna.

In this letter, written from New Orleans on March 3, 1943, Anna conveys her eagerness to leave. At the same time she expresses hope that her husband will follow through with the necessary financial support for the trip. She may not have known that her husband had just lost his job at Moore shipyard in Oakland. That was why he had asked her to postpone her arrival date. In a panic, he wrote to Franklin D. Roosevelt, enclosing Anna's letter and asking the president to investigate racial discrimination in the shipyards—the reason he gave for losing his job. Although these letters ended up in the Fair Employment Practice Committee case files, we have no record of whether Wilfred secured employment and sent for Anna.[41]

Since men usually preceded women, many migrant women traveled across the country alone, with female relatives, or with small children. Most, like Ethel, came by train—a four-day trip that the women recall with astonishing clarity, even to the point of remembering exact departure and arrival dates. Several factors contributed to the journey's significance. Most migrant women absorbed the popular images of California as the land of sunshine and movie stars. Olive Blue remembers seeing photographs of Treasure Island, midway between Oakland and San Francisco, which had hosted the Golden Gate International Exhibition of 1939–40 and for that reason had been converted into a fairyland of lush landscaping, exhibition pavilions, fountains, lights, and statuary. In Olive's mind, all of California was prosperous and exotic, a giant fairground. Cornelia James's and Ethel Tillman's imaginations were fed by geography books that contained equally colorful images of California, portraying it as a land of orange groves, palm trees, and endless summers.[42]

Migrant women also perceived California as a place of relative freedom for black people, a refuge from the harshest manifestations of Jim Crow. And since most migrant women were at a point in their lives where the limits imposed by the white world were particularly painful, California became a symbol of liberation. Theresa Waller clearly expected California to be a better place for black people—an image fostered by her white employers, who were originally from California and "treated me so nice, and talked to me like I was a person. And if I was late getting through cleaning the kitchen they would take me to the bus line and make sure I got on the bus. And they told me about California and how I would like it and everything. I was getting away from my environment."[43]

Filled with such images and expectations, migrant women began their journey in the shabby "colored" waiting rooms of train stations throughout the South. There they encountered discrimination and indifference from white ticket agents who charged unfair rates, refused to give information regarding arrival and departure times, or ignored black customers until all white travelers had been served.[44] From there they boarded Jim Crow cars located at the end of trains and crowded with servicemen, baggage, and other migrants. Many women believed that this would be their final encounter with Jim Crow, or at least a final brush with this particular type of humiliation. Like Theresa, they expected the West to offer them the opportunity to be "somebody," to be treated like human beings.

The journey, then, was perceived as a passage to a better place. Indeed, migrants who traveled by rail referred to their carriers as "Liberty Trains."

As these trains left the station, however, migrant women were forced to observe segregated seating and dining arrangements. This changed after the train crossed the Mason-Dixon line, the boundary dividing the "zone of racial separation" from that part of the country with an informal and less elaborate system of segregation. Migrant women recall feeling a mixture of excitement and glory as they crossed this boundary. Although they still had a long way to go before they reached their destination, they believed they had crossed into a world where most of the burdens of "twoness" would be lifted.

Ruth Gracon left Pine Bluff, Arkansas, in 1940 to join her husband in Oakland. Ruth recalls that "I just ran for it when I left Arkansas. It was beautiful, but making a living was a difficult thing." With no one but her new baby, Ruth boarded a California-bound train. "I remember crossing the Mason-Dixon line and being able to sit in a coach instead of the Jim Crow car. I think it was in Kansas City. The Pullman porter was really nice—said that I could sit anyplace now. Got off the train and got onto another, and they said I could sit anywhere. Rode all the way to California on that train."[45] Theresa Waller left Houston in October 1943 to join her husband, who had found work on the San Francisco waterfront. Theresa "rode out of Texas on the Jim Crow car . . . packed with military people." In El Paso, Theresa changed trains, and a soldier who rose to give her his seat said, "You can relax now, because we're at the Mason-Dixon line, and the Great White Father has to look up to you now."[46]

Although the journey was exciting, it was also emotionally and physically exhausting. Many migrant women had never left the towns and cities where they were raised. And despite its golden image, California raised fears as well as hopes. Throughout the journey, women carried anxieties about starting a new life in a strange environment: finding a job and housing, being reunited with loved ones after a long separation, and facing the possibility of temporary dependence on friends and relatives. Finally, women, particularly those with small children, found the trip physically exhausting. Weariness heightened the emotional intensity of the journey and eroded the composure of even the most confident.

Mary Lee, who had never been on a train, boarded a Jim Crow car in Shreveport to join her husband in Oakland. The train was delayed on several occasions, and she and other black passengers were forced to sleep in train stations because local hotels refused to accommodate black people. After seven days with little sleep and with "no idea what California would be like," Mary reached her destination in a state of nervous exhaustion. Lacey Gray's journey was equally trying. After boarding a train in

Lake Charles, Louisiana, with two infant daughters, Lacey drank some contaminated water and became ill. Some soldiers who shared the car came to her assistance, helping her change trains and caring for her daughters while she slept. Opal Smith, who was also traveling with two infants, relied on a female cousin during the train trip. Throughout the journey, the two women washed diapers and hung them to dry across the aisle. Since Jim Crow cars rarely contained sleeping compartments, they spent the entire four-day trip holding the children.[47]

A smaller number of migrant women came west by automobile, traveling with family members or friends in vehicles loaded with personal belongings and household goods. Since few hotels accommodated black people, these travelers camped by the road or took turns driving until they crossed the Mason-Dixon line. Young women who traveled with older relatives remember the trip as fun and exciting. Blanche Jennings, who had told all of her friends that she was going to California to be a movie star, left Missouri with her parents and two siblings in a car loaded with "everything imaginable." Her mother, who wanted her family to eat well on the trip and during their first weeks in California, packed canned fruit and honey-baked ham—produce from the farm they had just left. At the state line, agricultural inspection agents made them leave their food before crossing into California. This episode and the ascent over the Sierra Nevada were the high points of the trip for fifteen-year-old Blanche. Women with small children, however, had to cope with the demands of food preparation, washing, bathing, and child care during the long cross-country drive along Route 66. For them, the journey was exhausting.[48]

Whether they had traveled by train or by car, migrant women arrived in the East Bay area feeling a mixture of exhaustion and high expectations. But in the first hours following their arrival, high expectations were frequently replaced with negative impressions. The East Bay grew significantly during the war years and thus took on characteristics of a boomtown. Richmond, in particular, looked wild and unkempt, with government housing projects, trailer parks, cafes, bars, and clubs springing up on swampy vacant lots to the north and west of the city. New arrivals who were unable to find housing were sleeping in cars and parks. And everywhere, at all hours, people in work clothes—not movie stars—were going back and forth from their defense jobs.[49]

Ruth Cherry arrived in Oakland while her husband was at work. At the station, a serviceman, whom she "felt the Lord had put in my path," called a cab to take her to the room her husband had rented. He came home in work clothes, and she started crying when she saw him. "I had never seen him in coveralls and dirty. He was a barber by trade, and always clean." Theresa Waller was simply exhausted when her husband greeted her at the station. After they embraced, Theresa told him, "I'm so tired, I wish I'd stayed home." Her remark hurt him so much that it was several years before he could speak about the incident.[50]

Migrant women who had expected a land of sunshine and orange groves were immediately disenchanted with the weather. By most women's accounts, the years between 1940 and 1945 were unusually cold, foggy, and rainy. Willa Henry, who drove out with relatives, had sent her only winter coat by train with her other belongings. "The night we got there, my uncle took us out to eat at Slim Jenkins [an Oakland nightclub] and I thought I would freeze to death coming out of that warm climate."[51]

Others remember the rain and fog. Carmelia Chauvin recalled that it was raining when her train pulled into Oakland, and it continued to rain for another week. Lovie McIntosh, who arrived at the foot of Cutting Boulevard in Richmond, remembers the rain and mud. Her husband had rented an apartment in one of the new housing projects, and Lovie's first days were spent indoors while her husband worked at the shipyards. "I can remember the hills above Richmond looking so dismal. It was raining a lot then. War was over in Europe and Roosevelt had just passed. We were upstairs in the project and the wind would blow and blow, and I would cry and cry." Opal Smith, whose husband worked the night shift, remembers the fog rolling in after sunset on her first evenings in Oakland. She and her small children huddled in their tiny apartment, frightened by the strange sound of the foghorns.[52]

In the weeks and months ahead, migrant women would face enormous challenges and additional disappointments. Their encounters with racial discrimination would be particularly painful. Ruth Gracon remembers hearing "that things were going to be different out here, but they weren't like we thought they'd be. They didn't have 'No Colored' signs or anything like that, but they had other ways of telling you they didn't want you." Ruth and other migrant women soon realized that the divisions between white and black worlds also existed in California, requiring them to build new communities as well as new homes.[53]

There was a comforting continuity in the migration process, however, and migrant women used that continuity to buffer their initial disappointments and to create new homes and communities. Although many of these women had left their childhood homes for the first time in their lives, they carried substantial portions of their pasts with them: networking skills learned from their mothers; cultural and religious values regarding work, worship, and family loyalty; relatives and friends; family heir-looms; and the knowledge that others would soon follow. Moreover, few migrant women envisioned their move as a final separation from those who remained behind. Through letters, frequent return visits, and phone calls, women would continue to draw on the advice and cultural traditions of family and friends back home. Their cultural values would not only become the basis for individual and collective identity in their new environment but would also translate into successful efforts to counter the destructive impact of discrimination on their families and communities.

Chapter Three . . . . .

. . . . . I Never Thought I'd Have to Create All That

Making New Homes
in the East Bay Area

To newcomers and established residents, the San Francisco Bay shapes the region's character, defining geographic boundaries, moderating the area's climate, and refreshing the senses with its natural beauty. To the west, San Francisco and Marin Counties stand opposite each other at the mouth of the bay, bordering the Pacific and linked by the Golden Gate Bridge. Across the Bay to the east are the cities of Richmond, Berkeley, Oakland, and Alameda. Prior to the war, the East Bay served as a residential suburb of San Francisco, housing white-collar workers in comfortable, well-planned neighborhoods that extended along and up into the East Bay hills. Closer to the Bay, downtown businesses provided middle-class residents with a wide range of services, including movie theaters, restaurants, department stores, and specialty shops.

Along the waterfront, an ethnically diverse working class—including East Bay African Americans—filled jobs in a growing number of blue-collar industries, established separate neighborhoods, and patronized small business districts and gathering places. Conservative political leaders and their white-collar constituents aggressively protected the East Bay's racial and class boundaries, while celebrating how the "various elements of the city stayed in their localities and were fairly well satisfied."[1] Excluded from white-collar communities and upscale sections of the downtown area, working-class residents created tightly knit, self-sufficient neighborhoods. There, prewar residents enjoyed the friendly, small-town atmosphere of their surroundings. By 1940, however, wartime migration would begin to disrupt established patterns of stratification, as well as the small-town insularity of ethnic enclaves.

Wartime migration to the East Bay Area—by both whites and blacks—greatly exceeded the region's capacity to provide necessary goods and services to its old and new residents. Housing, transportation, schools, social services, and recreation facilities were stretched to the limit, exacerbating racial and class tensions among an increasingly diverse population. Poor white southerners from Oklahoma and Arkansas, skilled tradesmen from the Midwest, and working-class black families from throughout the South all came together and competed with existing residents and with each other for scarce resources. John A. Miller, area coordinator of national defense for Contra Costa County—which includes the cities of Richmond and Vallejo—captured the concern of city administrators in his report to the United States House Subcommittee on Congested Areas. "In 1940 Contra Costa County, California, had a population of 100,230 happy souls. . . . Proud, industrious, hard working, prosperous people who paid their bills in advance and laid a little away for a rainy day lived here. Then came the rude awakening. . . . Shipyards required ship workers. Ship workers required homes in which to live. Homes were built. People came to live in homes, trailers, tents, tin houses, cardboard shacks, glass houses, barns, garages, in automobiles, in theaters, or just in fenced off corners with stars for a roof. The population zoomed from 100,000 to 324,000."[2]

Charles R. Schwanenberg, city manager of Oakland, voiced similar concerns for Alameda County, which included the cities of Oakland, Berkeley, and Alameda; he noted that the county had grown from 513,011 in 1940 to 630,000 by April 1943. He went on to enumerate the resulting strains on housing, schools, police departments, public health services, sanitation facilities, and transportation, concluding that "the magnitude of the problem and the complex relationships of one to the other has been beyond the capacities of the municipalities to solve on the local level."[3]

Established white residents blamed all migrants for the disruptive effects of unplanned population growth. Poor and working-class white migrants from Texas, Oklahoma, and Arkansas, a frequent target of such hostility, were stereotyped as lazy, ignorant, and dirty. But even the greenest "Okie" was ultimately viewed as assimilable. Katherine Archibald, who observed the interplay of racial and class tensions within an Oakland shipyard, concluded that "despite occasional verbal skirmishes between Okie newcomers and the threatened defenders of a longer tenure, the Okies of the wartime immigration, even as I watched them in their first few shipyard years, promised to be quietly absorbed, eventually, into the matrix of California culture." Still, the process of absorption was gradual and fraught with tension. Marilynn Johnson clearly documents how southern white migrants, including working women and youth, became the target of wartime law-and-order campaigns in the East Bay. Moreover, their attempts to transcend social barriers by purchasing nice clothes, jewelry, and other consumer goods were ridiculed as wasteful, cheap, and tasteless. Nevertheless, white migrants did assimilate, and between race and newcomer status, race proved to be the more formidable barrier to community membership.[4]

White migrants and established white residents shared a common racial identity that softened or blurred their cultural and class differences. Whiteness was the newcomers' currency of assimilation, guaranteeing their eventual acceptance as permanent residents. In contrast, established white residents viewed black migrants as unassimilable, undesirable guest workers who would, they hoped, return to the South at the end of the war. White migrants eagerly joined forces with white old-timers to reinforce and elaborate on the discriminatory practices long used to keep native black residents socially, politically, and economically subordinate. These practices would not only maintain racial hierarchy, whites hoped, but would also discourage recent black migrants from staying in the East Bay.

In 1946 the Oakland Institute on Human Relations documented increasing racial discrimination directed against the East Bay's growing black population. Its report, titled "What Tensions Exist Between Groups in Local Communities," described how white property owners and real estate agencies attached restrictive covenants to property deeds, prohibiting owners from selling or renting to black people. These covenants, along with other restrictive real estate practices, concentrated the area's black population within the oldest, least desirable sections of East Bay cities, producing severe overcrowding and de facto segregation in schools. The report also documented high levels of employment discrimination and numerous cases of whites' refusing to serve black patrons in East Bay hotels, bars, and restaurants. Many business owners posted signs that announced, "We Refuse Service to Negroes."[5]

White residents justified such discrimination by portraying black migrants as a danger to "white civilization" and white womanhood. In workplaces and neighborhoods, whites exchanged stories about black sexual assaults on white women, public rudeness, and incompetence and laziness on the job. Others spread rumors that black people were taking over California, pushing whites out of everything from streetcars to jobs. The white press fueled this resentment and fear by zealously reporting any crime committed by a black person and printing reactionary editorials.

One editorial printed in 1944 by the *Oakland Observer* is worth quoting at length. The recent increase in racial tensions, the article claimed, had been "brought about by the influx of what might be called socially-liberated or uninhibited Negroes who are not bound by the old and peaceful understanding between Negro and white in Oakland, which has lasted so many decades. . . . Thus we see, in Oakland, white women taxicab drivers serving Negro passengers, and white women waitresses serving Negroes in white men's restaurants." The author went on to issue a not-so-veiled threat to black newcomers: "[I]f that is not a potential source of trouble, we do not know what is. Right there is where the Negro is making his big mistake. He is butting into white civilization instead of keeping in the perfectly orderly and convenient Negro civilization of Oakland. . . . It might be as well for the more orderly and respectable Negroes to tell the newcomers about the facts of life."[6]

White newcomers embraced the racist assumptions and attitudes expressed in this editorial in an attempt to distance themselves from "unassimilable" black migrants. Aligning themselves with the existing white population, white migrants used race to mute their outsider status and hasten their own assimilation. In other words, they became insiders by casting black migrants as permanently unassimilable. Indeed, white newcomers willingly shored up the foundations of white privilege in the East Bay, participating in discriminatory practices and remaining silent when they were blamed for the region's increasingly hostile racial climate. Again and again, established white homeowners, businessmen, politicians, and public servants justified what were actually long-standing patterns of discrimination by pointing to the supposedly ingrained racism of white southern migrants. Racial discrimination, they pretended, was something new, necessary to prevent conflict between white and black migrants. This preserved the myth of a golden past where white and black residents lived in racial harmony—a myth that traced the region's racial problems to the wartime influx of unruly blacks and reactionary whites.[7]

In reality, the prewar East Bay black population had endured numerous forms of discrimination: occupational and residential segregation; police brutality; lack of union representation; exclusion from hotels, restaurants, swimming pools, ice rinks, YMCAs, and USOs; de facto segregation in schools; and inferior public services such as trash collection, street lighting, road repair, and police and fire protection. Although it was small, the existing black population was hardly complacent. As early as 1915, Bay Area black residents established the Northern California branch of the NAACP, which was headquartered in Oakland. Protesting the Bay Area release of Birth of a Nation in 1915, it went on to support national issues such as the Dyer antilynching bill, the Glass extradition case, the Louisville segregation case, and the Scottsboro defense. Since many NAACP members were Pullman porters, the group also supported the efforts of the Brotherhood of Sleeping Car Porters to obtain better working conditions and wages. In 1923, Oakland and San Francisco NAACP members established separate chapters after the latter claimed that the NAACP had become too focused on East Bay issues.[8]

East Bay black residents went on to establish several other political and protest organizations before the war. By the early 1920s, Oakland citizens had founded Local 188 of the United Negro Improvement Association, which sponsored regular meetings, picnics, parades, lectures, and cultural programs. The Appomattox Club, also established in the early 1920s, began to organize black voters and groom young black professionals for political leadership. During the same period, neighborhood improvement clubs in Richmond, Oakland, and Berkeley pressed city governments for better police protection, street lighting, and recreation facilities. By 1928, after two years of lobbying, the Alameda County League of Colored Women Voters finally persuaded an Oakland hospital to admit black women as nurse trainees. Finally, just before the war, East Bay black activists organized "Don't Buy Where You Can't Work" campaigns against businesses that refused to serve or hire black residents. At the same time, the East Bay Women's Welfare Club began to pressure local schools to hire black teachers.[9]

These efforts to dismantle racial barriers were impressive, but they were severely limited by the small size of the region's prewar black population. For this reason, black residents created a large number of autonomous self-help institutions. The Fanny Jackson Coppin Club, founded in 1899 by a group of Oakland church women, established an orphanage, a day nursery, and the Home for Aged and Infirm Colored People. "Colored" YWCAs and YMCAs, founded in the early 1920s, provided vocational training, adult education, and a wide variety of social and cultural programs. During the Great Depression, the Linden Branch Y in West Oakland also offered job referrals, food, and clothing to needy citizens. Churches and lodges—some of which had been founded as early as the mid-1800s—also met the material, social, and cultural needs of their members. Finally, thriving business communities in West Oakland and South Berkeley gave East Bay black residents a measure of economic independence. In Oakland, for example, there were over one hundred black-owned businesses by 1929, including fifteen eating establishments, two undertakers, two insurance companies, sixteen real estate agents, five printers, sixteen barbershops, and thirteen beauty parlors.[10]

East Bay black residents thus had a long history of resistance to racial discrimination; however, their resistance was shaped and perhaps muted by the relatively small size of the prewar black population. Change came gradually, in small increments. In the meantime, autonomous institutions provided necessary services and united residents in a close-knit community. The large group of black migrants, who possessed a sense of entitlement that had been strengthened by the prodemocracy rhetoric of the war, threatened to disrupt both white residents' perceptions of racial harmony and black citizens' sense of community. A black resident of Oakland, interviewed by Douglas Daniels and quoted in *Pioneer Urbanites*, put it this way: " 'I think they were more aggressive, really, in many ways [than the older residents]. Less friendly. They tended to be more suspicious of whites . . . a little unpleasant in . . . the remarks they made about whites and that sort of thing.' "[11]

Since most black migrant women thought they were leaving a repressive environment for a more open one, it was extremely painful to learn that whites viewed their initial attempts to exercise basic freedoms as evidence of their "uninhibited" natures. Equally painful was that the existing East Bay black community accepted white stereotypes of the newcomers as immoral, rude, loud, and lazy. Emmaline Benedict, a black California native from a well-known pioneer family, remembers attending meetings "with some of the natives and the best people from the South, saying they ought to send them [the migrants] back." Emphasizing her social distance from the migrants, she went on to relate the following: "I remember one family. They moved in and that thing [their apartment] got to smelling. They didn't know a thing about plumbing or anything else, you know. And they were using the bathtub for the toilet and washing their face in the real toilet."[12]

Established East Bay black residents also highlighted cultural distinctions between themselves and newcomers. Virginia Cravanas, another California native, remembers that "we in California didn't know anything about black foods. That was brought out here by the southerners. They also brought in new music. And every street corner had a storefront church. Their religion was different from ours. Ours was quiet, theirs was holiness. As soon as a preacher felt he could preach a better sermon, a new church would spring up." Black old-timers believed that such differences reflected poorly on their community. Having struggled to present themselves as virtuous citizens worthy of equal treatment, old-timers worried that they would be lumped together with newcomers and lose their hard-won, although largely token, gains.[13]

Marguerite Williams, who was raised in the prewar East Bay, remembers that despite its discrimination, "there wasn't that feeling that white people were your enemy." Migrants, she maintained, "had an ingrown dislike of white people," which led to open conflict. Referring to the magnitude of the migration, Marguerite went on to explain that there "were so many that it was like aliens to us. . . . We would just watch them, because of their behavior and everything. . . . [Before the war] we all lived together in a little community. . . . There wasn't any racial fights. . . . It seemed like overnight people on the street would be fighting. You would go into the store downtown and the people wouldn't want to wait on you. That bothered me because I wasn't used to that."[14]

Some longtime black residents were more candid about prewar racial politics in the East Bay, explaining that the relatively small size of established black communities ruled out confrontational tactics in response to discrimination. Virginia Cravanas remembered that "before the war blacks had to do for themselves. In California we didn't have anything. We just got the crumbs. . . . We resented the influx [of migrants] because we thought we were doing the right thing. But we weren't doing a thing. We were really the bottom of the bucket, working as stock clerks and maids. Newcomers came in and called attention to what we were denied. When they came out here they felt this was the land of milk and honey, and they were going to get some because they never had anything anyway."

Virginia also touched on another source of tension between newcomers and old-timers: occupational status. Established black residents, both poor and middle-class, worked primarily as servants, cooks, porters, janitors, and unskilled laborers. A small elite, which consisted of doctors, lawyers, ministers, educators, and more prosperous business owners, "constituted that upper strata of the black middle class and resembled the white middle class in their occupations, values and lifestyle." There was, however, a great measure of fluidity among social groups. Poor residents could attain middle-class status by securing stable employment, upgrading their education, or devoting time to community service. The elite and members of the middle class frequently worshiped in the same churches and joined the same lodges and clubs. Occupational discrimination and the relatively small size of the prewar black population helped blur class lines, contributing to a sense of group harmony. Migrants, however, were primarily working-class industrial workers who refused to accept the type of menial service jobs that had long been filled by established residents.

Moreover, migrants cared little about existing class distinctions and codes of conduct. Indeed, their sheer numbers ensured that they, not the old-timers, would define social norms.[15]

Most longtime black residents had neither the desire nor the resources to integrate newcomers into their communities. Indeed, given the sheer magnitude of the migration, any assimilation would occur in reverse, with longtime residents blending into migrant communities. Although this eventually did happen, old-timers kept to themselves throughout the war years, attempting to preserve the largely illusory privilege attached to being a nonmigrant. Emmaline, Virginia, and Marguerite all describe highly insular enclaves of longtime residents within larger migrant communities. In 1940, for example, Oakland's black population numbered 8,462, the largest in the Bay Area and the second largest in California. By 1950, this population stood at 47,562, with migrants outnumbering prewar residents by more than four to one. Virginia remembers that she "associated only with certain people—the other early families. Most migrants stayed to themselves. They didn't accept us and we didn't accept them. Every time you'd turn around there would be more people in town, but we kept to ourselves." Eventually, Virginia admitted, "we had to learn their ways," but during the war years "we kept to ourselves." Katherine St. Clair, who belonged to an elite Oakland family, agreed, explaining that the established black community was initially shocked by the "drive" and determination of the newcomers. "We mixed in eventually, but it wasn't the newcomers that assimilated. It was the old-timers."[16]

When old-timers did interact with newcomers, it was frequently on an exploitative basis. Virginia's brother, who went into real estate during the war, pretended to be from the South when he conducted business with migrants, emulating their accents and mannerisms. One of Marguerite's relatives, who lived in North Richmond, got rid of her chickens, white-washed her coops, and rented them out to desperate migrants. "They weren't the only ones," commented Marguerite. Similarly, Katherine St. Clair's father profited from the wartime housing shortage, purchasing dilapidated Victorian homes in West Oakland and subdividing them into individual rental units.[17]

There were exceptions to this tendency, of course. Several longtime East Bay activists viewed migrants as potential allies. C. L. Dellums, local leader of the Brotherhood of Sleeping Car Porters, became vice president of the Northern California NAACP in 1937. Under his leadership, the organization took a stronger position on employment discrimination. After the war started, Dellums lobbied for the integration of Bay Area war housing, helped A. Philip Randolph organize the March on Washington move-ment, and helped forge an interracial coalition to fight discrimination in local defense industries and unions. Migrants, he perceived, would add new energy to these struggles. Similarly, D. G. Gibson, president of the Appomattox Club, and Frances Albrier, a black Democratic Party activist, embraced migrants as potential voters, anticipating that their numerical strength would revolutionize East Bay politics. Other established residents encouraged their churches, lodges, and service organizations to meet the needs of migrants. Tarea Hall Pittman, for example, helped local chapters of the National Council of Negro Women become more responsive to the needs of working women.[18]

Black business owners also welcomed the influx of migrants. Along with black landlords who profitably subdivided their property to accommodate newcomers, they prospered during the war years. Established business districts, like Seventh Street in West Oakland, expanded rapidly, supporting an increased number of doctors, lawyers, and entrepreneurs. Nightclubs along the avenue, such as Slim Jenkins' Place and the Swing Club, catered to migrants' musical tastes by bringing black blues artists to the East Bay. Similarly, entrepreneurs in Richmond opened new nightclubs and restau-rants that reflected the cultural preferences of their new clientele.[19]

For the most part, existing residents—white and black—and white newcomers subscribed to the myth that black migrants were culturally inferior and unassimilable. In reality, black migrants were as well edu-cated, more highly skilled, more likely to live in two-parent households, and more active in churches and labor unions than members of the nonmigrant black population. Moreover, as established black and white residents observed, black migrants were ambitious, determined to buy homes, start businesses, and obtain more training and education. Cultur-ally, black migrants were no more foreign than white migrants. But de-spite this profile, established residents and white migrants held onto the myth of cultural inferiority and used it to justify racial discrimination and economic exploitation, preserve real or illusory group privileges, and help one group attain insider status. The myth of cultural inferiority and difference persisted well into the 1960s, and it prevented any concrete, collective efforts to integrate black newcomers into the postwar social and economic order. The failure of policymakers to address seriously discrim-ination and provide black migrants with adequate housing and secure jobs both during and after the war created severe problems within new migrant communities—problems that only served to confirm or reinforce the myth of unassimilability.

Migrant women, who as soon as they arrived were labeled as undesirable, temporary guest workers, had to rely on their own cultural resources to make new homes for their families. In the East Bay, this was no easy task. White residents used restrictive covenants and discriminatory real estate practices to confine black migrants to the most rundown or undeveloped sections of Oakland, Berkeley, and Richmond. These neighborhoods, which were characterized by dilapidated, overcrowded housing and inadequate infrastructure and social services, required a substantial investment of labor to make them habitable. Through their emotional and physical labor, migrant women created comfortable homes for their families and established linkages among neighboring households. Their labor took several forms: the physical act of cleaning, repairing, and furnishing a new dwelling; the emotional work of managing a family's adjustment to a new environment; coordinating the tasks of household maintenance, including child care, laundry, meal preparation, personal hygiene, and house cleaning; and locating essential goods and services, such as banks, markets, medical care, and recreation facilities.

In addition, migrant women built and maintained supportive social relations within neighborhoods by helping the sick, sharing child care, pooling resources, and exchanging information about employment, housing, marketing, and social services. They also sustained family ties by organizing holiday celebrations and reunions, maintaining connections to relatives and friends back home, and providing temporary accommodations to new migrants. Finally, migrant women built permanent institutions that, in the absence of governmental assistance, provided their communities with necessary social services. Women performed these unpaid and largely unrecognized tasks in addition to working for wages. Their home- and neighborhood-building efforts, subsidized by their wage labor, subverted white notions of migrant transience and guest-worker status. Indeed, migrant women's actions spoke louder than their words, conveying the message "We are here to stay." Given the inhospitable conditions that greeted new arrivals—conditions that migrant women buffered or in some cases reversed—migrant communities were remarkably successful.

Migrants' search for housing typically went through three phases: temporary, transitional, and permanent. Initially, migrants stayed with friends and relatives or found short-term accommodations in crowded boardinghouses, trailer parks, chicken coops, tents, or automobiles. Male migrants who preceded female relatives frequently lived in this type of housing until they found better accommodations. However, many families that migrated as units also lived in these temporary, cramped quarters. Lacey Gray, whose experience was typical of women who came out with their husbands, remembers renting a single room in North Richmond. She, her husband, and two small children shared a single bed, but they felt fortunate to have found anything: "When we came to Richmond, there wasn't much housing at all."[20]

From there, migrants found more spacious housing in government war projects or privately owned apartment buildings. Lacey applied for government housing as soon as she and her family arrived in Richmond. After a month on a waiting list, they moved into a "brand new project." This development, like many in the East Bay, was block-segregated, with white and black residents assigned to separate sections of the project. Although she was disappointed and angry about the segregation, Lacey was delighted to have the additional space. "The project had a living room, one bedroom, and a kitchen. The living room was so big my husband and I slept there and gave our daughters the bedroom. And the rent was only $35 per month. That was water, gas, lights, everything!"[21]

From this transitional housing, migrants moved into permanent rental units or purchased their own homes. By the late 1940s, or sometimes sooner, many migrant families had saved enough to purchase homes. Their choices were severely limited by residential segregation, however. When Lacey Gray and her husband began to look for a home, real estate agents directed them to North Richmond, an unincorporated, remote, and swampy settlement; Parchester Village, an all-black township northwest of Richmond; and undeveloped sections of Richmond where the shipyards and housing projects had once stood. Lacey recalled this experience with bitterness in her voice:

> When we first started looking, the real estate agents took us out to North Richmond, and I didn't want a place there. So they took us out to Parchester Village and said that it was going to be black and white together. But they had one white lady living in a model home, and when black people had all moved in, she moved out. It was nothing but a black settlement. When they wanted to build a school out there Governor Warren wouldn't let them, because it would have been segregated. But he sent buses out and bused those children into the white community. So we bought a lot in an undeveloped part of Richmond where all the white people had moved out.[22]

The first months in the East Bay, spent in temporary, crowded housing, were the most challenging for migrant women. By 1941, all migrants had difficulty finding housing. Black migrants, however, faced the additional constraint of residential segregation, maintained by restrictive covenants, discriminatory lending and real estate practices, and government financing policies designed to "protect the character" of existing neighborhoods. Long before World War II, these practices had confined the existing black population to aging or undeveloped neighborhoods in the East Bay. These neighborhoods, which were already overcrowded and lacked basic services, accommodated migrants only with great difficulty.

Oakland's prewar black population, the largest in the Bay Area, lived in West Oakland; on Market Street, north of the San Pablo Avenue intersection; and along the Berkeley / Oakland border. West Oakland, one of Oakland's oldest sections, was the heart of the city's black community; it contained a number of small businesses, a large park and recreation center, several churches, and numerous service and social organizations. With the city's highest level of units in need of repair or with no private bath, West Oakland also provided the largest source of temporary housing for black migrants. Between 1940 and 1945, West Oakland's population density increased fourfold. And by 1952 this area contained 85 percent of the city's total black population.[23]

Until migrants found transitional housing in government projects or privately owned apartments, most of them rented rooms in West Oakland in the grand but dilapidated Victorian houses that existing owners or renters had profitably subdivided. Katherine St. Clair, daughter of a shrewd black entrepreneur, remembers how "father was into buying and selling, and when the war started he bought up property and converted it into apartments . . . all down in West Oakland. He would buy them at low cost and fix them up, converting houses into two or three apartments." Katherine Legge, a tenant selection supervisor for the Oakland Housing Authority, found severe overcrowding during her inspections. Reporting to the U.S. House Investigation of Congested Areas, she stated that "you nor anyone has any idea of the living conditions of Negroes working in defense industries. I can take you to see numerous families where 14 people live in one room." Other researchers found similar problems, reporting that "new arrivals to the city are taken in trucks to the Negro community and 'peddled out' to rooming houses." They also discovered several trailer camps with inadequate "sanitary provisions." In one West Oakland camp, they observed that "youths and adults, in several cases, are living five to six persons to a room."[24]

In Berkeley, migrants had even more difficulty finding temporary housing. White residents confined black citizens to small geographic areas in

West and South Berkeley and, through restrictive covenants and physical intimidation, vigorously defended the boundaries between black and white sections of the city. Moreover, Berkeley contained only one public housing project, which opened in 1941 over the objections of the Berkeley Chamber of Commerce and the Berkeley Manufacturers Association. Their opposition to the project, which mirrored that of most white residents, was based on fears that migrants would take over the city and threaten established patterns of race relations.[25]

Until this project opened, migrants found housing in the existing black communities of South and West Berkeley. Before the war, South Berkeley housed middle-class and elite black families that considered its tree-lined streets and single-family homes a step up from Oakland's black neighborhoods. The established residents of South Berkeley, like the black entrepreneurs of West Oakland, subdivided single-family homes and rented rooms to newcomers. This once-quiet residential area, which became uncomfortably congested within a five-year period, soon threatened to push beyond its traditional boundaries and spill into bordering white neighborhoods. In contrast to the settled residential atmosphere of South Berkeley, West Berkeley contained dilapidated, overcrowded housing stock in close proximity to heavy industry. Migrants who found temporary housing in this neighborhood—Berkeley's oldest and poorest—created an additional burden on an already-blighted section of the city.[26]

Richmond, of all the East Bay cities, provided the least temporary housing for newcomers. Numbering only 270 and inhabiting a marshy four-block section of North Richmond, its prewar black population had few vacancies even when existing housing was subdivided. And white residents, like those in Berkeley, resisted residential integration. Thus, until newcomers advanced to the top of a waiting list for government housing, they had no alternative but to settle north of the existing black community on unincorporated land near the city dump. There migrants squatted on vacant land, living in tents, shacks, and trailers, without the benefit of running water, electricity, sanitation facilities, paved roads, or garbage collection.[27]

None of the migrant women in my sample lived in this North Richmond shantytown. Most found temporary lodging in one of the East Bay's newly subdivided rooming houses or with friends and relatives who had preceded them. The degree to which women participated in the initial search for housing varied. Women who already had friends or relatives in the East Bay often made housing arrangements well in advance of migration. Even if these relatives were in-laws, women frequently served as housing brokers, securing temporary accommodations prior to migrating. The role of housing broker was an extension of women's unpaid, largely unrecognized family maintenance work; it was migrant women who maintained contact with the fictive and real kin who migrated first and would later house newcomers.

Lee Henderson maintained a close relationship with her brother even after he moved from their childhood home in Oklahoma to the East Bay in the late 1930s. As war industries generated new jobs, he wrote home, urging Lee to come and offering her a place to stay. Similarly, Estelle Peoples maintained a long-distance relationship with cousins who had moved to the East Bay before the war. They too wrote of wartime employment opportunities and offered temporary shelter. Estelle's efforts to maintain contact with her cousins paid off. When Estelle's husband moved west while she remained behind in Texas to settle their affairs, her cousins graciously welcomed him as part of the family. By the time Estelle arrived, her husband had a job, and they could afford to rent a place of their own.[28]

Migrant women also drew on friendships to secure temporary housing. Louisa Hall, the woman who lost her home in an Arkansas flood, maintained close ties with a minister who had moved to the East Bay early in the war. When he heard of Louisa's problems, he urged her to come west with her husband. And when they came, the minister provided both temporary housing and spiritual support as Louisa and her husband struggled to retrieve a sense of control over their lives. Ethel Phillips, who came to the East Bay while her husband was fighting in the Pacific, stayed with a young couple she had known back in Minden, Louisiana. These two friends had encouraged Ethel to join them in Oakland, and they shared their home with her until she found her own apartment.[29]

A second group of migrant women came west with husbands, friends, or relatives without prearranging where they would stay. Unless they were underage, these women, actively participated in the search for temporary housing. Their concerns—safety, cleanliness, nearness to schools, markets, health services, and laundry and cooking facilities—were infrequently addressed in the East Bay's tight housing market, but they shaped each family's final choice of accommodations. June Williams and her husband left St. Louis for the East Bay in 1942. Arriving in Oakland after a three-day train trip, they went directly to a relative's address. "We just showed up. He was a bachelor with a one-room apartment who gave us the bed and slept on the floor." The following day, June and her husband looked for housing, stopping people on the streets and asking if they knew of any vacancies. In a neighborhood that seemed ideal because it was within walking distance of markets and churches, June stopped a woman who was leaving a corner grocery. "She said she had a room she was going to rent as soon as she cleared it out." Aware of the acute housing shortage, June asked if they "could help, and we cleared it out the same day. And the next day we picked up our luggage and moved right in."[30]

A third group of women, who had no friends or relatives in the East Bay and whose husbands had preceded them, had to trust their spouses' choice of housing. Given the general housing shortage and the fact that none of the women I interviewed ended up in the North Richmond shantytown, many husbands took their wives' comfort and safety seriously. If a man found a single room for his family, he was doing well by wartime standards. Women who were initially shocked by their surroundings soon learned that all newcomers made similar concessions. Lacey Gray's husband, who left Longleaf, Louisiana, in July 1943, arrived in Richmond during the peak of the housing shortage. Fortunately, he found a room with an established black family in North Richmond, narrowly escaping the shantytown. When Lacey arrived two months later with their small daughters, all four of them lived in his room and shared a single bed. But Lacey soon came to see that they at least lived in a real house, even if they had to share a kitchen and bath with other renters. Mary Lee's husband also migrated first, leaving Shreveport, Louisiana, for a military assignment in Alameda. When Mary arrived, pregnant with their first child, they shared a single room that he had found in South Berkeley. The owners, having converted their single-family home into several units, rented to "young sailors and soldiers and their families." In this noisy, crowded house, where all the residents shared a single bath and kitchen, Mary struggled to create stable and comfortable surroundings.[31]

All migrant women, whether rooming with relatives or living in cramped, rented rooms, experienced physical and emotional hardship during the temporary housing phase. Until women secured more permanent housing—a process that took from one to twelve months—they struggled with minimal resources to care for their families. Bathing, cooking, cleaning, caring for children, and doing laundry required ingenuity, versatility, and additional labor in the absence of proper facilities. Moreover, women had to devote more time and effort to emotional housekeeping—maintaining family peace and mental health—in an environment characterized by its newness and lack of privacy. Along with these household maintenance tasks, migrant women learned to negotiate transportation, and they found jobs, markets, banks, churches, schools, and health services. Using the skills learned from their mothers, migrant women built relationships with other women, reestablishing the social supports and institutions that had sustained their communities back home. Best Johnson remembered the most important lesson she learned from her mother: "Caring and sharing. Doing for your family and other people too." She and other recent migrants used this reciprocal ethic to relieve the burdens associated with temporary housing and to build the foundations of more permanent communities.[32]

Women's efforts to create stable friendships and homes were heroic, given what little they had to work with. Wartime housing investigators documented some of the difficulties migrant women faced. One family, unsuccessful at finding better housing, lived in a basement that contained "no bathroom, no tub, and the whole family seem[s] to wash in the kitchen sink. The place is infested with rats, and when it rains the place is immediately inundated because neither doors nor windows can be shut tightly. . . . The place is unaired and dimly lighted. For these [sic] extremely unsanitary, dirty, overcrowded place the family pays weekly $16.25." The migrant woman living there "implored [the researcher] to do something about the situation." Another family occupied a "substandard frame dwelling [with] no bathroom, no toilet or no hot water. They use the next door neighbor's toilet and shower. This toilet is shared by the tenant upstairs over the neighbor." In one rooming house, eight families shared a single kitchen and bathroom. In others, women attempted to create "makeshift kitchen arrangements in their one or two rooms by placing a small gas burner in one corner of the room, using a crate box placed under or outside the window for refrigeration, and having little or no provision for the storage of food commodities." Such conditions were the norm. Over 40 percent of new arrivals lived in buildings without a bathroom. Of those who did have bathrooms, one-fourth lacked showers or tubs. Most dwellings did have kitchens, but "the most characteristic arrangement was for all families . . . to share a common kitchen."[33]

Migrant women creatively transformed these surroundings. June Williams decorated a bleak rented room with her own needlework and with secondhand furniture from nearby thrift stores. Mary Lee made tables and chairs from orange crates and covered the floor with kelly-green linoleum. Then she painted the crates and walls to match the floor, and bought a matching spread for the bed. Women also did their best to retain traditional dietary patterns, although few markets carried familiar vegetables, meats, or cornmeal until the migration peaked in 1943. Willa Henry remembers being "so green and upset trying to shop at first. I found some of the things I was accustomed to, but back home we had fresh pork and chicken and greens and black-eyed peas. I went to the Tenth Street Market and asked for some okra and they looked at me as if I was nuts." Ethel Tillman, who longed to have space for a garden so that she could grow familiar vegetables, shared ideas about food substitutes with neighbor women.[34]

Women who came out earlier helped more recent migrants find markets, banks, health care, churches, and schools. In these places, migrant women made additional friends, and these friends connected them with other resources. The Housewives Market in Oakland, whose sights, sounds, and smells were reminiscent of home, was one such gathering place. Similarly, West Oakland's black cultural and recreation center—De Fremery Park—and the nearby Well Baby Clinic brought migrant women together. Church, however, was the center of migrant community life. Estelle Peoples's female cousin showed her how to ride the trains and buses and where to shop. But most important, the cousin took Estelle to church, opening up a lifelong source of friendship and social support. "Most members had come from somewhere else," Estelle recalled, "and I started making friends there right away." Indeed, 85 percent of the migrant women in my sample reported that church was their single most important source of friendship and mutual aid.[35]

Although most migrants expected a greater degree of equality in the East Bay and arrived with a sense of entitlement, they still confronted unfamiliar racial mores. Migrant women, uncertain how flexible these mores were, turned to more established migrants for advice. Acclimated migrants encouraged them to challenge any discrimination they encountered. Theresa Waller's first friend, who roomed in the same house, "had experienced discrimination and was set on not putting up with it here. But I held back. I didn't want any confusion, because where I came from, no matter whose fault it was, we were always to blame. It's nothing you can say to make the officials think that you're telling the truth or were mistreated. So you just shut your mouth and let it end just as quick as it can. Seeing my friend be assertive helped me let loose and go into any place I felt like going into."[36]

From the moment they arrived, migrant women turned to other women for assistance and advice. These early relationships helped recent migrants gather information and resources to create a home base from which they and other family members could search for employment and more permanent housing. Indeed, neighbors, fellow church members, co-workers, and even acquaintances often provided newcomers with information on fair rental rates, landlord obligations, vacancies, and how to apply for government housing. For example, one day when Mary Lee was about to give birth to her first child and was depressed at the prospect of bringing her newborn home to a single rented room, she "was walking down the street with tears in my eyes when a lady stopped me and asked me what was wrong." The woman, who became Mary's close friend, was the housing secretary for the government housing project in West Berkeley, and she "told me about an opening there." Olive Blue was sharing a rented room with her child and unmarried sister when she heard about government housing from co-workers at the Kaiser shipyards. They moved in soon and stayed until Olive's husband returned from the service. By then they had enough combined savings to buy their own home.[37]

Most migrants moved from temporary housing into one of several government housing projects in the East Bay. Under federal legislation passed in 1940, prewar public housing units were converted into wartime projects. Simultaneously, federal agencies used Lanham Act funds to build new war-worker housing throughout the region. Although they were built and maintained with federal funds, these projects were managed by local housing authorities, whose boards were dominated by conservative businessmen. For example, housing authorities placed black migrants in temporary projects slated for demolition after the war. In contrast, they reserved permanent public housing for white applicants who were viewed as "responsible citizens, good workers, healthy, well adjusted families." Finally, even temporary projects were administered on a segregated basis. Some contained buildings or units reserved for black tenants; others were completely segregated by race, and all-black projects were located far from white neighborhoods and in the least desirable sections of town. Thus, while war housing was an improvement over the substandard, makeshift accommodations in North Richmond or West Oakland, it was also a way of marginalizing and containing the black migrant population.[38]

Oakland housing authorities managed three low-rent housing projects, which had been planned before the war as part of the city's early redevelopment efforts, and eleven temporary wartime projects. Of this total, four were racially integrated, three completely nonwhite, and seven for whites only. Demand greatly exceeded supply. During the first quarter of 1943, Katherine Legge of the Oakland Housing Authority reported that "I have 60 applications per day, 40 of which are Negro, and I can't house one of them." By the end of the 1944 there had been little improvement. In December of that year, the housing authority reported 735 applications for housing, but only six placements.[39]

By the end of the war the integrated and nonwhite projects, concentrated in West Oakland, housed approximately 1,500 nonwhite families; all but a few of these families were black. In sum, the housing authority intentionally confined black migrants to West Oakland, complementing the discriminatory housing policies of private citizens and real estate agencies. By 1945, largely because of these policies, the majority of black migrants lived in seven highly congested census tracts. During the postwar years, the city demolished this housing as part of its West Oakland redevelopment plan.[40]

Opposed to any expansion of the city's black population, white citizens of Berkeley resisted a federal plan to construct war housing in West Berkeley. Their efforts failed. In 1944 the Federal Public Housing Agency built Codornices Village, accepting white and black tenants but segregating each group in separate units or blocks. Although they had failed to keep black migrants out of the city entirely, white Berkeleyans could take comfort in the fact that Codornices Village went up in West Berkeley rather than in all-white sections of the city. The project was also designated as temporary, relieving white fears that migrants would become permanent residents.[41]

Richmond's war housing, located in southwest Richmond on vacant tracts of land near the shipyards, was also designated as temporary and administered on a segregated basis. The Richmond Housing Authority assigned black residents to separate buildings within each project, and racial "balance" was maintained through quotas: the ratio of black and white residents was held at one to four, although the authority's own regulations stipulated a quota of "one Negro in every three rentals."[42]

Of all the East Bay cities, Richmond was most successful at containing black migrants within separate, temporary housing developments. By the end of the war, white migrants either secured permanent housing in Richmond, returned home, or relocated within the Bay Area. Black migrants had nowhere to go, but they were determined to stay. By 1952, 90 percent of Richmond's black population still lived in temporary housing.[43]

Public housing allocated to black migrants was flimsily constructed and deteriorated rapidly from overcrowding, lack of maintenance, and underprovision of necessary services. Many projects were built on swampy, poorly drained land that was muddy for most of the year and flooded during the winter. Garbage collection was inadequate, contributing to unhealthy conditions and high rates of disease among residents. The west side of Codornices Village, for example, faced the Southern Pacific rail line and the city dump. Housed in the units that faced west, black residents endured fumes from burning trash and the clatter of passing trains, while whites enjoyed the quieter, cleaner portion of the project. Similarly, black migrants in Richmond were concentrated in units built on swampy land adjacent to the shipyards and railroad tracks, while whites lived in those nearest the downtown and white residential neighborhoods. Such disregard for public health and safety signified and reinforced the temporary status of black migrants, placing them outside any system of mutual obligation, although their labor was essential to the war effort.[44]

Despite these deficiencies, migrant women preferred the projects to the single rented rooms they had recently vacated. Women also expressed satisfaction with indoor plumbing, space heat, hot and cold running water, and modern cooking appliances—amenities many black southerners had never had. Indeed, several women commented that the projects were the nicest place they had ever lived. Lacey Gray, whose two-room company house in Louisiana had lacked indoor plumbing, liked her apartment in the projects. For $35 per month, which included utilities, she received more space than she had ever had: a living room, bedroom, kitchen, and full bath. Myrtle Eaton was similarly impressed with her apartment, located only half a mile from Kaiser Yard No. 3, where she worked as a welder. Her wages—$1.20 per hour—easily covered rent and household expenses. This housing was considerably more affordable than the $8 to $17 many families had paid for a single room.[45]

Above all, government housing was woman-centered, spatially conducive to the formation of helping networks. In addition to housing large concentrations of migrants, projects contained recreation centers, laundry facilities, and common yards that women defined as communal. In these common spaces, women assisted each other with orientation tasks like finding markets, churches, and social services. Moreover, transitional housing in government projects also afforded greater stability and facilitated more complex exchanges and joint projects, such as shared child care, common gardens, group celebrations, and loans of food and income. Women also opened up their homes to more recent migrants, providing the same assistance they had received upon arrival. Men undoubtedly used communal space as well, centering their activities on recreation and the exchange of job information, both of which complemented women's efforts to build a sense of community in the projects.

Finally, the experience of women in my sample challenges common assumptions about projects—assumptions based on popular images of postwar, low-income housing developments that warehouse the poor at a safe distance from white neighborhoods and newly redeveloped shopping and business areas. Migrant women's positive experience with multifamily war housing suggests that such developments may be better suited to women's needs than suburban, single-family homes would be. War projects, which housed upwardly mobile, economically secure migrants, had few of the problems associated with postwar, low-income developments. Indeed, women thrived in them. Thus, income level rather than spatial design determined how one experienced this type of housing. Ethel Phillips, who sent back to Louisiana for her son and daughter as soon as she secured government housing in Alameda, has good memories of that project. "I liked life in the projects. It was communal. No one ever took anything, stole anything. People left their doors open."[46]

Ethel Tillman, who moved from Vicksburg, Mississippi, with her husband, ten children, and an aunt, "made friends with neighbors right away." Her popularity grew along with her generosity: "We sponsored dozens of other families while we were still in the projects, putting them up until they could find a house and a job." Many of these people were strangers who requested assistance at the Tillmans' church. "We have fond memories of the different people who came through—family, strangers, couples and children, single men and women."[47] Ethel and her aunt also shared food with their neighbors, provided medical advice, and helped care for the children of working mothers.[48]

Cornelia James, whose family moved into a Richmond project from a boardinghouse, remembers a "sense of community" there. She went on to note that "people could trust each other. [The project] had a recreation center where they had dances for kids, reading rooms, tennis courts, volleyball courts, a baseball field, pool, and card room. You had a place to go and meet people. Now, all you have is church."[49] Lovie McIntosh also remarked on the rich social life in the projects—one that drew her into institutional involvements with other women. "The lady whose wall was connected to ours was from Texarkana. I got acquainted with her and soon picked up other friends. I gather friends real easy. So we got to know people, and it was really nice. They were all people who had migrated. Some was from Texas, and some was from Mississippi, but there was several families from Arkansas, which was really nice. And I got involved with the church right up the street, and began to do PTA work too."[50]

Many migrant women describe their years in the projects as happy and fulfilling. Projects did foster a "sense of community," bringing large numbers of migrants together in a semicommunal setting that was particularly suited to women's needs. But these years also brought economic prosperity, compared to what migrants had experienced in the prewar South, and an unprecedented amount of disposable income. During the five-year period between the time the first projects were built (1941) and the end of the war (1946), migrants made "good money." Because they came from families that prized economic independence and home ownership, migrants opened savings accounts, and most women continued to be frugal consumers. Ethel Tillman, surprised at the abundant selection of secondhand clothes at the Salvation Army thrift store, bought "beautiful adult clothes and cut them down into dresses, pants, and suits" for her children. For Ethel, this was a luxury. Although migrants continued to observe familiar patterns of saving and thrift, their efforts actually placed them beyond the edge of poverty. For the first time in their lives, many could simultaneously save and afford a higher standard of living. Thus, from a social as well as economic standpoint, life in the projects represented progress.[51]

Cornelia Duvernay and Carmelia Chauvin, twin sisters from New Orleans, lived with their mother, two sisters, and four children in an Alameda project. Cornelia and their mother stayed home with the children, while the three remaining sisters worked as welders at Bethlehem Steel. On Sundays their mother would cook for friends, much as she had done in the South: "Mama would cook, and the friends would join us. In Alameda we had lots of friends from Louisiana, and it was really fun. She shopped at the Housewives Market and could get Creole ingredients there. And our brother in New Orleans would send us crates of shrimp and crab. We had guys from the base who were from Louisiana come over. Mama would cook, and we'd have beer and dance."

Neighbors, observing how much fun the family had, "just couldn't believe that we all lived together. They would say women can't live together like that, but we did."[52]

In the decade following the war, most migrants moved from women-centered projects to permanent housing. Many purchased single-family homes in existing black and racially mixed areas or in formerly white neighborhoods just beyond the prewar black/white residential boundary line. Between 1950 and 1960, the number of black homeowners in Berkeley grew from 1,909 to 4,160. During the same period, Richmond's black homeowning population increased from 329 to 2,191, and Oakland's from 4,133 to 11,552. By 1960, nearly 50 percent of black-occupied homes in Berkeley were owned. In Richmond, this figure was 58 percent, and in Oakland, 42 percent. In Berkeley, a higher percentage of African Americans owned homes than whites. Migrants who could not afford to buy homes found rental housing in permanent low-income projects or in private rental units.[53]

Black renters and homeowners faced a tight housing market in the postwar years. White residents and realtors vigilantly protected white neighborhoods from black encroachment. At the same time, East Bay cities adopted redevelopment plans designed to eliminate temporary war housing. When these units were destroyed, migrants had fewer housing options than they had had during the war. In Oakland, for example, postwar housing construction was most heavily concentrated in white areas, and existing black neighborhoods suffered a net loss of housing units. Whether it was intentionally designed to remove migrants, or simply resulted from poor planning, postwar redevelopment compounded migrants' housing woes. Their tenacity, in the context of forced removal and ongoing housing segregation, certainly confirmed one researcher's conclusion that few migrants ever planned to return to the South. Richmond's total population, for example, declined between 1947 and 1960, from 101,579 to 71,854. However, the number of black residents increased from 13 percent to 20 percent of the total, while the proportion of white residents declined.[54]

By 1950, 78 percent of Richmond's black population lived in temporary war housing slated for demolition by the newly created Richmond Redevelopment Agency. Although the city was legally required to provide replacement housing, few tenants were informed of this obligation. Those who did request replacements were transferred to other temporary projects also slated for demolition. In contrast, the city reserved its permanent, low-rent projects for white tenants. Indeed, as demolition of primarily black projects progressed, the city reclassified an all-white temporary development as permanent. Clearly, Richmond's leadership viewed white migrants as more worthy of permanent citizenship.[55]

Black migrants had fewer options. Those with savings purchased lots in North Richmond or on vacant tracts of land in the southern and western sections of town once occupied by war housing and industry. In the early 1950s, two private developers built a "racially unrestricted" tract of single-family homes in an unincorporated area north of Richmond. This tract, called Parchester Village, became an all-black development—a counterpart of postwar, white, planned suburban communities. The city of Richmond annexed this development in 1963. Those who wished to purchase in white neighborhoods still faced discriminatory real estate practices, although restrictive covenants were no longer legal. Families that circumvented biased realtors confronted violent opposition from white homeowners. One family successfully purchased a home in the all-white Rollingwood neighborhood of Richmond. The night of their move, three hundred white residents gathered outside their house and shouted threats. Although the police provided protection, the family endured threatening phone calls and remarks from hecklers in passing cars for several weeks.[56]

Those who could not afford to buy had to find rental housing, which was even more scarce now than it had been during the war. Contra Costa County built one low-income, integrated project in North Richmond in 1949. And the city built another, Easter Hill Village, in South Richmond. However, the number of families these projects accommodated was insignificant compared with the number of black tenants—10,431—who had been displaced.[57]

Residents of Codornices Village, Berkeley's only war-worker housing project, also faced eviction during the postwar years. In 1954, the federal government notified residents of the village that they had six months to leave. At that time, 88 percent of the village's residents were black. Berkeley, unlike Richmond, had no control over the decision, although the city could have acquired the project from the government and extended its life. But the city in fact welcomed the demolition. Five years earlier, in 1949, the city council had refused to consider the development of low-income housing within its borders, despite the availability of federal aid for that purpose. Had the city built permanent, long-term housing, the residents of Codornices Village would have had an alternative to eviction and displacement.[58]

The only other housing available to migrants was in South and West Berkeley. Those who had savings bought homes in these sections of town, sometimes in white neighborhoods that bordered the black sections. In turn, white residents moved out, gradually expanding the borders of black Berkeley. Profit-minded realtors, black and white, helped migrants purchase homes in bordering white neighborhoods. Katherine St. Clair's father, who during the war had made a living purchasing and subdividing West Oakland Victorians, turned to "block-busting" after the war ended. Working in partnership with a white realtor, Katherine's father found migrants who were willing to buy homes in white neighborhoods. The white realtor would arrange the sale, knowing that neighboring whites would bring him their business as they bought homes elsewhere. Katherine's father then sold vacated houses to other black buyers. Such partnerships were limited to certain sections of Berkeley. Katherine remembers that the white realtor would not have integrated neighborhoods in North Berkeley or the hills. In fact, "he was very prejudiced, but he used Daddy and Daddy used him."[59]

Migrants who could not afford homes found an expanding rental market in South Berkeley and West Berkeley. As building materials became available after the war, white and black housing speculators demolished older, single-family homes and built multifamily units. Katherine and her husband, participating in this postwar housing boom, bought two eight-unit buildings in Alameda that had formerly housed servicemen. "You could buy one for $500, but you had to tear it down from the roof to the foundation." She and her husband took the buildings apart and used the materials to build new apartments in South Berkeley. But the St. Clairs were small-scale landlords who lived in their own building. Other builders engaged in "the worst kind of destructive real estate speculative activity" and thereby undermined the stable character of many historic, all-black neighborhoods in Berkeley. By the time zoning restrictions stopped this process in the early 1970s, whole neighborhoods of small, single-family homes had been replaced with cheap, high-density rental housing. Had this development been scattered throughout the city, in white as well as black neighborhoods, its impact would not have been as concentrated.[60]

By the end of the war, 85 percent of Oakland's black population lived in West Oakland, the East Bay's largest black community. There migrants bought or rented homes close to churches, lodges, De Fremery Park, and black business strips along Market and Seventh Streets. Although approximately 11 percent of the city's black population still lived in public housing in 1947, the remainder had either purchased homes or secured permanent rental housing in relatively affordable West Oakland neighborhoods. Residents there enjoyed a richer institutional life and sense of community than anywhere else in the Bay Area.

However, after World War II, Oakland's city council designated West Oakland as a blighted area and targeted it for redevelopment. At the behest of real estate, construction, and business interests, the city proceeded to demolish existing public housing projects as well as entire neighborhoods of single-family homes, black institutions, and businesses. These were replaced with housing developments designed to lure more affluent residents into the area. During the same period, a freeway divided the neighborhoods of West Oakland and isolated a large section of the community from other sections of the city. Next, half of the black commercial strip along Seventh Street was razed to accommodate a rapid transit system. Finally, hundreds of acres of homes and businesses were demolished to accommodate a new postal complex.[61]

Displaced residents, who numbered well over 10,000, had difficulty finding housing in other sections of the city. It was not until 1966 that East

Bay citizens had a legal basis to fight housing discrimination. Most found housing in East Oakland, formerly a white, working-class section of the city. But as one researcher observed, new residents "did not find a system of social organization that existed in West Oakland. East Oakland did not have well established Black neighborhoods that had a history of cooperation and community organization. The Blacks who moved to East Oakland were strangers, and it took time for a community to develop." Thus, migrants who had located permanently in West Oakland, buying or renting homes after moving out of transitional housing, were forced to move yet again. In East Oakland, which had no black businesses or institutions, new residents had to create a community from scratch.[62]

For migrant women, the move from transitional to permanent housing brought a distinct set of challenges. Without the semicommunal spatial design of wartime housing projects, women had greater difficulty meeting friends and engaging in joint projects. Those who bought homes had to literally and figuratively speak over fences. Those who moved into rental housing lived with a high degree of impermanence, seeing neighbors move in and out as their economic fortunes improved or declined. This, too, created barriers to friendships and helping networks. While women did become stabilizing forces in their neighborhoods, providing numerous services and resources, they increasingly turned to institution-building to create and maintain community. Migrant women's institutional work, the topic of Chapter 5, not only linked isolated households but also helped stabilize neighborhoods with large transient populations.

Having a more permanent home base also allowed migrant women to reinforce their connections with family members who remained in the South. During the temporary and transitional housing phases, women maintained contact through letters and phone calls. But once settled in homes of their own, women began what became a life-long pattern of extended return visits. Table 10 shows the frequency of these visits among women in my sample.

Indeed, a consumer survey conducted in 1960 suggests that well after migration peaked, women were much more likely than men to travel away from home on vacations, returning to the South to attend reunions, care for the sick and aged, and help settle family conflicts. Moreover, migrant women continued to extend their resources to newcomers. Between 1955 and 1966, for example, an additional 18,000 new migrants moved from the South to Oakland. These newcomers reinvigorated migrant culture, reinforcing distinct dietary preferences, speech patterns, spiritual traditions, art forms, and folk beliefs.[63]

			Table 10. Frequency of
More than yearly	12%	5	Migrants' Return Visits
Yearly	33%	14	to the South
Every two to five years	35%	15	
Infrequently	16%	7	
Never returned	4%	2	
Total	100%	43	

The pattern I have outlined in this chapter—from temporary to transitional to permanent housing—is a general one. Some women bypassed the temporary phase completely. Others went from temporary to permanent housing, skipping the transitional phase. The tasks I have identified with each phase also represent a general pattern. Orienting tasks, for example, were not strictly confined to the temporary housing phase; each move necessitated reorientation. Moreover, the process of learning about one's environment does not have a discrete ending. Rather, it consists of layers of awareness and familiarity that accumulate over a lifetime. Nor was institution-building always confined to the permanent housing phase. Some adventurous, self-assured, and enterprising women started organizations while in transitional housing.

In addition, the process of becoming familiar with one's environment, creating helping relationships, and building enduring, family-supporting institutions is not a product or outgrowth of different types of housing. These tasks were accomplished by people who creatively used the physical resources associated with their surroundings. The women themselves transformed substandard, temporary housing into a relatively stable base from which they could secure better housing and other basic necessities. Finally, in the context of mass institutional opposition, women's efforts to create and maintain stable homes must be conceptualized as a form of active resistance against those who tried to prevent them from creating permanent homes in the Bay Area.

In the next chapter, I turn to women's paid labor, which is very much connected to their unpaid work in the home. "Home" as a physical entity and state of mind was neither public nor private space. Rather, it was a center that supported other life-sustaining activities: social exchanges, institution-building, and wage labor. Indeed, the familiar dichotomy between public wage labor and private homework all but disappears in East Bay migrant communities. Women who were engaged in both paid and unpaid labor used one to reinforce the other. Migrant women, for example, invested their wages in home improvements and labor-saving appliances. Their wages, along with their unpaid labor, made a house a home. The home, in turn, provided a myriad of services—from laundry and meal preparation to emotional succor—and thereby enhanced worker stability and satisfaction. Neighborhood social contacts, another product of women's unpaid labor, provided child care, medical advice, information on jobs and housing, and other services that directly benefited workers. In turn, women's workplace contacts provided information and resources that enhanced home life.

In order to withstand policies designed to discourage permanent settlement, migrants built and strengthened connections between home, work, and community, much as they had done in the segregated South. Rejecting the integration of newcomers and adopting policies of removal and containment, the East Bay's white community forced migrants to build their own communities with their own resources. One woman, commenting on the work this project required, stated that "lots of things in the South are just born in you, but when you come here it's like you have to create it. And I never thought I'd have to create all that."[64]

A woman defense worker is
the focus of Dorothea Lange's
photograph *Oakland—10th Street
Market*, Fall 1942. (Copyright
the Dorothea Lange Collection, The Oakland Museum,
The City of Oakland. Gift of
Paul S. Taylor.)

Dorothea Lange's photograph
*Metropolitan Oakland (10th Street
Market) during War Times*, ca.
1942, shows a migrant couple
shopping in Oakland's down-
town area. (Copyright the
Dorothea Lange Collection,
The Oakland Museum, The
City of Oakland. Gift of Paul S.
Taylor.)

In Dorothea Lange's *Richmond—Housing for Shipyard Workers*, February 1944, a migrant woman sits in front of her trailer. Housing shortages forced many migrants into substandard, unsanitary, or overcrowded housing. (Copyright the Dorothea Lange Collection, The Oakland Museum, The City of Oakland. Gift of Paul S. Taylor.)

Above: *Woman in Welder's Mask, Richmond*, 1943. Dorothea Lange's sensitive portrait of this young woman reflects the pride and confidence that new employment options often generated. (Copyright the Dorothea Lange Collection, The Oakland Museum, The City of Oakland. Gift of Paul S. Taylor.)

Facing page, top: *Richmond, McDonald Avenue*, ca. 1942, by Dorothea Lange. African American migrants dramatically altered the racial composition of Richmond's population and demanded equal access to the city's services and public space. (Copyright the Dorothea Lange Collection, The Oakland Museum, The City of Oakland. Gift of Paul S. Taylor.)

Facing page, bottom: *Shipyard Workers Waiting for Bus, Cutting Boulevard, Richmond*, ca. 1942, by Dorothea Lange. This photograph illustrates the increased diversity of the wartime working population, as well as the relative cleanliness and structural soundness of federal housing projects (center and right background) designed for war workers. (Copyright the Dorothea Lange Collection, The Oakland Museum, The City of Oakland. Gift of Paul S. Taylor.)

Below: *McDonald Street, Richmond, Calif.*, ca. 1943, by Dorothea Lange. Wartime economic opportunities produced a sense of prosperity among both newcomers, like this migrant woman, and established residents. (Copyright the Dorothea Lange Collection, The Oakland Museum, The City of Oakland. Gift of Paul S. Taylor.)

Facing page: *McDonald Street, Richmond, Calif.*, 1942. This portrait by Dorothea Lange captures the self-confidence and assertiveness that newcomers displayed as they demanded access to the East Bay's resources. (Copyright the Dorothea Lange Collection, The Oakland Museum, The City of Oakland. Gift of Paul S. Taylor.)

Women Line Up for Paychecks, Richmond Shipyards, 1942–43, by Dorothea Lange (Copyright the Dorothea Lange Collection, The Oakland Museum, The City of Oakland. Gift of Paul S. Taylor.)

Chapter Four

. . I Always Desired Independence, Never Wealth

Migrant Women
and Wage Labor

As migrant women created homes for their families with their unpaid labor, they also contributed to family income through wage work. Indeed, most women began to look for paid employment soon after moving to the Bay Area. Thus, the physical and emotional stress of relocation was often compounded by the demands of beginning a new job. But unlike decent housing, jobs were relatively easy to find. Migrant women heard about them from friends, relatives, neighbors, newspaper advertisements, employment bureaus, and fellow passengers on trains and trollies. Word of employment was everywhere, electrifying the atmosphere of streetcars, markets, theaters, diners, and dance clubs.

Jobs were not only easy to find; they were also good. In the past, most gainfully employed African American women worked in domestic service, but during World War II migrant women found different, higher-paying jobs. For the first time in their lives, many had other options: industrial jobs in defense industries, clerical work in an expanding governmental sector, service employment on military bases and in defense plants. In 1940 almost two-thirds of employed black women in the Bay Area worked in private domestic service. By 1943, however, that number fell as women took better jobs in durable goods production.[1]

At the end of the war, black women lost their defense jobs, but few returned to private domestic service. By 1948, well after defense industries closed, only one-fifth of black working women held domestic positions, compared to 66 percent in 1940. Most went on to fill factory jobs (16.6 percent), clerical or sales positions (12.6 percent), and service-sector occupations (34.2 percent). Thus, despite cutbacks in defense in-

dustries, black women still held onto a significant number of manufacturing jobs. Meanwhile, government agencies accounted for the increase in
clerical jobs filled by African American women. On the other hand, few
women went into private-sector clerical or retail occupations. According
to a U.S. Department of Labor study, "Negro workers apparently did not
participate in the postwar expansion of retail trade."[2]

Limits to Opportunity

Even as the war produced greater economic opportunities for migrant
women, their economic status in relation to other workers remained the
same. As Karen Anderson observes, "Whatever the hierarchy of preference[,] . . . black women could always be found at the bottom," both
during and after the war. So although black women shared some of the
overall advances made by women during the war, they continued to
occupy the lowest rungs of the job ladder, suffering racial as well as
gender discrimination.[3]

During the war, defense industries hired white women first, training
them to fill better-paying, less dangerous jobs. A Department of Labor
study revealed that "there was a considerable scattering of white women
in a broad range of jobs, a very large number appearing in the clerical
occupations. The racial minorities[,] however, were markedly concentrated in a limited number of occupations. Thus, 63 percent of the Negro
women were engaged as welders trainees and laborers. . . . In contrast only
6 percent of white women were engaged as laborers, 9 percent worked as
welder trainees, and 9 percent as electrician trainees." By the time black
women were hired, white women had already received training and taken
the best jobs, "working as inspectors, painters, shipfitters, electricians,
welders, machinists, assemblers, track drivers, tank sealers, loaders and
unloaders." White women not only worked at better-paying jobs but also
held jobs longer. Just as large numbers of black women were hired in
1943, war production peaked, and within a year it began to decline.[4]

By 1945, therefore, most migrant women had already lost their defense
industry jobs, enjoying the windfall of new opportunity in war-related
employment for a brief two-year period. Having earned between $.90
and $1.50 per hour—several times what they had made as southern do-
mestic workers or schoolteachers—most of these women hoped to find
other industrial jobs. For them, work was more than a patriotic duty; it
was an economic necessity. A Women's Bureau survey of Bay Area women
found that 95 percent of nonwhite women employed during the war

years planned to continue working after the war. In contrast, only 67 percent of white women expressed the same desire. Clearly, holding onto good jobs was a priority for more African American women than white women.[5]

Migrant women did find other jobs, but rarely at wages comparable with those defense work offered. Although only a few returned to domestic service, most continued to be underrepresented in clerical, professional, managerial, and skilled occupations. In 1948, only one-fifth of black women in the Bay Area held clerical, managerial, or professional jobs, compared with three-fourths of all employed Bay Area women. Those who did find clerical jobs usually worked for the government. The postal service, for example, employed several women in my sample.[6] Indeed, government employment continued to expand throughout the postwar period, providing better job security, wages, and benefits than all other Bay Area jobs open to migrant women. In Oakland alone, government employment expanded 28 percent between 1960 and 1966, and 29 percent of the city's civilian, employed black population drew government paychecks by the end of that period. However, not all of these jobs were clerical; large numbers of migrant women worked for the government in custodial positions.[7]

Most migrant women worked in unskilled factory or service jobs. By 1960, one in ten migrant women worked in semiskilled industrial occupations, primarily in laundries, food processing industries, and apparel factories. The food processing industry, which expanded during the war, employed large numbers of migrant women in the postwar period. Although this work was seasonal, highly routinized, and low-paying, many migrant women appreciated the flexibility it provided; it allowed them to work around husband's and children's schedules, run their own side businesses, and engage in volunteer activities. Other migrant women found employment in the garment industry, usually sewing for independent contractors on a piecework basis. Like food processing industries, garment factories provided little job security but afforded desirable flexibility and autonomy. The majority of migrant women, however, worked in public- and private-sector service industries during the postwar period. By 1960 over 50 percent of black women workers in the Bay Area worked in service occupations, compared with 17 percent for all employed women. While the percentage of black women in private domestic service had declined, more now worked as custodians, cooks, and nurse's aides in institutional settings.[8]

Despite the fact that most migrant women did secure employment after the war, unemployment among nonwhite women still remained high, measuring 11 percent as late as 1960. Black women were also more likely to be underemployed, working at temporary or seasonal jobs. Although their overall labor force participation rates were higher than those of all women, they worked fewer weeks out of the year. Black women's incomes were also substantially lower than white women's. In 1959, black women earned an average of $1,627, compared with $2,177 for white women, $3,944 for black men, and $5,436 for white men.[9]

In brief, the war provided migrant women with a short-lived taste of the good life but with only a lingering aftereffect. Although they filled the lowest-paying, least desirable jobs in the shipyards, defense employment represented a tremendous improvement over the domestic service jobs they had previously held. As one migrant woman commented during the war years,

> I'll tell you. You see, I am a colored woman and I am forty-two years old. Now you know that colored women don't have a chance for any kind of job back there except in somebody's kitchen working for two or three dollars a week. I have an old mother and a crippled aunt to take care of, and I have to make as much as I can to take care of them. It costs so much to live these days. I went down to the government office in Marshall there and they said maybe I could find a war-job out here. I got my neighbors to look after my mother and aunt and came out here on the bus. I went to work for Kaiser and saved enough to bring my aunt and mother out here. I owed Mr. Baker four hundred dollars back home. I made enough to pay back all of it. He returned fifty dollars to me.[10]

But the war boom did not last. Between 1945 and 1950, migrant women looked for other jobs, and many such women were unsuccessful. Migrant women recall the immediate postwar years as a time of great personal and collective hardship. While most eventually found employment, it was in the lower-paying, unskilled industrial and service sectors. Few migrant women returned to full-time domestic jobs, but still fewer escaped from gender and race-based occupational segregation.

Migrant men's experience mirrored that of migrant women, necessitating a two-wage family unit even during the prosperous war and postwar years. Thus, most migrant women did not necessarily work because they wanted to; rather, they worked because their wages were essential to immediate survival. Male migrants were forced into jobs well below their skill levels during the war. A 1943 Department of Labor study found that "fully a fourth of the Negroes . . . who reported their typical occupations as skilled, held semiskilled or unskilled jobs in the local war plants." The study went on to observe that "the distribution of the men within several skill categories also afforded some striking group contrasts. No representatives of the racial minorities appeared in the professional posts and very few in the clerical. Just under half of the whites were employed in skilled jobs, substantial numbers as welders, electricians, machinists, pipe-fitters, and shipfitters. In contrast to the 42 percent of the whites, the semiskilled and unskilled occupations included fully four-fifths of the Negroes and 71 percent of the 'others.' "[11]

The Fair Employment Practice Committee (FEPC) regional field records provide additional evidence of discriminatory hiring. Samuel Hudson, for example, came to the Bay Area as a skilled plumber and steamfitter, having worked for two firms in Greenville, Mississippi; at McKissack and McKissack in Tuskegee, Alabama; and at the Charleston, South Carolina, navy yards. Like Marcellus Knox—a plumber from Austin, Texas, with sixteen years of experience—Hudson could not secure skilled employment at the Richmond shipyards, because the Steamfitters and Helpers Union Local 590 would not admit black members. Boilermakers and Machinists Union locals also prohibited or placed restrictions on black membership, severely limiting access to other skilled jobs in Bay Area defense industries. Frequently, however, industries observed their own discriminatory hiring practices. In 1944, Milas Johnson, a skilled meatpacker and World War II veteran, was refused employment at Oakland's Armour Company because "we can't take colored. . . . We don't have the facilities." Milas, who had worked for Armour in Kansas, promptly filed a complaint with the FEPC. Cases like these led another group of researchers to observe that "this distribution runs contrary to the idea that the in-migrating Negroes were lacking in industrial experience or that they were for the most part common laborers or domestic or other types of servants. This distribution suggests the exceptional character of the in-migrating group—that it was above average in occupational background and education, and that the group had abilities and potentials for which there was no outlet in the areas from which they migrated."[12]

Following a period of postwar unemployment, most migrant men found jobs in semiskilled or unskilled industrial occupations or in the service sector. Industrial occupations included longshore and warehouse work, primary metals production, sanitary services, shipbuilding, construction, assembly, and packing. Those in services worked primarily as janitors, porters, cooks, waiters, bartenders, taxicab drivers, chauffeurs, and parking attendants. Only one in eight worked in the skilled trades as craftsmen, foremen, and kindred workers, and even fewer were engaged in white-collar occupations. Still, by the mid-1960s, unemployment rates for the generation that had migrated during the war were lower than those of any other age group, suggesting that the wartime move was still producing some positive aftereffects.

The sons and daughters of migrants and those who migrated after the war had greater difficulty finding and retaining jobs. At the end of the war, industries began leaving East Bay cities and relocating to larger and less expensive industrial sites in Bay Area suburbs; this process accelerated between 1950 and 1965. Postwar white flight out of Richmond, Oakland, and Berkeley coincided with industrial relocation to the urban fringe. Between 1960 and 1966, for example, Oakland lost one-quarter of its manufacturing jobs. As these jobs—traditionally a source of upward mobility for minority workers—left the city, whites who moved to the suburbs filled them, but they also continued to commute to Oakland to work in the dwindling number of inner-city industrial jobs. Thus, the decrease in manufacturing jobs was compounded by an increase in the number of people who continued to work in Oakland but lived elsewhere. Deindustrialization, which gained public attention in the 1980s, began in the postwar years within increasingly black inner cities. Only when plants began closing in white communities, though, did capital flight become a "national" problem.[13]

While male migrants were less vulnerable to this shift than younger workers because of their seniority and longer employment histories, they were still segregated into occupations that were highly vulnerable to recessionary and seasonal shifts in supply and demand. In 1960, for example, 58 percent of nonwhite men in the Bay Area worked fifty to fifty-two weeks, and 16 percent worked half a year or less. In contrast, 67 percent of all men worked fifty to fifty-two weeks, with only 12 percent working twenty-six weeks or less. Moreover, migrant men made lower wages both during and after the war, providing less of a cushion during periods of unemployment and underemployment.[14]

As manufacturing jobs left the core areas of East Bay cities after the war, the East Bay's older housing stock, located in predominantly black neighborhoods and stretched beyond capacity from wartime migration, rapidly deteriorated. In Oakland, for example, postwar housing construction was concentrated in nonblack areas, while black neighborhoods suffered a net loss of housing units. In the absence of a sustained governmental commitment to provide jobs and housing for black communities, working-class migrant women and men helped stabilize their neighborhoods in the hard economic times following the collapse of the wartime industrial boom. Their helping ethic, learned from their parents and expressed through the institutions they created and through individual acts of kindness, helped East Bay black communities survive the structural economic shifts of the postwar period.[15]

Negotiating the Double Burden

During the war, migrant women found jobs in a wide variety of East Bay industries: shipyards, canneries, hospitals, military supply depots, railroads, and service occupations. The most coveted jobs, however, were skilled and supervisory positions in the shipyards. Migrant women, who faced both gender and racial discrimination, seldom received these "good" jobs. Even after the shipyards began recruiting black workers, union discrimination prevented many men and women from finding skilled jobs in defense industries. The Boilermakers Union, which controlled the largest number of shipyard crafts, negotiated closed-shop agreements with East Bay shipyards early in the war. At the same time, it excluded black workers from its locals, effectively blocking their access to skilled crafts. In early 1942, the Boilermakers finally created a separate auxiliary for Oakland's black shipyard workers. However, it was not until 1943, following protests organized by Frances Albrier, a longtime East Bay black activist, that the union established a black auxiliary at the huge Kaiser shipbuilding facility in Richmond.[16]

Once cleared by their auxiliaries, black women faced other barriers to equal employment: white men dominated highly skilled and supervisory positions; white women, who had entered the shipyards earlier, monopolized gender-specific clerical, skilled, and semiskilled jobs; and black men received the better-paying semiskilled and unskilled positions. Toward the end of the war, some migrant women did find jobs as trainees or helpers in shipbuilding crafts, but a majority worked in other industries or as shipyard janitors, laborers, food service workers, and restaurant attendants.[17]

Filling the least desirable, lowest-paying jobs in the wartime labor force, migrant women created an alternate source of status and identity as homemakers, church women, and community workers. Defining their labor on behalf of community and family as their "real work," migrant women resisted categorization as menial or marginal laborers. Although women's wartime jobs represented a step up from domestic service, they were still at the bottom of the occupational ladder. By emphasizing their role as wives, mothers, and community workers, migrant women were reinforcing a value system that had long been a feature of black family life.

Unlike many of their white counterparts, black women had a history of negotiating and reconciling the double burden of wage labor and domestic work. Long before the war, black women's labor market activities were necessary to family survival, complementing domestic well-being rather than conflicting with it. As Sharon Harley asks in her study of black domestic workers between 1880 and 1930, "How else were children to be fed, clothed, housed, and educated if mothers did not contribute to family income?"[18] The economic necessity of women's wage labor, however, existed within a larger social framework that simultaneously forced black women into menial job classifications and defined marriage and homemaking as appropriate female vocations. As Harley indicated, black working-class women extricated themselves from this dilemma by muting the importance of their paid labor and stressing the significance of their domestic roles: "Not only was women's unpaid labor in the home a great source of worth and pride, it also provided them with a sense of autonomy and control absent for them in the labor market environment."[19]

Care must be taken, however, not to attribute too much agency to black working-class women. At least part of their decision to place greater value on the domestic role was a function of social pressure to preserve male authority and breadwinner status. In a society that equated male virtue with economic success, a woman's unspoken agreement to minimize her role as a worker was essential to marital harmony and survival within the family unit. Moreover, migrant women's oral histories reveal some of the personal costs of negotiating dual roles, as well as exceptions to the rule that women placed family concerns above work commitments.

Even in the most successful marriages, women's paid labor produced ongoing tensions and conflicts. World War II, a time of major change for the migrant women in my sample, brought these tensions into sharp focus. Defense jobs, which paid much more than women had ever made in the South, gave women an irrepressible sense of pride and accomplishment. Many of these women had left home for the first time; consequently, they also felt an enhanced sense of self-sufficiency and independence. Young migrant women used to pinching pennies could now afford lovely clothes and the price of admission to nice restaurants, theaters, and nightclubs. In the boomtown, rags-to-riches atmosphere of the wartime East Bay, traditional gender roles could feel stifling. Black women also received more social permission to take pride in their wage work when the government began promoting female labor as a patriotic duty. During the war their labor was not only necessary but also state-sanctioned.

Nevertheless, government sanction did not instantly modify personal behavior. Many women had married just before migration. Their new relationships, already tested by the move, now faced the additional challenge of adjusting to shifting gender roles and expectations. The majority of marriages in my sample survived, but some were destroyed by lack of trust, conflicting interests, and unmet expectations. In some cases husbands decided to return to the South, while their wives insisted on remaining.

Henrietta Bolden, for example, arrived in California near the end of the war and found a job cleaning railroad cars for Southern Pacific. Before they came to California, she and her husband lived on a farm outside of Guthrie, Oklahoma, farming on shares. Henrietta remembers their Oklahoma life as one of unremitting toil, "picking cotton, chopping cotton, keeping a garden, and feeding chickens." To supplement their farm income she also worked as a domestic servant, earning a meager $1.50 per week. To this day she "wouldn't want to have a farm." Six months after arriving in California, her husband wanted to return to Oklahoma. Henrietta reluctantly returned with him, "but I just couldn't stand chopping cotton and told him I was coming back." Returning to Oakland without him, Henrietta went back to work for Southern Pacific. "The country girl had come to California, seen the bright lights, and run wild."

Henrietta remembers Oakland as a fun place during the prosperous war years, filled with nightclubs and ballrooms that would "bring people from the South to perform." And she made sixty-five cents an hour, so she had the money to dress up and go out. "I would buy nice clothes with shoes, hats, and gloves to match" and go restaurant- and club-hopping with friends up and down Seventh Street. There, "men would stand on the corners and whistle and say, 'Heaven is having a recess today, because here comes one of the angels.' "[20]

Olive Blue, who moved to California while her husband was serving overseas, found work at the Kaiser shipyards. She signed up to be a scaler—to smooth out welds by removing stray drops of metal. She was recruited to issue tools and mark time cards instead, because she wrote clearly, but scaling paid better, so Olive convinced her supervisor to give her back her old assignment. "After a while I began to show other ladies how to work. I worked days, swing, and grave, and rotated shifts. I enjoyed it, but didn't stay long. My mother came out to visit and she liked to die . . . said she wouldn't go back as long as we [Olive and her sister] were working in the shipyards." In the meantime, Olive's mother found out that the post office was hiring women, and she encouraged her daughter to apply. "So that's what I did—went to San Francisco and took the exam. I always feared what the Bible said, and that was to obey your parents." Olive not only passed the civil service exam and received the job but also began giving classes in her Richmond housing project, teaching others how to take the test. "My sister got into it [the post office] and friends got into it, and it was just nice." After her husband returned from the service, he wanted to go back to the South. Olive was enjoying her job and wanted to stay, and the couple negotiated an amicable divorce.[21]

Other marriages were destroyed by lack of trust or conflicts over women's independence. Carmelia Chauvin's husband returned from the war a "changed man." Back in New Orleans, Carmelia had married a member of her father's social club. The prospective groom, a seaman, had demanded an answer before his upcoming stint at sea, and Carmelia, thinking that "there was no way in heaven he'd be back in time," said she would marry him if he returned to port by June, "because I wanted to be a June bride." To Carmelia's disappointment, he did return on time, and they married; but by August he had been drafted and sent overseas.

While he was gone, Carmelia joined her older sister in California; she moved there with her mother, another sister, and two nieces. Once in Oakland, Carmelia tried to find work as a typist, but very few businesses would hire black clerical workers. Finally, she and a sister were hired at Bethlehem Steel, where they worked as welders after completing a short training course. Carmelia characterized the work as "fun." After work, she and her sister, an uncle, a cousin, and a brother-in-law, all of whom worked the swing shift, walked home together.

At the housing project where Carmelia lived with her sisters and mother, life was good. "Guys from the base who were from Louisiana would come over and Mama would cook, and there would be beer and dancing. It was a fun time until my husband came back and then it was downhill. We didn't have much of a relationship because we got married in June and he was gone in August. And he was gone for three years and when he returned he accused me of everything you could think of. And I didn't do anything." Carmelia, who had found a high-paying job and established independent friendships in her husband's absence, paid a price for her self-sufficiency. Shortly after his return, Carmelia's mother gave a party and invited the many friends they had met since coming to California. Later that evening, Carmelia's husband hit Carmelia, beginning a pattern of violence that eventually sent Carmelia to the hospital. After she was treated and released, her husband returned to New Orleans. Later he came back to Oakland, where he lived with his sister. He died in 1958, leaving Carmelia with three small children to raise on a single salary. Fortunately, Carmelia found a job with the government following the war; she retired from that position only after thirty years of service.[22]

Opal Smith's independence also created problems in her marriage. She moved to California from Texas in 1943, a year after her husband had come out. Although he made enough in the shipyards to support their growing family, Opal wanted to work for "extras." As Christmas approached, Opal asked her husband if she could take a temporary job to buy a tree and presents. He reluctantly agreed when she promised to quit following the holiday. "But I never stopped. Came out in September or October of 1943 and started work that Christmas at the Postal Concentration Center sorting mail for servicemen. And after the war I went over to San Francisco, rerouting mail to the servicemen who had come home." Opal worked nights so she could get her children off to school and pick them up in the afternoon. While they were gone, Opal cleaned the house, did laundry and grocery shopping, and prepared the evening meal to convince her husband that she was still a dedicated wife and mother. Nevertheless, her husband grew progressively more jealous, accusing her of "running around" with the men where she worked. In 1946, her husband lost his job at the shipyard. The following year they divorced, and he moved back to Texas.[23]

Most married couples in my sample, however, welcomed the opportunity to add to family income and eagerly embraced women's wartime employment. The added income provided by women's paid labor enhanced rather than detracted from family stability, particularly given that married women continued to take primary responsibility for child care, cooking, cleaning, laundry, and shopping. As long as women remained homemakers—even if they had to work double-time to do it—men retained their breadwinner status. Few of the women I interviewed challenged this arrangement; they prized their homemaker status and willingly maintained their husband's designation as primary provider and family head, despite the obvious strains of working two jobs.

Child care was a particular concern of married women. Berkeley and Oakland provided facilities relatively early, but Richmond school officials resisted establishing programs that would add to their administrative burdens during and after the war. In 1943, Richmond finally agreed to establish several day nurseries, but their facilities and those in Oakland and Berkeley had difficulty attracting black children. Kaiser's facilities, open around the clock, were well-attended. However, limited hours, high costs, and inconvenient locations led to underuse elsewhere. Besides, black migrant women had long relied on friends and relatives to provide child care. Children were viewed as part of a communal trust and thus were only reluctantly placed in the care of outsiders.[24]

In 1943, Ethel Tillman left Mississippi with her ten children and an aunt; she traveled west to join her husband, who had come to the East Bay a year earlier. Ethel's husband, a skilled pipefitter, had obtained a job at Mare Island Naval Shipyard in Vallejo. Ethel also found employment there, sorting scrap metal into different piles according to its composition. While Ethel worked the swing shift, her aunt cared for all ten children and for many others whose mothers also worked in defense industries. During off hours, Ethel had her hands full, shopping, washing clothes, preparing meals, and making certain the children were doing well in school. The Tillmans also sponsored several other families from the South, providing housing and food until they found places of their own. This hospitality imposed an additional burden on Ethel, who took most of the responsibility for housekeeping.[25]

Unlike Ethel, Lee Henderson had no friends or relatives to help with child care, but she found an imaginative alternative. She and her husband moved from Oklahoma to Oakland in 1941. Once in the Bay Area, Lee worked as a domestic servant "until they got the shipyards going." Then she attended welding school and secured a job at the Kaiser yards in Richmond. Her husband worked at Oakland's Moore shipyard. With their joint income, the Hendersons soon bought a house in Berkeley. But in 1943 Lee had a baby and was forced to quit her job. However, she quickly came up with an alternate source of income that allowed her to stay home with the baby. From her own experience in the shipyards, she knew that workers disliked the food served in cafeterias and on catering trucks and missed home-cooked meals. So she started packing lunches for men and women who worked in the yards, and she "made good money doing that."[26]

Ruth Cherry had fewer options. Her need for paid employment forced her to make painful sacrifices. Shortly after she joined her husband in Oakland in 1945, he quit his job in the shipyards because of a life-threatening heart condition. Since the shipyards had stopped hiring new workers by the time Ruth arrived, she settled for a lower-paying cannery job in order to support her husband and infant daughter. But cannery work was seasonal, forcing Ruth to supplement her wages by providing in-home child care to white families during slack seasons. When her husband moved back to Louisiana, Ruth had to place her daughter in a preschool so that she could continue to send money to her husband and provide a home for her child.[27]

Married women who delayed childbearing or never had children negotiated work and family obligations with fewer hardships. Oma June Scott, for example, grew up in Austin, Texas. As the war effort got under way, Oma began hearing about plentiful, high-paying defense jobs in the Bay Area, and soon after her high school graduation, she and her new husband moved to California. Once settled, they sent for Oma's mother, sister, and brother-in-law, but no sooner had they reestablished their family than Oma's husband was drafted. Oma went to work in the shipyards and moved in with her mother, who had saved enough from her own job to buy a house. When Oma's husband returned, the young couple used their joint savings to purchase a home. And by the time Oma had her first child she had already received a layoff notice from her job. For Oma and her husband, as well as other young couples, wartime employment provided an economic cushion for the postwar years.[28]

Similarly, Theresa Waller and her husband came to California in 1943 from Houston, Texas. After finding full-time jobs—he as a longshoreman on the San Francisco waterfront, and she in an Oakland cannery—they saved to buy a house. Without children, Theresa felt more social permission to identify as a worker and derive status from her occupation. Not surprisingly, she expressed deeper satisfaction with her wartime job, and more bitterness over losing it in late 1945, than women with greater family obligations.[29]

A small percentage of married women—8 percent in my sample—did not work during the war, deferring to their husbands' insistence that a woman's place is in the home. Best Johnson came to California with her husband two days after they married, arriving in Richmond in October 1944. Mr. Johnson soon found a job in the Kaiser shipyards, and he told Best that he wanted her to stay home. The Johnsons then began a family; a new child arrived every two years between 1945 and 1964.[30]

Marlene Lewis and her husband moved to California after several years of work as migrant farm laborers. "Wherever the money was, that's where we were," she recalled. But once they arrived in the East Bay, her husband found work in the shipyards "and wanted me to stay home." She went on to explain that "I thought women should stay home too—that you just had children." In spite of these values, Marlene did not stay home. In 1943 she returned to school and earned her high school diploma. Then, after scoring in the ninety-eighth percentile on the civil service exam, she went to work at the Oakland Naval Supply Center.[31]

Single women, particularly those without children, were largely free of the role conflicts and double workloads that married women faced. For them, the war years were particularly joyful and exciting. Unlike married women, they could freely enjoy the bright lights of the wartime East Bay and unapologetically take pride in their new status as war-industry workers. Willa Henry finished her first year of college in Texas, then came out to California to join other family members who had migrated earlier in the year. She initially intended to work for the summer and return to college, but she ended up making "more money than I had ever earned in my life." Willa attended welding school and remembers that "all kinds of women were taking those classes . . . but we [migrants] were not thinking of patriotism. We were thinking of money."

After she completed training in vertical, horizontal, and overhead welding, Willa went to work in the Kaiser shipyards on the graveyard shift. She then "got an easier job as a shipfitter and went on day shift"; she remained there until she was laid off in early 1945. Hoping to polish her secretarial skills, she then applied to a local business college, but she was told that "they did not accept colored students because part of their policy was to guarantee graduates jobs, and they had problems placing black students." However, she soon found employment as a "limited war service mail clerk," sorting letters and packages at the Oakland Army Base and the San Francisco Post Office. This position lasted until 1946.

Willa was "never ashamed of coming from the South, because money talks." She would buy nice clothes with her shipyard money and walk down Oakland's Broadway with "my head held high." In the evenings she would go to the swing clubs along Seventh and Eighth Streets or take the "F" train from Oakland to San Francisco. There she and her friends would see the "big-name" southern black musicians, many of whom had not appeared in the Bay Area before the war.[32]

Frankie Patton, another single migrant, had been a schoolteacher back in Guthrie, Oklahoma. In 1942, she arrived in California and joined her younger sister, Lee Henderson, who had moved out a year earlier with her husband. Frankie came thinking she would teach, "but Oakland schools were not hiring black women" in 1942. Two years later the school district faced a massive influx of migrant children and tried to recruit her, but Frankie said "no thanks." By that time she had found work in the Alameda shipyards, painting ships for sixty-five cents an hour—much more than she would have made as a teacher. Like Willa, Frankie enjoyed the Bay Area's nightlife. In 1942, however, "there wasn't much entertainment; more culture came in in the mid-1940s." Early in the war Frankie and her friends entertained each other in their homes, hosting dance and dinner parties. Later, as more migrants arrived, they went to "hear the big bands and see the big acts at Sweet's Ballroom in Oakland and the Golden Gate Theater in San Francisco."[33]

For married and unmarried migrant women, war jobs provided the opportunity to enjoy Bay Area entertainment, to dress and eat well, and to realize the dream of home ownership. Many also experienced enhanced status as workers and a reprieve from the demeaning and unrewarding demands of domestic service, although often at the expense of marital harmony and established gender roles. But while war-related jobs were clearly an improvement over those that migrant women had held in the past, white workers continued to monopolize the best jobs and supervisory positions. Evidence that many women did in fact obtain a sense of identity from their wage work is found in their resistance to various forms of occupational discrimination.

Faith McAllister, for example, "never saw a black leaderman in welding. I had a black woman friend who was a leaderman, but only over those black ladies who swept up." Her observation was accurate. In 1943, 102 black workers, including at least 30 women, filed a complaint with the FEPC, claiming that their employer, the Permanente Metals Corporation of Richmond, failed to upgrade and promote them, and in some cases asked them to train the white employees who became their supervisors. Just a month later, 173 workers, including 27 women, filed a similar complaint against Richmond Shipyard No. 1. Instead of protecting black workers, labor unions were part of the problem. Defense industries with government contracts operated on a closed-shop basis. Thus, workers needed union clearance to work at skilled trades. However, several unions either refused to admit nonwhites or segregated them into Jim Crow auxiliary unions. As late as July 1944, for example, Machinists Local 824 of Richmond refused to clear black workers, stating that "if they were forced to take Negroes into the union, or to clear or refer them, the men would walk out of the plants and that they as union officials would turn in their badges and go out with the men." As the following letter by Mrs. Etta Germany indicates, migrants bitterly protested this type of discrimination:

Mr. President,
Honorable Sir,
I wish to call your attention to a very disgraceful and UnAmerican situation that now exists in the Boilermakers and Welders Union Local 513 of Richmond, Calif. I am a Negro girl. Three weeks ago I and lots of

others enrolled in the National Defense Training Classes to become welders. I applied for a job at the yards several times. But each time myself and others of my race were given the run around. . . . [Be]cause of being Negro I was not allowed to join the Union. Now Mr. President there are a great many Negroes in Defense Training as myself who upon completion of the course will be subjected to the same treatment as myself. . . . We are all doing what we can to assist in winning the war. I sincerely feel that this is no time for our very own fellow citizens to use discrimination of this type.[34]

Once hired, migrants faced hostile co-workers. In Oakland's Moore shipyard, white workers—male and female—viewed black migrants as an "invading mob" and routinely circulated stories of black incompetence and stupidity. Shipyard management often encouraged such stereotypes. For example, an employee handbook that was designed to introduce new workers to the Richmond yards contained offensive racial caricatures and jokes. Many migrants noted that white women were often the worst offenders. Effie Walling, a white welder at Mare Island in Vallejo, betrayed the high level of racial hostility when she commented that black women "weren't good workers at all." She went on to claim that "the women of the black [race] were very belligerent against white women."[35]

When migrant women encountered harassment, they often had no-where to turn. Faith McAllister, harassed by her white supervisor, ex-plained that "it was no good complaining because who would you com-plain to? The same kind of fellow that he was?" Faith went on to sum up the wartime work experience of most migrant women: "Discrimination was hard, but we've been doing it for years and years. At least we got paid for putting up with it out here."[36]

Some migrant women responded to racial harassment and discrimina-tion by turning inward, adopting a dignified and reserved attitude toward white co-workers, and creating their own support networks. Katherine Archibald, a white observer at Moore shipyard, described the daughter of a prosperous black Texas farmer; this woman had taught school in her home state before migrating to the East Bay. More educated and skilled than many of her white co-workers, she was nevertheless denied a clerical job at Moore. Instead, management hired her as a restroom matron. The woman took the position but radiated moral and intellectual superiority while on the job. Many, however, refused to accept such treatment. Bea-trice Morris, for example, applied for an opening as a power-machine op-erator at the California Manufacturing Company in Oakland. They hired her but placed her in a less skilled job. When she asked to be reclassified as a power-machine operator, she was told that "the white power machine operators objected to having a Negro seated among them." She immediately quit her job and filed a complaint with the FEPC.[37]

Women also joined men in protesting the auxiliary union system. Until 1945, when a Bay Area shipyard worker successfully challenged the legality of such unions in the state supreme court, black workers were forced into Jim Crow auxiliaries as a condition of employment. There they paid dues but were denied an equal voice in union elections and policy decisions. In 1943, for example, twenty-one burners at Moore Shipyard, representing an additional one hundred workers, walked into the regional FEPC office to protest the loss of their jobs: they had been fired for refusing to pay dues to the Boilermakers Auxiliary Union A-26. However, the FEPC had no authority in such cases, since auxiliary unions were still legal.[38]

Most longtime East Bay black residents shunned defense industry employment, perceiving greater stability in their existing jobs. But many established black labor leaders and community activists, responding to the potential numerical strength that migrants could add to their movements, became ardent advocates for better jobs, housing, and social services. The Communist Party–affiliated East Bay Shipyard Workers Committee, founded in 1942 by an established black resident, attracted a large migrant membership, educated migrants about unions, lobbied against housing and job discrimination, and fought for the right of black auxiliary members to elect their own representatives. Similarly, the Bay Area Council Against Discrimination, founded during the war, drew its leadership from over seventy organizations, including the Brotherhood of Sleeping Car Porters and the Marine Cooks and Stewards Union. Its housing and labor subcommittees joined with white liberals and black ministers to conduct voter registration drives among black migrants, and the groups forged a progressive, prolabor coalition that would successfully challenge probusiness, antimigrant East Bay conservatives in postwar elections. Thus, while most established black residents remained hostile toward newcomers, labor issues created an arena for cooperation between migrants and prewar black leaders. Ultimately, their coalition would benefit all East Bay black residents, regardless of their origin.[39]

Although migrant women benefited from such advocacy, it did not immediately erase the pain and humiliation they suffered both on and off the job. Migrant women recall that they remained second-class citizens no matter how much money they made in their wartime jobs. Estelle Peoples remembered an indignity she suffered on the way to work: "I was going to work one morning and I sat beside this white lady and she jumped up and I said, 'My God, I thought I left all of that at home.' And I didn't move, but that was when I began to notice that things weren't that different here." Mary Lee, who worked at a food processing plant "canning beets and carrots for fifty cents an hour as opposed to a dollar a day back in Shreveport," remembered taking the train into San Francisco with a friend to enjoy a meal at one of the city's finer restaurants. As they left, a waiter followed them outside and dropped all of their dishes into the gutter. For women such as Mary, having a good job heightened rather than assuaged the sting of discrimination.[40]

Postwar Employment Trends

By 1945, as defense industries demobilized and turned remaining jobs over to men, migrant women employed in shipbuilding began to lose their jobs. Throughout the East Bay, but particularly in Richmond, black unemployment rates climbed steadily from the end of the war to 1950. In 1950, Richmond's nonwhite unemployment rate stood at 29 percent, compared with 13 percent for the white labor force. The jobless rate for black women stood at 39 percent—significantly higher than that for black men (25 percent), white men (10 percent), and white women (13 percent).[41]

Many migrant women viewed postwar unemployment as a product of white economic policy, designed to encourage migrants to leave the Bay Area. Lovie McIntosh, a migrant who organized postwar boycotts of stores that refused to hire black workers, explained that "Richmond never recovered from postwar unemployment. If good jobs had continued to be available, the community would have been a lot different. By not providing jobs, whites were trying to freeze the black community out."[42] Lovie's assertion is certainly consistent with the data on postwar hiring practices. A 1954 study by the California Department of Employment found that "only 30% of Richmond's employers hired workers on the basis of merit alone. Another 30% did not hire any Negroes, regardless of their qualifications, and an estimated 40% hired Negroes only for certain jobs and did not provide equal opportunities for advancement."[43] A Bay Area–wide study by the California State Employment Service came to the same conclusion, reporting that black residents, if fortunate enough to find employment, were confined to low-paying, unskilled jobs, regardless of their education and skill level. The study went on to state that the jobs available to black workers provided less security during recessionary periods than did the managerial, sales, clerical, skilled trades, and professional positions open to white workers.[44]

Despite these barriers, the migrant generation remained in the East Bay and struggled to maintain the fledgling communities they had established during the prosperous war years. Throughout the 1950s their jobless rates gradually declined, and by the 1960s the migrant generation had the lowest unemployment rates of any other age group. In Oakland, for example, unemployment for migrant women had declined to 8 percent by 1966, but it stood at 16 percent for a younger generation of black women, those between twenty-five and thirty-four years old. During the same period, unemployment rates for migrant men declined to 6 percent but remained high for youth who had come of age as the East Bay began losing large numbers of industrial jobs. It appears that migrant women and men, after an initial period of unemployment, were able to secure remaining jobs in the declining industrial sector because of their relative seniority and work experience. And as deindustrialization accelerated in the 1960s, their experience and seniority continued to place them at a competitive advantage over younger black workers just entering the job market.[45]

Migrant women's postwar employment was central to the relative economic stability of the black working class, frequently providing at least half of a family's income. Even when women's employment was irregular and more supplemental to that of the primary wage earner, their wages enhanced family security and quality of life. In my sample, women's postwar jobs fell into two categories: irregular, part-time, or seasonal work in garment factories, canneries, and domestic service; and full-time, long-term employment, usually in the governmental sector. During childbearing years, some women chose employment strategies in the first category, trading job security and higher wages for greater flexibility. However, most women took such jobs because they had no alternative. Other, more fortunate migrant women found employment in the second category and embarked on stable careers that often lasted their entire working lives.[46]

Women who took jobs in the first category employed a number of strategies to enhance their earning power or balance work with family obligations. Louise Steele, a welder during the war, found a part-time job altering women's clothes at a department store during her children's school hours. Believing that "two people have to work . . . even mothers with small children," she supplemented the income from this job by taking sewing into her home. This arrangement allowed her to earn full-time wages while accommodating family needs. Later, as her children entered their teens, she found full-time work in the garment industry.[47]

Lacey Gray worked early morning hours at a bakery when her children were small, supplementing what her husband earned as an elevator operator and doorman at a bank. When Lacey and her husband divorced, she supported her teenage daughters by combining work during the day, party catering during the evenings, and a custodial job at an industrial plant.[48] Similarly, Mary Lee took seasonal, part-time jobs in canneries while her children were young but began to work full-time after they started school. Employed by Del Monte, Mary worked twelve-hour shifts during peak canning seasons, from 6 P.M. to 6 A.M. Then she would help her children get off to school, clean the house and do the laundry, and sleep until they came home. Her husband, who worked days in a cleaning and pressing plant at the Alameda Naval Base, watched the children in the evenings.[49]

During the war, Opal Smith worked nights at her postal job so that her schedule would not interfere with her family obligations. In 1946, when her husband lost his defense job and returned to Texas, Opal's younger sister moved in with her and provided child care in the evenings. After all of the residual wartime mail had been rerouted, Opal lost her job. Now single, jobless, and with young children to support, Opal invested her savings in a house: she lived in the bottom and rented out the top. She then supplemented her rental income by selling cosmetics door-to-door. When her children were older, Opal found a full-time day job at Oakland Naval Supply Center and married a man who worked in maintenance at the University of California. Both Opal and her second husband kept these jobs until they retired.[50]

Many migrant women went directly from wartime jobs into long-term, full-time employment with the government or private sector. Although the majority of these women also had family obligations, they viewed their jobs as too valuable to pass up. Government jobs, in particular, provided a level of pay and security rarely offered to African Americans by private industry. As a consequence of their full-time, sustained employment, this group of migrant women identified with their jobs and saw themselves as workers. While most continued to take primary responsibility for children and domestic chores, they clearly took pride in their wage work. However, women rarely stressed their monetary contributions to family income. Instead, they focused on the characteristics they had been raised to value: competence, hard work, dependability, and economic independence.

After losing her war job, Estelle Peoples was hired by the State of California as a professional custodian. Estelle worked for the state until her retirement in 1970, and she "loved her job and co-workers." She particularly enjoyed working alone, setting her own pace, and having individual responsibility for a certain area. Estelle recalled that this job allowed her to be her own boss.[51] Olive Blue, after losing her wartime post office job, found work at Oakland Naval Supply Center and remained there until her retirement in 1984. Loved and admired by her co-workers, Olive had this to say about work: "I think we should love what we do. . . . Do it whether it is great or small. Do it well, or don't do it at all."[52]

June Williams, whose husband was injured in a defense plant during the war, went to work as a practical nurse at a local hospital in 1945. She worked there for the next thirty-two years, although her husband eventually recovered and found a construction job. Together June and her husband bought a house, financed regular visits back home, and took the children on camping trips up the Sacramento River. "By living frugally and saving, we were able to do well."[53]

Ruth Gracon went to work for Del Monte cannery in 1946 while her oldest daughter and a neighbor provided child care. She worked there for the next thirty-five years. Each season, she explained, was marked by a different fruit: "started with apricots, then peaches, then pears, then tomatoes, and cherries in the winter." Her husband, who worked at the Alameda Naval Air Station, also fixed radios and televisions on the side. Their combined wages allowed them to buy a house in Berkeley and support a family of ten children. Now widowed, Ruth recalls that "neither of us ever wanted to retire."[54]

A small percentage of migrant women, unable to find long-term, full-time employment or successfully piece together part-time work, relied on public assistance during periods of unemployment. As a whole, working-class women—even those with good jobs—viewed welfare as a temporary safety net, providing job insurance during times of unemployment, sickness, or the absence of reliable and affordable child care. Those women who used welfare did so because they lacked other alternatives; it was their strategy of last resort, adopted out of necessity. Unlike the black middle class, the working class lived with the prospect of poverty and joblessness. This vulnerability produced a greater level of identification with those in need, along with a tolerance of a wide range of survival strategies.

Henrietta Bolden, a divorced woman with four small children, lost her job with Southern Pacific in 1948. She worked wherever she could, cleaning homes, hotels, and motels. But during periods of unemployment, illness, or inability to afford child care, Henrietta went on public assistance. She remembers how difficult it was to "make things stretch" and maintain a sense of dignity while under the supervision of case workers. "One way I would make things stretch was by buying clothes from the Goodwill and altering them for my children. I always wanted them to look nice. I'll never forget the day this social worker came by when the children were going off to school and asked, 'Do they dress like that every day?' And I told her, 'Yes, they do.' And she said to me, 'It looks to me like you're living awful good on the money.' And I said, 'You mean to tell me I'm living good off the money when I'm buying clothes from Goodwill?' She shut her mouth after that."[55]

Similarly, Cornelia Duvernay relied on public assistance because domestic work did not cover health insurance, food, clothing, and rent. "I did domestic work when I could find it, but basically raised my kids on welfare. And they did all right. One is a lawyer, and the other an accountant." After her children were older, Cornelia found a full-time permanent job with the Oakland public school system and remained there until she retired.[56]

Despite their precarious position in the labor market, many migrant women displayed a high degree of identification with their jobs, responding to poor wages and working conditions with both collective and individual forms of resistance. Ruth Cherry, who found a janitorial job at the University of California following the war, helped organize fellow workers and obtain student support for their union. Ruth remembers what it was like before they unionized. "Lots of single women worked there with so little job security. Supervisors could fire at will. It was then that I realized how hard-hearted people were during that campaign; what we wanted was so basic."[57]

Willa Suddeth went to work for a fledgling electronics company following the war, and she helped organize her mostly female co-workers. After a successful union drive, Willa became a shop steward, attending classes in labor relations three nights a week. During this period she initiated a program within the company to hire more minority workers, and she struggled to make her union more responsive to working women's needs. She eventually became her union's paid community service coordinator, connecting union members with personal problems to the appropriate service providers. Willa saw herself as continuing a family tradition of labor activism: in the South, her father and uncles had belonged to an all-black trade union. "The only way my family ever got along was through unions," she recalled.[58]

Lucille Moss found a job as a practical nurse at Kaiser hospital following the war and worked there for the next twenty-five years. When hospital workers organized, she "was right there with them. And when we went out on strike, I couldn't walk the picket line because of a knee injury. But I made soup and coffee and brought it out to the strikers."[59]

Migrant women who found themselves in occupations that were traditionally difficult to organize adopted individual forms of resistance. After raising her children, Louise Steele found work sewing clothing on a piece-work basis in a San Francisco garment shop. During a meeting where workers and management negotiated the price of a new garment, one of Louise's co-workers turned to her and said, "This shop is the only one where management actually bickers over pennies, isn't this so, Louise?" When Louise vocalized her agreement, one of the shop owners called her "stupid." Louise quickly fired back, "I beg your pardon, you're stupid yourself." The owner then retorted, "You're fired." But Louise, eager to have the final word, responded, "No, I'm not; I quit." Later, her supervisor contacted her and said she could have her job back if she apologized to the owner in front of her co-workers. But Louise refused, stating that she would return only if he "begged her pardon in front of the other workers."[60]

Many other migrant women also refused to remain where they felt unfairly treated or degraded; instead they used education to improve their job skills and move into more rewarding occupations. Best Johnson worked as a practical nurse at a convalescent hospital—a low-paying, demanding occupation. After work, she attended night school and eventually obtained a credential in early childhood education. She then found a more satisfying job as a Montessori schoolteacher. Similarly, Louisa Hall took care of white children while she finished her high school degree. She then studied special education in college, took the civil service exam, and was hired by the State of California as a teacher's aide in special education classrooms.[61]

Marlene Lewis, who worked as a farm laborer before migrating to California, also completed her high school degree in the Bay Area. Her husband, who had found a high-paying shipyard job, insisted on being the sole breadwinner but did not object to her educational ambitions. After the war, Marlene took the civil service exam, passed with an almost perfect score and, over her husband's objections, took a job at Naval

Supply. Like many other migrant women, Marlene demonstrated a remarkable capacity to recognize and take advantage of opportunities for occupational mobility. Raised in an environment where survival often hinged on initiative, improvisation, and decisive action, few migrant women had time for self-doubt. When asked how they summoned the courage to take such personal risks, most women responded that they never paused to think about failure. "We knew what we had to do, and we did it."[62]

Migrant women's relationship to paid labor was complex. While many identified themselves as workers and obtained considerable pride and self-esteem from their jobs, few participated in a more general workplace culture. The subtle and overt racism of white co-workers continually diluted the potentially unifying impact of class. Thus, most migrant women viewed themselves as workers but not as members of a unified working class or industrial proletariat. To be sure, small numbers of male migrants—particularly those who belonged to more racially inclusive unions, such as the International Longshoremen's and Warehousemen's Union—developed strong identifications with their trade and fellow workers. But most migrants, male and female, worked in low-paying service industries or as semiskilled and unskilled industrial laborers.

Occupationally segregated into low-paying, traditionally nonunion jobs, the migrant generation did not identify with the white workers who monopolized the better-paying blue-collar jobs. Instead, they turned to other working-class black workers in their churches and neighborhoods to form a race-based analysis of their position in the labor market. At the same time, their work served to define the boundaries of black working-class culture, placing them in a distinct socioeconomic category separate from both the black middle class and the poor.

In this culture, migrants could strive for economic independence but not for personal wealth and advancement. Prizing thrift, frugality, and simplicity, the working class criticized the black middle class and elite for their perceived selfishness, elitism, and condescension. Conversely, members of the working class regarded the poor as less fortunate versions of themselves, not as social or moral inferiors. Above all, migrants "appreciated those who moved ahead, but kept their common touch," remembering where they came from and their connection to those who remained behind. This meant rejecting ostentatious displays of wealth, pretentious mannerisms and speech patterns, and other distinguishing markers of privilege.

Migrants also valued work as a moral good: even the lowliest of jobs was worthwhile if performed well, and calling a person a hard worker was paying them a high compliment. Thus, few migrants looked forward to retirement. When they were forced to quit their jobs because of ill health or old age, most remembered their working years with pleasure and pride and devoted their remaining energy to nonpaid family, church, or community work.

In the end, working-class culture and identity—shaped both by men and by women—was more a product of lived experience in the home, church, neighborhood, and community than a product of the workplace. It was also transmitted, consisting of values, skills, mannerisms, tastes, and preferences passed from one generation to the next. Thus, working-class migrants saw their cultural inheritance as uniquely southern and carefully transplanted it out West. In the process, East Bay culture—black and white—took on a new southern character.

Chapter Five . . . . .

. . . . I Never Denied Where I Came From

Migrant Women and
Their Cultural Work
in the East Bay

During interviews, migrant women stated quite forcefully that their cultural traditions were distinctly southern and thus gave them a separate identity and a common bond with other migrants. Many established black residents also came from the South and probably shared many of the class, ethnic, and regional characteristics that were used to define migrants as foreign and unassimilable. However, wartime racial tensions associated with mass migration and increased competition over resources masked similarities between old-timers and newcomers. More than they had in the past, established residents wished to disassociate themselves from "uncouth" migrants, who were being blamed for disrupting the "harmonious" prewar social order. And migrants, feeling marginalized, held even more strongly to what they believed set them apart. Thus, cultural differences between the two groups may have been either more perceived than real or accentuated by wartime hostilities.

At the same time, we should not ignore the possibility that prewar black residents, whose population was smaller, adopted white, middle-class notions of respectability and decorum to mute cultural differences and promote racial equality. As Douglas Daniels noted in *Pioneer Urbanites*, established Bay Area residents "emphasized the American and San Francisco aspects of their identity, concealing their Afro-American background when it would disadvantage them." Ironically, their efforts to assimilate helped foster a climate of civility between the races but failed to dismantle structural barriers to full equality. Early black residents did enjoy more social fluidity—they rarely encountered overt white hostility and violence—but they could only achieve this peace by staying in their place and helping perpetuate the myth of relative racial harmony and liberalism.[1]

In contrast, wartime migrants were unselfconsciously southern; they bore distinct cultural markers, including speech patterns, dress, dietary preferences, musical tastes, modes of worship, and a self-help tradition forged in the segregated South. Many established black residents worried that they would be lumped together with uncouth migrants and, as a result, greeted newcomers with hostility. In his wartime survey, Charles Johnson found that 82 percent of established black residents believed that migrants threatened their own opportunities for advancement.[2]

These fears, which were not entirely unfounded, point to significant cultural distinctions between the two communities. Whether recent, long-standing, real, or imagined, such differences shaped both personal and collective identity during and after the war. Aurelious P. Alberga, an established resident interviewed by Douglas Daniels, commented that migrants' "English, naturally, was very, very bad." He went on to remark that it would take several years "before they seemed to get Americanized." Another longtime resident interviewed by Daniels observed that migrants and established residents were "just like two different peoples." Old-timers whom I interviewed commented on different religious preferences, mannerisms, and hygiene. Migrants also had different musical tastes and dietary preferences. Those who came in the early 1940s had difficulty finding black southern dietary staples: cornmeal, okra, collard greens, black-eyed peas, and traditional seasonings like filé. Blues, spirituals, and secular folk songs, "shunned" by existing residents "as relics of slavery," were also carried out West and popularized by migrant audiences.[3]

Finally, migrants appeared to have an heightened sense of race consciousness. Although established residents developed independent institutions, they observed that newcomers were more self-reliant and suspicious of whites. To an even greater extent than old-timers, migrants were forced to build relationships and mutual aid associations that buffered the impact of racial discrimination. Indeed, Willa Henry, from Elmgrove, Texas, observed that "in the South black people had to be self-supporting. That's why you see so many more professionals there. They had their own businesses and schools. The blacks in the South had learned to work for themselves. The natives [in the Easy Bay] didn't even have their own businesses." While racial discrimination was hardly absent in the East Bay, it was muted enough to prompt one established resident to remark, "We all just—we didn't know we were Negroes or anything." At the same time, migrants were also more critical of established race relations and determined to make changes—characteristics that impressed and inspired the area's more visionary black leadership.[4]

Despite what old-timers thought of them, working-class migrants viewed their southernness as central to their individual and collective identity. Rather than rejecting where they came from, they used their common origins to cement new friendships, preserve family bonds, and build community institutions. Southernness thus became the building block of migrant communities, providing a concrete sense of identity in a largely hostile environment. Indeed, just as existing residents created hostile stereotypes in response to increased migration, migrants created positive representations of southernness to stabilize their presence in the East Bay and to create a bond of identity. Rather than rejecting where they came from in the naive hope that they would be accepted, working-class migrants adopted southernness as a source of strength that distinguished them from the established black and white populations.

By "southernness," migrants were referring to a way of life that they had learned from their elders, including beliefs about right and wrong, tastes and preferences, aesthetic sensibilities, speech patterns and mannerisms, perceptual orientations, etiquette and ritual, skills, and crafts. But southernness also had a less tangible quality that migrants characterized as "feeling part of a place." A sight, sound, touch, or smell could evoke powerful physical and emotional associations with the South—associations that bound migrants together on an immediate, sensual level.

In either case, southernness was a highly fluid concept. Tastes and preferences, values and rituals were continually reinterpreted and modified over an individual's lifetime. And memories evolved and mutated to accommodate shifts in individual and collective identity. What remained, however, was the perception of something as solidly "southern." In this sense, whether migrant culture remained or ever was actually southern is immaterial. Migrants' perception of themselves as southern was what counted, because it provided a positive group identity in an unwelcoming environment. The transmission of culture—in this case, southern culture—was thus essential to the formation of working-class migrant identity. This common identity in turn facilitated the formation of permanent migrant communities and community institutions.

As they transplanted their southernness and built institutions that reproduced it, migrants transformed the East Bay's existing white and black communities. Southern migrant culture simply swallowed the tiny prewar East Bay black population, ultimately erasing its favored and distinct position with the white community. As "unassimilable" and "aggressive" migrants replaced the "good" black citizens who knew their place, whites attempted to preserve their political, economic, and social privilege by limiting migrants' access to decent housing, medical care, jobs, and education. Migrants fought back, and the resulting struggles shaped East Bay politics from World War II to the present. Ultimately, southernness proved impossible to contain. Even before the war ended, it was everywhere: on supermarket shelves and in the voices murmuring out on the fishing pier, sounding from storefront churches, curling fragrantly out of women's kitchens, and thriving in gardens. And as the underpinning of working-class identity, it was absolutely essential to the success of the migrants' postwar civil rights battles.

In migrant communities, both men and women conveyed cultural norms and values to the young. Women, however, played a unique role—one that stemmed from their culturally sanctioned role as wives, mothers, church women, and caregivers. Although it was unpaid and was ignored in the existing migration literature, this work was recognized and rewarded within migrant communities; it provided women with a source of respect, self-esteem, and authority that their paid labor often failed to confer. Finally, cultural work transmitted working-class values while serving the immediate economic needs of migrant families and communities. As such, it crossed the boundaries of public and private spheres, taking place within the home but also extending into neighborhood and community.[5]

The kitchen and the meals generated by women's devotion to cultural tradition stood at the center of black southern family and community life. Migrant women's childhood memories center around Sunday dinners, church suppers, summer picnics, and lavish meals marking graduations, baptisms, marriages, reunions, birthdays, and holidays. Their mothers, who were often employed as domestic workers or caterers, knew how to cook and reserved their best efforts for their friends and families. Louisa Hall grew up on an eighty-acre family farm, shared by her parents, her father's sister and brother, their spouses, and several cousins. They produced all of their own food—chickens, eggs, milk, cream, butter, beef, pork, fruits, vegetables, berries, corn, and cane syrup—and ate very well. "We had lots of celebrations, including a big barbecue on the Fourth of July, when we made ice cream. And every Sunday we had a big picnic or dinner and could invite our friends."[6]

Opal Smith remembers her mother and aunts preparing weekly church suppers. "Back in the country, church was the only place to go on Saturday and Sunday. We would have picnics on Saturday and spend all day at church on Sunday, followed by a big dinner." Sunday dinners were also a fixture of Ethel Tillman's childhood, but they were served at home instead of at church. "We had a tightly knit family. My father had two sisters who were close to us, and every Sunday dinner would rotate between my aunts and mother. And all other family were welcome."[7]

Cornelia Duvernay and Carmelia Chauvin, raised in New Orleans, also recall huge family meals. "Aunts and uncles came over, Mama would cook, and we would have a good time in our little place." But their mother, as we have seen, also cooked for the neighborhood, serving gumbo, stuffed crabs, potato salad, and fried chicken in their backyard for a small fee. In this manner, she helped her family survive the depression.[8]

Migrant women learned that food held families together, served as a conduit for cultural transmission, and helped extend and maintain supportive social ties. Indeed, food and the talk that took place around the table *were* culture. Paule Marshall remembered how her mother and friends regularly gathered around the kitchen table to reflect on their relationships and work and to offer each other support and affirmation. Their words, shared over the kitchen table, conveyed wisdom as well as a deeper cultural sensibility. For Marshall, "it wasn't only what the women talked about—the content—but the way they put things—their style." Later she attributed her success as a writer to "the rich legacy of language and culture they so freely passed on to me in the wordshop of the kitchen."[9]

But "kitchen talk" also conveyed darker lessons about racial cruelty and survival. Theresa Waller recalled her mother and neighbor women discussing how they "worried after" their sons, "because naturally menfolk had a hard time in segregated areas." By harboring such talk, the kitchen served as a "site of resistance," a place where sons and daughters learned how to survive in the Jim Crow South while receiving affirmation of their blackness.[10]

By watching their mothers give and share food with others, migrant women also learned the ethic of "caring and sharing." Willa Suddeth recalled how her grandmother would put together bags of food for families that had experienced a death, birth, illness, or job loss. "Seeing my family help others motivated me to get involved . . . to help other people." Ruth Cherry, raised in rural Louisiana, recalled how the government gave cows to her parish during the depression. "My mother and other church ladies would get together and can the meat and then share it with people in the neighborhood." She went on to describe how "friends back home would help each other out if one person ran out." This ethic, she maintained, was distinctly southern. "What you have, I have. What would hurt one, would hurt the other. Hospitality they call it, but it was the only way we made it through."[11]

Given the cultural importance of food, migrant women learned to cook at an early age. Lucille Moss, raised in New Orleans, accompanied her aunt to the big open-air French market. There Lucille learned how to test foods for freshness and select the proper ingredients for Creole dishes. Each day after school "I would come straight home, do the breakfast dishes, and cook dinner for the family." Her aunt, a professional caterer and dressmaker, would supervise. In addition to "doing everything [her] brothers did," Ethel Phillips learned how to sew, cook, and can. By the age of twelve, she was cooking for the entire family, standing on a box to reach over the big woodstove.[12]

Most migrant women were accomplished cooks by the time they left the South. And once in the East Bay, they actively reestablished their culinary traditions, seeking markets that carried the proper ingredients, experimenting with food substitutes, and sending home for seasonings and ingredients that could not be obtained in California. Ethel Tillman, who migrated early in the war, "decided that we just had to have some cornbread," and she used Cream of Wheat as a substitute for cornmeal. Cornelia Duvernay and Carmelia Chauvin's mother found most of her ingredients at the big Housewives' Market in Oakland, but they sent back home for crates of shrimp and crab.[13]

Those who arrived toward the end of the war usually found everything they needed to create familiar meals. Oma June Scott recalled that "moving out here did not change our eating habits. Stores had everything we had in Texas, and an even better selection of fruits and vegetables." She went on to mention that her culinary repertoire expanded when she moved into Oakland's Italian neighborhood. Although "they moved out when we started to move in, . . . I learned how to cook spaghetti thanks to the Italian mothers at the PTA."[14]

As more migrants moved to the Bay Area, followed by immediate kin and extended family members, southern-style dinners served to bring people together. Best Johnson and her husband moved to Richmond in 1944, joining his brother and sister-in-law, who had arrived a year earlier. Then Best's sister, mother, and two brothers moved to the East Bay. Soon children were born, including ten who belonged to Best and her husband. As the family expanded, Best's mother kept them from drifting apart by serving weekly meals in her home, a ritual she continued until her death in 1973.[15]

But food did more than keep families together; it fostered supportive social relations as well. Migrant women met friends while shopping in markets and cooking for church and school functions, neighbors, and co-workers. And once they made friends, women used food to formalize and consolidate relationships. Cornelia Duvernay and Carmelia Chauvin's mother, for example, brought friends into their home with her communal Sunday dinners at their Alameda war housing project. Ethel Tillman, who brought her great-grandmother's Wedgwood serving platter all the way from Mississippi, also attracted friends with food. She and her aunt "were good cooks . . . and would share with neighbors anything we had."[16]

Gardening, like cooking, was a skill migrant women viewed as uniquely southern. Kitchen gardens have long been a feature of rural life. However, among black southerners, gardens carry a historical meaning rooted in African tradition, the experience of slavery, and the economic hardship of Jim Crow. In West African societies, women grew produce and controlled its exchange in the marketplace. Once in North America, African women continued this tradition within the context of slavery. When plantation owners permitted slaves to have small garden plots, the crops grown in those plots supplemented meager slave diets, adding essential nutrients and welcome variety. Communal gardens also served as social centers where families shared gossip and made joint decisions. During and after Reconstruction, gardens continued to supplement family diets, providing black residents with a small margin of independence. Although the gardens were no longer communal, they still served an exchange purpose, yielding produce that could be bartered or used to build reciprocal relationships.[17]

Migrant women—even those who gladly abandoned farm life—planted kitchen gardens out West, despite the risk of reinforcing unflattering stereotypes that portrayed newcomers as country bumpkins. Most learned to garden at a young age, helping their mothers tend kitchen plots. On southern farms, men grew cash crops like cotton, corn, cane, and live-stock, while women cultivated large vegetable gardens for home consumption and exchange. But even when families left farms for southern towns and cities, women continued to produce food in backyards, vacant lots, pots, and barrels. Whether they were urban or rural, women derived status from sharing their produce. Food, which was already charged with cultural significance, acquired greater value if it was home-grown, for such food represented a form of human labor that directly sustained life.[18]

Onnie Lee Logan, a black midwife from Alabama, recalled that "we had three big gardens. String beans, butter beans, turnip greens, English peas, sweet potatoes, Irish potatoes, okra, ever'thing. Tomatoes, three or four different kinds of squash." She went on to remark that "plenty of 'em didn't have as much food as us. Mother didn't give 'em time to come. She would take 'em vegetables, she would take 'em meal, flour, piece of meat, whatever. . . . Love, care, and share, that's what we did. We had it and my daddy and mother they shared with the ones that didn't have it. Mother would send a piece and share."[19]

Whether rural or urban in origin, migrant women remember this tradition. Lacey Gray, who grew up on a farm in Longleaf, Louisiana, attributes her health to good food from her mother's kitchen garden. "Mother never used pesticides or chemical fertilizers," she said, "and we never had problems with insects either. Used cow manure on big crops and chicken manure on the kitchen garden." Similarly, Mary Lee, raised in Shreveport, Louisiana, remembers eating a mostly vegetarian diet from the garden. Her mother, a laundress for white families, grew vegetables and herbs and used her wash water to fertilize and moisten her plot. Mary remembers, "Mother shared a lot with neighbors."[20]

When migrant women moved to the East Bay, they transplanted their gardening heritage. Cornelia James remembers how her mother and a cousin "from back home in Arkansas" started a vegetable garden on a vacant plot of land in their Richmond war-worker housing project. "Mother helped people out, shared garden produce with anyone who wanted any," and, as a consequence, made friends quickly. Similarly, Faith McAllister's mother, who followed Faith to Richmond during the war, "always had company here and back home." Faith went on to explain that "Mother loved to cook . . . made good peach cobblers and apple pies. And we had a vegetable garden in both houses, which she and I cared for." Ethel Tillman and her aunt also took gardening seriously. After buying a house in Berkeley, they "would raise a vegetable garden and plant enough to take care of other families. Always did canning. Would can garden produce and seasonal fruits." Although they performed this labor from their home, Ethel and her aunt called it "public work," signifying its broader cultural and social value.[21]

African American quilts, like kitchen gardens, had African roots. Unlike European American quilts, those made by black southern women often exhibit strong, contrasting colors, irregular, offbeat patterns, and multiple strips that create a sense of movement or visual rhythm. These aesthetic features, which stem from West African textiles, were adapted to the European quilt medium during the Diaspora.[22] For the women who made them, quilts served a variety of purposes. Like gardens, they brought women together and served as objects of exchange. Pecolia Warner, a black Mississippian interviewed by William Ferris, recalled that her mother would organize quilting bees. "We was in the country then, and no house was very far apart. So Mama would have them at our house, or she would go to my auntie's or my cousin's, and she would help them quilt. I was a little girl, but I'd be following her, because I wanted to learn how to do that. I used to say, 'If I ever get grown, I'm going to quilt myself.' " Later, Pecolia made her own quilts and passed some of them on to less fortunate neighbors. "When someone gets burned out, you know, I'll donate them some quilts. I don't necessarily altogether piece them up for myself. I like to help people with them." Similarly, Willa Suddeth remembered how her mother would sew with other women during the winter and pass quilts on to needy neighbors.[23]

Mothers also used quilting to teach their daughters the virtue of hard work. Henrietta Bolden "never set down with idle hands. Always was mending, piecing a quilt, or crocheting." Ethel Phillips, who referred to her sewing skills as "motherwit," remembered piecing quilts out of scraps under her mother's watchful eye. Pecolia Warner credits quilting with keeping women out of trouble. "See, when women is doing something like making a quilt, they're not out in the streets. They're not out in the jukes and taverns. They got something at home to occupy them without going in those places."[24]

Migrant women transplanted their quilting tradition to the East Bay and in recent years have earned artistic recognition from filmmakers and public and private collectors. However, they continue to quilt primarily for friends and family and to keep a dying tradition alive. After our taped interview, Henrietta Bolden spread a multicolored quilt out on her living room floor and explained her special fondness for the nine-patch pattern, which "has followed us down the years." Her daughters, busy with jobs and family responsibilities, lack the time, patience, and interest to quilt. Similarly, Oma June Scott took delight in sharing her handiwork and commented that quilting has kept her busy since retirement. She now teaches quilting and other crafts at senior centers to keep the tradition alive.[25]

Many migrant women came west with a knowledge of traditional folk medicine, which, like gardening and quilting, had African origins. In African medical lore, illness stems from an individual's failure to maintain bodily or spiritual harmony. Natural illness, which results from an internal physical imbalance, can be corrected with plants, roots, and herbs.

Unnatural illness, which results from the evil acts of others or from an individual's inability to cope with life's stresses, can be cured with incantations, charms, and ritual. When they were transplanted to the United States, these beliefs blended with Native American herbal lore and European medical practices.[26]

In Africa and the United States, healing was an accepted extension of midwifery. In plantation households and slave quarters, black women not only presided over births and deaths but also drew on their knowledge of medicinal plants and ritual to cure everything from teething pain to broken hearts. During and after Reconstruction, this knowledge continued to have practical value for communities that were routinely denied access to white medical institutions.[27] Most healers were deeply religious, attributing their powers to a special relationship with God. Thus, traditional healing practices, even those dealing with unnatural illness, were completely compatible with Christianity. Finally, healing was often a skill passed from one generation to the next, learned from mothers and grandmothers and preserved as a family tradition.[28]

After moving to the East Bay, migrant women cultivated or foraged for plants used to make curative teas and poultices. They also transplanted healing rituals, preventive lore, and an irreverence for the medical profession. Ethel Tillman, who learned about folk remedies from her mother and aunt, rarely relied on doctors once she moved to California. "When we moved here we became members of Kaiser and would go to their doctors, but we used our own remedies for common illness. For colds you make a syrup from beef tallow, mutton tallow, honey, and onions. Mullein tea is used for colds and fever. We used beech-bark teas in the South for colds. People used to come from far and wide to have us cure swollen glands. You heat a fork until it's red hot and then hold it as close to the gland as you can stand it. Put a piece of fat meat on a pine stick and burn it so the pitch and fat mingle, and use it to cure boils. Make a poultice and change it every day."[29]

Similarly, Lacey Gray learned about healing from her mother, "who made things out of herbs, and mixed animal fat and kerosene for puncture wounds." For Lacey, however, good health began with uncontaminated produce. "We could use natural remedies because we had a good diet. Today, people get sick from all the chemicals in their food." Lacey also recalled the competence of midwives who delivered all of her sisters and brothers and her own two children. Mary Lee, too, remembers how "Mother knew all about herbs and natural healing. She went into fields and got things for fevers, colds, and babies teething. Fig leaves were for fever. You would wrap a body in a sheet lined with fig leaves. Fig juice was good for skin inflammation. We gave teething babies a string of garlic cloves. Garlic was also good for colds, along with catnip and rose hips. Never went to a doctor." Mary, who now lives next to a regional park in Richmond, forages there for wild greens and medicinal plants.[30]

Louise Steele expressed a common suspicion of medical professionals. Her grandmother, who ran a home laundry back in the South, burned her arm one Christmas Eve, and "it was June before she could put her clothes on and half of this time she was not even aware. The doctor doubted that she would be able to work even if she lived, but she went on to raise my mother and me." Louise then proceeded to describe how doctors diagnosed this same grandmother with tuberculosis and advised her against nursing her daughter. "They said she had T.B., but she lived to be one hundred years old—living on well after those doctors were dead and gone."[31]

Louise and other migrant women use these stories to illustrate the limitations of standard medical practice and to highlight the role of destiny, which, in Louise's words, is "left to the man up there." They also point to the role of individual strength and determination in the healing process. And given their belief in the work ethic, it is not surprising that migrant women also praise hard work and service to others as "a way to keep your mind off troubles and illness. . . . Helping others makes you realize you are blessed . . . that you have nothing to complain about." Olive Blue, like Louise, stresses the importance of the right attitude to emotional and physical health: "Just keep hate out of your life. Shortcomings is given into each life and into each life some rain is going to fall. Some days is going to be dark. And many times we'll weep. 'But weep not like those who have no hope, because weeping comes in the night, but joy comes in the morning.' "[32]

Heeding their own advice, migrant women frequently adopted the role of informal medical care providers in their families and neighborhoods. They viewed their work on behalf of the sick and aged as distinctly female and southern, rooted in a kind, tradition-based lifestyle that fostered respect for elders and compassion for the helpless. The value of their caregiving, however, is obscured by the very ideology that surrounds it. As members of poorer communities, migrant women routinely provided medical services and advice normally extended by physicians and hospitals. In the South, where medical facilities were separate and unequal, women's unpaid caregiving was even more essential. Thus, migrant women, like their mothers before them, bore much of the cost of family and community health care. And because such work took place within the home and was thus conceptualized as neatly cut off from the public sphere, its economic value and its costs to the caregiver remained hidden. Framing this labor as "southern" or as an extension of "homemaking" privatizes it, reinforcing the view that caregiving is removed from the economic realities of capitalist production.[33]

Migrant women rarely complained about the personal costs of caregiving, however, viewing it as their duty and obligation. When caring for aging parents, most reflected that this was their way of giving back what had been given to them. Louise Steele's relationship with her grandmother illustrates migrant women's commitment to caregiving. After moving to Richmond and securing employment, Louise brought the grandmother who raised her out to California from their small hometown in Louisiana.

Several years later, when her grandmother became ill, Louise developed hypertension. She had been trying to provide in-home care while maintaining her full-time job. When she refused to work overtime, her supervisor warned her "that it was either putting my grandmother in a home or losing my job. And that said a whole heap to me, to put this job ahead of the only woman who was Mama to me. And I just stared at him, because my grandmama taught me that if you're going to say the wrong thing, don't say anything." Louise never did receive time off to care for her grandmother, but she was forced to take disability leave because of her hypertension. As the grandmother grew worse, she only reluctantly allowed Louise to care for her. "She was an independent woman and it was hard for her to let others care for her. During this period she had to relinquish her power—her always doing for others—and allow me to do for her."[34]

Some migrant women even returned south for extended periods to care for sick relatives. Marlene Lewis, for example, spent eight years back in Arkansas caring for her mother and aunt. "I was the only girl in the family who could do that, and I buried both of them." Similarly, Olive Blue returned to Louisiana for three years to nurse and ultimately bury her older brother.[35]

In a world of chronic economic hardship and uncertainty, the bonds of reciprocal obligation between parents and children grew strong indeed. Thus, the death of a parent often precipitated a major emotional crisis for the surviving caregiver. In Louise Steele's case, the death of her grandmother brought her back to her southern roots. Although she had been raised in the Baptist church, Louise attended Catholic services for most of her adult life because "mass lasted only an hour. Didn't want any part of that Baptist church, because back then Baptist churches had services all day." But Louise returned to her childhood church "immediately after my grandmother passed. . . . The spirit led me—told me that my roots was in the Baptist [church]."[36]

Migrant women also cared for the sick and aged outside of their families. Lovie McIntosh and her husband befriended another migrant couple during the war and maintained the friendship over the next forty-five years. Recently the man died, leaving his Alzheimer's-stricken wife without care. Lovie stepped in, providing her with daily supervision and assistance. Similarly, Ethel Tillman cares for sick members of the Vicksburg Club, a social and mutual aid association started by Mississippi migrants that the Tillmans joined shortly after the war.[37]

In addition to caring for the sick and aged, migrant women maintained extended family relationships. This work, which women identified as part of a southern helping tradition, took several forms: taking in children, bringing out relatives from back home, visiting those who remained in the South, and organizing family reunions. Along with the responsibility for home-based elder care, migrant women routinely took grandchildren, nieces, nephews, and younger siblings into their homes. Here again, women provided an unrecognized and unpaid service commonly performed by paid service workers in the public sector. Migrant women, however, viewed children as the freshest link in the web of reciprocal obligation that bound families together. To break this connection by entrusting children to the state, which had historically neglected the needs of black communities, was unthinkable.

Marlene Brown, who came to California as a thirteen-year-old in 1944, now cares for her disabled mother and three grandchildren in her mother's home. Recalling that "families where I came from were close-knit," Marlene took early retirement from her job and now devotes herself full-time to caregiving obligations. She is particularly serious about her grandchildren's education, volunteering in the classroom and taking an active role in providing after-school learning opportunities. Similarly, Oma June Scott and Mary Lee "adopted" grandchildren, assuming full parenting responsibilities well after their own children had left home.[38]

More commonly, migrant women have helped daughters and sons with child care. Olive Blue, for example, cares for her great-grandchildren before and after they go to school. She also takes responsibility for their religious training, reserving a special affection for a great-grandson who is a youth usher at her church. Olive is particularly pleased that he "thinks of my house as his own." Like most migrant women, Olive defines mothering in a broader sense: her "children" include nieces, nephews, and grandchildren as well as young people from her church, neighborhood, and workplace. During her thirty-five years at Naval Supply, she "met a lot of boys off the shift at sea" who ended up calling her "Mom" or "Grandma." In church, where her status as a mother is formally recognized, she also reaches out to young people, believing that "it is harder for kids today than it was for her." Older people, she feels, "must not worry whether young people will like them; kids need advice. And I tell them to find the right way and walk in it even when things get hard and you get discouraged."[39]

Like Olive, Lacey Gray feels a special responsibility toward the young: "My motto to youth is to patternize your life after someone who is doing good." To this end, she gives advice freely, "correcting young people who I see littering, fighting or stealing. If they are in my neighborhood, I'll go right out and talk to them . . . tell them I love them, but that if they don't respect their parents they are shortening their days."[40]

Theresa Waller, believing that children "are the future and that parents need the help of the community," takes neighborhood children into her home. She recalls her loving relationship with her father—how he "played with me and gave me attention"—and has attempted to give this same attention to other young people. Although she never had children of her own, several neighborhood children call her "Mom." And two neighbors who are now adults include her in their family gatherings as an adoptive parent.[41]

To Theresa and other migrant women, taking responsibility for others' children is consistent with their own southern childhoods. Olive Blue remembered that "if mothers in the past left their kids, all they'd have to do was tell a neighbor and those kids would be looked after." Theresa Waller recalled how "we understood that if our parents weren't home, the neighbors would keep an eye on us. They had permission to spank us . . . and if anything happened, my mother would hear about it and we would get it twice." Thus, child care was both private and public, taking place in the home but extending into neighborhood and community as well. Children, migrant women recognized, were a communal resource; if they did not internalize the southern self-help tradition, migrant communities would collapse. It should be noted that neighborhood parenting was not unique to migrant communities. Most older, working-class ethnic Americans have similar memories of interfamilial accountability. However, in the Jim Crow South, and later in the East Bay, the outsider status of migrants reinforced the notion that children were cultural capital.[42]

The blurring of public and private spheres also occurred when migrant women opened their homes to family and friends who followed them to the Bay Area from the South. Women's labor unquestionably supported the wartime and postwar expansion of the East Bay's black population by providing economically vulnerable migrants with room, board, and advice on where to find employment and permanent housing. But migrant women also extended hospitality to family and friends who "ran out of luck" after settling in the East Bay. Poverty, migrant women believed, had little to do with individual character. In their lifetimes they had experienced enough hardship and discrimination to know that little separated them from the ranks of the poor. As industrial jobs left the Bay Area during the postwar years, migrant women quietly addressed the human costs of unemployment and lowered expectations by providing food and shelter to those in need.[43]

Ethel Tillman and her husband sponsored numerous migrant families during the war, and they now share their home with a middle-aged son who has had difficulty finding a full-time job. Ruth Gracon, who raised eleven children while working in a cannery, now provides a home for a grown daughter who is mentally ill and unable to work. Oma June Scott took her pregnant seventeen-year-old granddaughter in after the young woman was rejected by her own parents. Now seventy, Oma plans to care for the baby while her granddaughter finishes school. Similarly, Mary Lee shares her home with a recently married granddaughter whose husband is in the military. She hopes that her assistance will allow the young couple to save enough money to buy their own home. Then she plans to open her house to single mothers who are recovering from drug addictions.[44]

In practicing this southern tradition of hospitality and kindness, migrant women both provided necessary services to their families and communities and passed the caretaking ethic on to a younger generation. But as they focused on strengthening their new communities in the East Bay, they continued to maintain direct connections to the South. They not only identified themselves and their values as southern but also actively fostered ties to the communities they had left through frequent return visits and annual or semiannual family reunions. In this sense, "community" transcended geographical boundaries; by returning regularly to their birthplaces, migrant women brought the West to the South and the South to the West. Thus, southernness was not a finite essence trapped in memory but a fluid, renewable resource.

None of the women in my sample expressed embarrassment over southern black folkways. Home, even in light of segregation's petty meanness, was regarded as a source of stability and virtue, heralding back to the terrible sweetness that characterized women's childhood experiences. There, even if only in the imagination, the church remained strong, children respected their elders, neighbors left their doors unlocked, and the community took care of its own. Eager to share this sweetness with the younger generation, many migrant families sent children south for extended vacations.

One woman named Adelaide, who was born in Houston in 1938, moved to Oakland with her mother and stepfather in 1941. Her grandmother, who had moved to the East Bay earlier in the war, bought a house and renovated the basement in expectation of their arrival. After the move to California, Adelaide contracted rheumatic fever and had to be home-taught for two years. At age seven, she was ready to return to school, but she had made such rapid academic progress that her teacher wanted to advance her a grade. Adelaide's mother, however, decided that this was not in her daughter's best interest, and instead she sent Adelaide to Texas for a five-month visit with her "father's people."

In Houston, Adelaide undoubtedly developed lasting ties to extended family and southern folkways. But she also confronted the pain her mother had attempted to leave behind. Experiencing segregation first-hand, she was swiftly and cruelly initiated into the collective struggle for dignity that had propelled so many migrants out of the South. At the same time, she fostered the ambitions of her peers. After seeing one of Adelaide's East Bay school photographs, a young friend asked whether she really attended school with white children. This almost unfathomable reality, portrayed in black and white, must have shaken already hardened assumptions about the inevitability and morality of segregation.[45]

Other migrants entrusted their children to southern relatives during hard times. When Maya Angelou's parents decided to end their marriage, they sent their two young children back to Stamps, Arkansas, to live with a grandmother and uncle. Maya Angelou later "discovered that the United States had been crossed thousands of times by frightened Black children travelling alone to their newly affluent parents in Northern cities, or back to grandmothers in Southern towns when the urban North reneged on its economic promises." But regardless of why or how children returned to the South, they came away with a stronger connection to their southern roots—to the values, loyalties, odors, tastes, and visual contours of the world that their parents had left behind.[46]

Family visits usually took place in August, a traditional time of rest and spiritual revival that followed the harvest. In her study of a small southern community, Elizabeth Rauh Bethel observed that midcentury migrants made annual visits home to "renew old friendships and catch up on the news, to establish once again the spiritual connections of their child-hoods." When they arrived, migrants brought gifts that made life easier for southern relatives and awed friends and family with the material evidence of their prosperity. After their welcome, migrants settled into a routine of picnics, visiting, and church-going. Women joined their aunts, mothers, and sisters in the kitchen, creating platters of food that brought kin together, while indulging in kitchen talk that bridged months of separation. When they left, seasonal visitors carried back the smells and tastes of home in tightly packed jars of preserves and bundles of smoked sausages and hams.[47]

Weddings, births, deaths, and illness also drew migrants home—women more frequently than men, because of traditional female roles. As family and community caregivers, women maintained the bonds of love and reciprocal obligation that extended beyond the East Bay back to their places of origin. But these bonds, like those that women created in their new communities, needed continual maintenance, ranging from regular phone calls and letters to annual visits. Visits were particularly important, because they allowed migrant women to provide direct assistance to sick or dying relatives; celebrate births and weddings, which brought new members into the extended family; and strengthen existing family bonds with parents, siblings, and other kinfolk. In exchange, migrant women received material and emotional support during hard times, and the promise of a home to return to if life became too difficult out West. Even if women never used these resources, the knowledge that they were in place heightened personal security and well-being.

Long-distance relationships, as a form of social security, benefited en-tire families and, by extension, strengthened migrant communities. They also provided a renewable source of southern identity, which contributed to the cohesiveness of migrant communities and the cultural richness of the East Bay Area. Many migrant women are now coming full circle and planning to move back home, drawn by those very relationships they faithfully maintained. The Jim Crow South of their childhoods, they note, no longer exists. Now the South seems like a kinder place to live, a refuge from the growing economic problems and collapsing infrastructure of East Bay inner cities.

Although all of Oma June Scott's relatives moved to the East Bay, she returned to the South to visit friends every two years. "We have lots of friends who stayed back in Texas, and we stay with them when we go back. In fact, the only vacations we took were back to Texas." Oma went on to relate how homesick she was when she first moved to Oakland. "All I could do was save those paychecks so that I could get back there. We even bought property—two lots—in order to move back and build." Oma and her husband decided to remain in California, but they continue to make trips back to Texas and intend to be buried in a cemetery "on the property my husband's family has owned since slavery."[48]

Opal Smith returned to Canton, Texas, every four years while she worked, but she now goes back every two years for family reunions. In Canton, she stays on the family farm, originally purchased by her grandfather but now owned jointly by Opal and her siblings. Her brothers, who migrated to the East Bay during the war, moved back to the farm several years ago. Two sisters, who remained in California after migrating, are presently trying to convince Opal to move back to Canton with them, but Opal feels that her two daughters still need her.[49]

Lacey Gray returned to Louisiana yearly for vacations, funerals, and to "carry a brother back to be buried in the family cemetery." Now that her children are grown, she returns home every November, avoiding the hot weather and staying for two to three weeks. Like Opal, Lacey jointly owns family land and "thinks about going back to live." Her father, who bought the land, "came from sharecroppers and never wanted it to be sold, so it will just pass from one generation to the next." When Lacey visits, she "attends the church built on family land" and stays "in the old house with my two sisters. That's what I like to do; I don't do anything else."[50]

Henrietta Bolden, from Guthrie, Oklahoma, "went back to visit in 1946 and about every year after that except for the ten years between 1956 and 1966," when she divorced her husband and had to raise her children alone. Now that she is retired, she returns twice a year, staying with her brother and cousins in Guthrie. Henrietta, however, has no plans to move back; her four children, grandchildren, and five great-grandchildren live in the East Bay and keep her involved in family activities.[51]

Some migrant women, particularly those whose immediate and extended kin also migrated to California, visited less frequently. When they did return, they often expressed surprise at the changes that had taken place in their hometowns. In 1986, Ruth Gracon went back to her small hometown outside of Pine Bluff, Arkansas, to visit a distant cousin. "She had a cateress fix dinner for us and lived in a big, beautiful house. My husband said to her that she had really moved up in life, because when we were kids, we'd have to come through the back door of a place like this."[52]

Henrietta McAlister, who migrated to California in 1945 with most of her family, returned to Laurel, Mississippi, in 1975 to visit some childhood friends. Henrietta "couldn't believe how much it had changed. I was amazed to see black kids attending what used to be an all-white school on the north side of town. This was the part of Laurel we used to run through." Henrietta went on to observe that she "was just thrilled with the changes down there, and wished I had been there to help." Similarly, Willa Suddeth returned to Shreveport to attend a high school reunion. "It was completely changed. We had the reunion in a part of town we had been excluded from, in a formerly all-white hotel." Now Willa is thinking about moving back to live on the family farm, which was originally purchased by her grandfather. Her brother, who returned home from California following his retirement, has offered to build her a house next to his.[53]

Migrant women like Willa never stopped identifying themselves as southerners. Although most appreciated the opportunities the East Bay offered their generation, they steadfastly refused to give up what they defined as their southern traditions: cooking, gardening, healing, caregiving, and actively fostering friendships and family bonds. This work, performed almost exclusively by women, provided all migrants with essential goods and services. Moreover, it reproduced cultural values and practices that gave migrant communities a positive, shared identity.

At the center of women's cultural work was the notion of hospitality— an ethic of helpfulness that, in the words of one migrant woman, "was the only way we made it through." Having directly experienced poverty, or at least lived uncomfortably close to it, migrant women survived by forging ties of reciprocal obligation and by avoiding any behavior that would "set them above" others.

Because so much of their cultural work was organized around building reciprocal relationships, it usually took the form of person-to-person exchange. Expressing resentment toward the black middle class and elite, migrant women tried to distinguish between types of giving. Henrietta McAlister, for example, stressed that her mother was not a "club woman" but one whose humble generosity to friends, neighbors, and fellow church members gave her considerable stature in the community. Similarly, Olive Blue pointed out that middle-class women "were different from us. They belonged to clubs and things." Her own mother, a seamstress, taught Olive how to be "the person who always knew everyone . . . always knew how people felt and what problems they were having. I just liked to know . . . just wanted to know." It should be noted, though, that practice and social ideals did not always conform. In the East Bay, some migrant women achieved middle-class status and became "club women," although they rejected this designation and maintained that their work was different.[54]

Although much of their charitable work took place outside of institutions, migrant women took an active and visible role in churches, civil rights organizations, school desegregation efforts, electoral politics, and grassroots community-organizing efforts. This work, too, was part of a self-defined southern tradition. Lovie McIntosh, a feisty migrant woman and former Richmond community organizer, observed that "if I had stayed in the South I would have been in the frontlines of the civil rights movement. And I did my share before I left." She went on to explain that she came from an activist family: "My paternal grandfather worked for a railroad company and was never one to take a backseat. Because he didn't depend on white people in town for his job, he stood up. And in the South, if you stood up you could lose your life, but at least you would preserve your dignity." By focusing on migrant women's collective action, the next chapter illustrates how this southern cultural tradition of "standing up" contributed to social and political change in the East Bay Area.[55]

Chapter Six

. . . If We Didn't Do It, It Just Wouldn't Get Done

Migrant Women and
Collective Action in
the East Bay

Middle-class black women's activism has been well documented by historians, but the community work of working-class and poor black women remains largely hidden. Class bias explains some of this invisibility, but not all of it. Equally significant is how and where poor and working-class women conducted their community work. Unlike those of middle-class "club women," their activities frequently occurred outside of formal organizations or political institutions. Instead, these women saw their community activism as an extension of their private caregiving.

Whether working with the PTA, registering voters, running church-based service programs, organizing boycotts and marches, or staffing grassroots community agencies, migrant women refused the titles and recognition of formal leadership. These, they maintained, would remove them from the very communities they were a part of. Like the low-income community workers interviewed by sociologist Nancy Naples, migrant women "did not separate their issues from their neighbors', but rather demonstrated a 'capacity for empathy' and caring in the continued attachment to their communities." Operating outside of formal leadership structures, migrant women activists gained the admiration, trust, and respect of their communities. They—not social workers, politicians, or "club women"—became the official representatives of their friends and neighbors. And they did so precisely because their own identities, aspirations, and needs matched those of their communities. Shared experience rather than formal authority gave activist migrant women community recognition and credibility.[1]

Migrant women learned this style of leadership, marked by the absence of hierarchy and an attachment to community, from their mothers and other female role models in their southern hometowns. The majority of women in my sample (85 percent) reported a close relationship with a community activist: a woman whose caregiving activities extended beyond immediate family members into their communities. These activists not only engaged in the cultural activities described in Chapter 5 but also in service-oriented community work. By doing so, they taught migrant daughters concrete organizing and networking skills. But equally important, older activists transmitted a sense of civic obligation and faith in the power of individuals to change society. Migrant women entered adolescence and adulthood with powerful role models—women whose identities and personal power derived from a "continued attachment to their communities."[2]

Charles Payne details a distinctly female leadership style shared by the migrant women in my sample. Ella Baker, raised in a rural farm family, recalled how "the world of her childhood as a kind of 'family socialism,' a world in which food and tools and homes were shared, where informal adoption of children was taken for granted, a world with a minimal sense of social hierarchy in terms of those who have, having the right to look down upon, or to evaluate as a lesser breed, those who didn't have." In her world, women exhibited a nonhierarchical, nonegocentric organizing style based on coalition-building and decentralized leadership. And it was this model that Ella Baker used throughout her extraordinary organizing career.[3]

This black, southern, female-centered leadership style stood at the center of locally based, midcentury civil rights struggles—from the Montgomery bus boycott to the Student Nonviolent Coordinating Committee's voter registration activities. However, it also left the South, traveling west and north with migrant women and ultimately informing the antipoverty and welfare rights movements, the community action programs of the 1960s, school desegregation struggles, and neighborhood-based efforts to meet the social and economic needs of original migrant communities. While few migrant women matched Ella Baker's truly exceptional gift for organizing, most shared her desire to do some good in the world. Moreover, migrant women like Baker saw themselves as following a tested recipe for social change, based on a "minimal sense of hierarchy" and group-centered leadership.

In one sense, East Bay white residents were right: migrants were troublemakers. Having moved west to find a better life, they were willing to use every lesson learned from their mothers and grandmothers to make reality conform to their expectations. Willa Suddeth, who came from an activist family in Louisiana, recalled that "people from the South were the ones who changed California." Migrants, she maintained, not only had high aspirations but also had "a history of pulling together as a community." Ruth Cherry, another migrant from Louisiana, agreed: "Because of discrimination back there, black people had their own businesses and stayed with their own. They [native Californians] didn't have the same level of community here. . . . They didn't work together in the same way." Willa Suddeth went on to observe that "southern black women were always in the forefront of change—in the home and in the community." Henrietta McAlister, another migrant woman, supported this contention and offered an explanation for it:

> Women made the community. The crux of whatever has been a part of the black evolution and revolution has been on the black woman's shoulder because the men were so crushed. They weren't allowed to do or say anything without being intimidated. And if we didn't do it, it just wouldn't get done. And men knew better, because they had to work. They had to take care of their families and knew that if they stepped out of bounds that wouldn't have been possible . . . or else they'd have to vanish, to get out of town as quickly as they could or they'd get killed. So the black woman had to be the backbone.

While Henrietta's thesis is flawed—men actively resisted racial discrimination, and women also had to fear intimidation and economic retribution—it echoes a common theme in migrant women's oral histories. However modest women were when it came to reporting their contributions to family income, they held nothing back when describing their community activism. Like their cultural work, described in the preceding chapter, collective action for social change clearly was sanctioned behavior for working-class women.[4]

Church

For migrant women, the church was an arena of personal and political transformation, a source of individual sustenance and collective liberation that transcended the boundaries of public and private spheres and met both spiritual and material needs. During worship, women renewed their relationship to a just and forgiving God who, despite human failings, offered the promise of redemption and regeneration. Sermon, prayer, and song, the key rituals of the Sunday service, allowed women to enter into an intimate, loving conversation with God. Alone, yet enveloped in the warmth, color, perfume, and passion of fellow worshipers, they poured out their sorrows and fears and opened themselves to God's redeeming message like "empty pitchers before a full fountain." When the service came to a close, women felt reconnected to their communities, even more determined to look "up and not back," and were certain that God stood with them in struggle.[5]

Just as significantly, the church brought individuals into a mutual aid association that used the talents and skills of its constituent members to benefit the whole. In the Jim Crow South of women's childhoods, churches served as employment and housing bureaus, schools, social centers, community meeting halls, and centers of political organizing and protest. Members buried the dead and took care of the sick, poor, and aged. And the faithful enforced community norms, correcting the young, admonishing backsliders, and ostracizing chronic offenders. In this manner, the church served as an overarching kinship system, meeting the needs and reinforcing the values of its constituent families.

As an extension of the family, the church adopted both the survival strategies and kinship terminology of its members. "Mothers" and "sisters," for example, used the same skills to care for their "church families" as they did to protect home and kin. Indeed, it was women who ran churches, raising money to pay for the building and compensate the pastor, caring for the sick and elderly, bringing in new members, preparing church suppers, teaching Sunday school and Bible study, and filling the majority of pews each and every Sunday. In other words, maintaining kin relationships—at home and in the larger church family—was women's work. As Joseph W. Scott and Albert Black have noted, "Church values and norms are those of female-centered kin networks, [which] emphasize the preservation of home and family."[6]

Not surprisingly, the church was the most frequently reported site of collective action for migrant women. It was where they learned to speak out and work with others and where they continued to find an outlet for their "public" concerns. Funeral programs eulogizing former church members provide touching portraits of migrant women's church work. Precious Jackson-Handy, a member of Beth Eden Baptist Church in Oakland, received the following tribute:

Precious Jackson-Handy was born March 10, 1916 in Mansfield, Louisiana. She was married to J. L. Handy on August 1, 1937. After moving to Houston, Texas in 1940, they were blessed with their first three loving children. They migrated to California in 1945 and was blessed again with three other loving children. Precious Handy became a member of Beth Eden Baptist Church in 1946. Serving over the years as president of the Young Women's Progressive Club Number One, Chairperson of Ada Circle, member of the Deaconess Board, member and teacher of the Mixed Bible Club, Lamanette of the Layman League and Secretary of the Children's Department of Sunday School for nine years.

The program then goes on to describe her community work with the Order of Eastern Star and a local chapter of the National Council of Negro Women, and it concludes with a poem written by the deceased:

I'd like to think that when this life is done
That I had filled a needed post
That here and there I'd paid my fare
With more than idle talk and boast. . . .[7]

Other funeral programs provide equally elaborate detail about migrant women's religious histories, celebrating their cradle-to-grave commitment to church-based community values. Ella Ward's eulogy begins with a description of her childhood in Bessemer, Alabama. There, Ella's mother, ill and near death, attempted "to teach her children about Jesus . . . during the last days of her life." At seven, Ella converted, and shortly after that her "Mother Nancy departed this life, leaving her two small children in the hands of her brother, Hardy Wyatt, and his wife Bunch, who reared the children in an atmosphere of Christianity and love." Raised by her aunt and uncle to be a good Christian woman, Ella married Nash Green Carlisle and had seven children by him. In 1928, when they moved to Birmingham, Alabama, "in order to provide better educational conditions for their large family," the Carlisles joined the Sardis Baptist Church. Ella, following the tradition in which she had been raised, "carried her children to Sunday School, church, and Baptist Young People's Union on Sundays, and sent them to prayer meeting on Wednesday nights for children, while she attended the adult division." Ella also sang in the choir as a soloist and taught Sunday school classes.

During her years at Sardis, Ella's family was forced apart by the economic hardship of the Great Depression. While her husband and two oldest sons moved north in search of work, Ella worked as a domestic servant. "She would walk long distances to and from work to save five cents car fare for her children, stand working long hours, come home and attend domestic duties, and attend nightly services and meetings at the church." Her eulogy went on to describe how "in times like these Ella would stay on her knees at her bed sometimes for what seemed like hours, praying while her children made frequent visits to her there for their needs."

Ella's marriage did not survive the long separation of those years, but she soon found a better life out West. One of her sons, St. Elmo, moved to the East Bay early in the war and sent for his mother and younger siblings. After settling in Berkeley, Ella joined Beth Eden Baptist Church and married Ivory Ward, superintendent of Beth Eden's adult Sunday school. "Having been a Sunday School teacher, Eastern Star member, a chorister, a soprano soloist, and a missionary worker, Ella joined these activities at her new church home."[8]

In referring to Beth Eden as Ella's "church home," the eulogy reflects the complexity of women's religious activism. Defined as a "home," the church provided a socially sanctioned and status-conferring outlet for energetic and talented women. William E. Montgomery relates the story of a woman whose husband wanted her to limit her public activities: " 'But whenever it came to church affairs, especially in raising money for the church he quietly puts his hands in his pockets and steps aside, leaving it for the women to do.' " Although the church reinforced existing gender roles, it extended women's sphere of influence beyond the home. Through their church, "mothering" women such as Precious Handy and Ella Ward obtained support and affirmation from an entire community and developed an image of themselves as competent, successful, and strong. Ola Beatrice Woods, a migrant from Hope, Arkansas, believed she was following a long tradition of strong black church women when she commented that "It's been considered a man's world all through history. But I can go back to the Bible to prove that it wasn't supposed to be. In fact, Christ's first missionary was a woman."[9]

The church, like home and neighborhood, was a center of the African American community, transmitting traditions and values and providing its members with spiritual and material resources. As such, even the most conservative parishes functioned as temporal sites of spiritual resistance, preserving life and meaning under the most dehumanizing conditions. Thus, women's efforts to establish and maintain churches reflected their desire for permanence and stability in the face of chronic hardships imposed by deeply rooted structures of racial and class discrimination.

When migrant women arrived in the East Bay Area, they immediately located or set about establishing churches. Indeed, some women followed their hometown ministers out West and became charter members of new congregations. Louisa Hall, for example, moved to California from Arkansas after she and her husband lost their home in a flood. Their minister, who had preceded them, rented part of his home to the displaced couple, and the Halls helped him start his own church. "Now the church is huge." Eventually Louisa became a lay speaker at her Oakland congregation—she was "the first woman to do so." Today she volunteers at its senior center and its support program for crack-addicted mothers and infants.[10]

Richmond, which had only one black church before the war, housed dozens after migrants arrived. Cornelia James's brother, an Arkansas native, founded Richmond's second black congregation early in the war, filling its pews with other migrant families. His was the church where Best Johnson and Olive Blue felt most at home after leaving the South in 1944 and 1943, respectively. Shortly after Best and Olive arrived, Cornelia's brother left for Los Angeles to start a new church, leaving his congregation in the hands of an unpopular minister. As a consequence, several members, including Best and Olive, began a new church in 1945. Today both women remain dedicated to the church they helped build. Over the years, Best Johnson served on the Deaconess Board and chaired the Nurses' Aid Committee. Today she works with the Missionary Society, cochairs Deborah's Circle, and serves on the Devotional, Pastor's Aid, and New Members Committees. She is also active in religious education; she regularly attends church-sponsored seminars, conventions, and classes. "I've always been active. If I'm not doing something, I don't feel right."[11]

For Olive, church became the basis of her social life. "Don't know anything about cards, betting, dancing. Never was a moviegoer. Church kept me busy. Went to church six days a week: Sunday to services; Monday to the Missionary Society; Tuesday to the Usher Board; Wednesday to Sunday School; Thursday to Choir; and Friday to the Baptist Training Union." Although she has scaled back her activities, she still serves as the church secretary, the president of Pastor's Aid, and a member of the Christian Aid Board.[12]

Other women, particularly in Oakland and Berkeley, joined existing congregations, swelling church memberships and changing the form and content of worship services. Churches that once served the East Bay's established black communities, many of them small and financially unstable, grew prosperous from the influx of migrant worshipers. But in exchange for their support, migrants demanded and obtained positions of power and responsibility in their adopted institutions. In churches and elsewhere in East Bay black communities, newcomers simply outnumbered existing residents, forcing old-timers to assimilate into migrant culture. Taylor Memorial M.E. Church in Oakland, for example, grew from 150 members in 1940 to 1,008 in 1954. During that same period, the church was rebuilt and completely financed; its members burned the mortgage on November 28, 1954. In its dedication brochure, the church acknowledged the source of its new prosperity. "California's total population increased 50% between 1940 and 1950. But the Negro population galloped ahead at the rate of 400%. . . . The greatest challenge is right here in Northern California. Oakland, for example, has a total population of nearly 400,000. 50,000 of that number are Brown Americans. In 1940 there were only 8,000 Negroes in Oakland. The increase has been over 6 for 1."[13]

Similarly, St. Paul A.M.E. Church in Berkeley noted its wartime surge in membership. Organized in 1926, the church struggled to survive over the next two decades. Then, between 1942 and 1943, its membership grew from 72 to 185; women represented 72 percent of the total congregation. In August 1943 the church burned its mortgage, following the complete renovation of the building, the purchase of a new pipe organ, and the construction of a new parsonage. Progressive Baptist Church in Berkeley, founded in 1935, also reflected this general pattern of expansion: "In its early history the church found it difficult in making arrangements for the payment of bills because of its small membership and financial status. It encountered many trials and tribulations, but continued to show evidence of progress, because it was rooted in God." Progressive's twentieth-anniversary brochure then went on to note that "In the nineteen forties when Christians migrated from various states to California, this church was a shelter and place of rest for God's people." Having begun with 35 members, the church grew to 1,245 by 1955. During the same period, it bought five lots, remodeled the church, bought an organ and three pianos, and built a dining room. Stressing that "no church is greater than the community she serves, nor the community greater than she is," Progressive proudly pointed to its active support of the NAACP and its contributions to college scholarships and religious camps for "delinquent boys."[14]

Migrants also inherited churches vacated by fleeing white residents. Golden Gate Methodist Episcopal Church, for example, disbanded in 1947 as its members moved out of the area. "World War Two came in 1941. The Golden Gate congregation, numbering less than 50 was drastically effected. Second generation church families began to move out of the area. A new Negro population gradually replaced them. Some effort was made to adapt to the new trend; but finally the church's strength wilted before the encroaching 'American Dilemma.' " After discontinuing services in 1947, Golden Gate reopened as the Downs Memorial Methodist Church and rapidly built a mostly black membership that soon exceeded the capacity of the old sanctuary.[15]

During the war years, the success of churches—old and new—rested on their appeal to migrants. This required providing social services as well as accommodating southern styles of worship. Cooper A.M.E. Zion Church in Oakland attracted migrants with its music programs. Reverend G. Linwood Fauntleroy, who was appointed pastor in 1944, transformed Cooper from a staid, sleepy church into a vital, growing institution. "Much joy was felt, for here we had finally secured the man that was much needed on the Coast. Young, energetic, extremely talented in music, and with a family who shared with him his musical abilities." The fiftieth-anniversary program notes that Fauntleroy's abilities made Cooper a "beehive of activities" and generated enough money to renovate the church and pay off its mortgage. "Such accomplishments in improving and furnishings for the church in a four-year period were unheard of, and sounds fantastic, for this young Pastor's works have been referred to as 'dazzling.' "[16]

However, it was largely migrant women who created and sustained such success stories by forming the loyal and active core of East Bay churches. Estelle Peoples, for example, joined Cooper in 1948 because she liked the music. "I came from a musical family, and stayed at that church because Reverend Fauntleroy was a minister of music." She went on to observe that "most members had come from somewhere else . . . Louisiana, Texas, Arkansas . . . from all over—not too many natives." At Cooper, Estelle sang in the choir, worked with the Nurses Society and the Missionary Aid Society, and "won four trophies for my fund-raising activities." After forty years of loyal service, Estelle left her church: "Didn't like the new minister at Cooper because he left his children and wife. I never had seen such carrying on in a church." Given her fund-raising history, Cooper was certainly poorer for having lost her.[17]

During World War II, women's church work, like their work in homes and neighborhoods, helped migrants settle into new communities. In addition to providing newcomers with information about jobs and housing, churches were often migrants' first source of friends. Following the war, churches continued to provide vital services to migrant communities. Oakland's Allan Temple Baptist Church, for example, sponsors an after-school enrichment program for inner-city children, raises money for college scholarships, owns and operates a retirement home for senior citizens, and runs a credit union, blood bank, and senior citizens' meal program.[18]

Finally, as permanent social service–providing institutions, churches undermined the white community's attempts to "freeze out" newcomers. As one white observer noted, established East Bay residents "expected much of its momentary overpopulation to go back where it came from, and shied away from encouraging this overpopulation to remain." In Berkeley, for example, white resistance to newcomers "led the [city] council to reject a proposal by the chairman of the planning commission, in February 1950, to make a survey of housing to determine how many people were in effect camping in Berkeley under lower than acceptable shelter standards." Such a survey, the council maintained, "might lead to a campaign for public housing," which in turn would lower the misery quotient and encourage migrants to stay. Thus, women's work in churches, by softening the impact of intentional neglect of their communities, forcefully announced migrants' determination to remain. Indeed, the physical presence of churches stood as a visible, concrete reminder that newcomers had firmly planted themselves in the East Bay.[19]

Politics

The political arena, to a greater extent than elsewhere, brought the migrant community into contact with established white and black leadership. Before the war, East Bay city politics was dominated by a conservative, antilabor business elite. The wartime boom brought unprecedented prosperity to the region, a development welcomed by local businesses. However, it also stimulated in-migration, including an influx of African Americans, whom business leaders regarded as undesirable guest workers. Migration—white and black—also highlighted the need for public-sector intervention to ease overcrowded housing, schools, transportation lines, and recreational facilities. The business community, which preferred private-sector solutions that could be selectively applied to weed out undesirable newcomers, actively resisted necessary improvements.[20]

In contrast, progressive labor activists actively built coalitions with white liberals and newcomers, stressing the need for civic improvements, better schools, housing, new job opportunities, and postwar city planning. Within black migrant communities, established labor leaders like C. L. Dellums and Matt Crawford and seasoned Democratic Party activists like Frances Albrier and William Byron Rumford registered newcomers and mobilized them in support of liberal agendas, which included a commitment to fair housing and employment legislation. By 1946, for example, the Alameda County NAACP was operating twelve voter registration schools out of private homes, churches, and community centers, using sample ballots to familiarize newcomers with California voting procedures.[21]

These coalitions that were built during the war did not immediately overturn East Bay conservative political machines. The process was gradual, occurring in stages and at different times within East Bay cities. However, in each community, African American migrants played a central and often decisive role in this political transformation. Women's political behavior must thus be placed within this broader context of migrant activism and coalition politics.

Few of the women in my sample voted in the towns and cities of their birth, but all of them knew that white southerners had unfairly deprived them of that right. When they arrived in the Bay Area, migrant women looked forward to joining the political process, viewing their vote as another way of meeting the needs of their families and communities. Henrietta McAlister, from Laurel, Mississippi, remembers that "we couldn't vote down there . . . not even a local NAACP chapter; it was just too dangerous." She went on to remark that "I registered to vote as soon as I came, and then decided to register others. Went door to door. . . . The white power structure in Richmond thought they could get rid of black residents by taking down the [war-worker housing] projects, but there were so many of us."[22]

Lovie McIntosh, Henrietta's close friend, came from an Arkansas family with a long history of activism. Although she did not vote back home, she recalls "walking into Little Rock's Woolworth's with high school friends and demanding service. . . . I always felt entitled." She then remarked that "there was a long tradition of protest before the Brown decision." When she arrived in Richmond, Lovie "immediately began to vote. Met a woman who had come out earlier and was involved in voter registration." Lovie "hooked up with her right away" and, like Henrietta, helped register other migrants.[23] Lacey Gray, who migrated to Richmond from rural Louisiana, may have been registered to vote by Henrietta or Lovie. "I didn't vote in Louisiana. My first opportunity came out here, and it was a great one. I remember they were registering people to vote out in front of stores." Since then, she has "never missed an election."[24]

Migrant women not only sought the franchise out West but recognized and objected to the South's subversion of the electoral process. Gracie

Potter recalled that her father had voted in Pelican, Louisiana, but "he could only vote Democrat and the polling place was the country store owned by the white guy who extended credit. So you can hardly call that voting." When she migrated to Oakland, Gracie "volunteered at the polls for eleven years in my father's memory."[25] Willa Suddeth, also raised in Louisiana, remembered an uncle who worked with the NAACP trying to register black voters. Like Gracie, Willa felt that she owed it to those who remained in the South to vote.[26] Texas, Theresa Waller recalled, had a poll tax that prevented her family and most of the black people she knew from voting. She went on to state that "you better believe I voted out here; voted every chance I got."[27] But voting was not always easy in the East Bay, either. In 1946, the Alameda County NAACP received complaints from new arrivals that clerks in the registrar's office were administering tests similar to those used in the South to obstruct black voting. After being approached by the NAACP, the registrar promised to investigate the matter and to warn clerks that such tests were a violation of policy.[28]

Undoubtedly, some migrants arrived in the Bay Area without any knowledge of the electoral process. But accounts of such "innocence," like stories about migrants who washed up in toilets or persisted in riding at the back of the bus, were products of antimigration sentiment, spread by established white and black residents to discredit newcomers. As this study has repeatedly stressed, the majority of migrants were relatively well educated and came to the Bay Area for more than economic opportunity. Once here, migrant men and women were informed and active voters. Indeed, a 1960 consumer survey of Bay Area black residents reported that 90.8 percent of women read one or more newspapers on a regular basis, and 94.8 percent of that number read the news section.[29]

Whether politically active from the start or "educated" by established residents, migrants altered local and state politics, joining white liberals and labor activists to undermine entrenched Republican leadership. As early as 1948, for example, migrants in Berkeley and Oakland, in coalition with white liberals and labor, elected California's first black assemblyman, William Byron Rumford, who went on to initiate the state's Fair Employment Practices Act and the Rumford Fair Housing Act. His campaign organizers recognized "that the largest single element contributing to that victory was the arrival in Oakland, Berkeley, and in California as a whole since 1940, of the hundreds of thousands of Blacks."[30]

In 1950, the same white-black coalition elected Berkeley's first liberal mayor; in 1961 it elected the town's first black council and school board members and, at the same time, took control of the city council. According to one observer, the 1961 election "was the election that changed the whole orientation of the City of Berkeley and gave an open flavor to its politics."[31] In Oakland, a progressive coalition elected four white members to the nine-member city council in 1945. It would take several years, however, before Oakland's progressives elected their first black leaders; black political participation, initially encouraged during the war years, blossomed in the 1960s as migrants gained additional experience and influence through War on Poverty programs that encouraged community activism and control. By 1964 Oakland had elected its first black city council member; by the late 1970s, its first black mayor; and in 1983, its first black majority on the city council.[32]

Richmond's migrants flexed their political muscle in 1947, supporting Louis Richardson in his bid for a seat on the city council. Richardson, a black migrant and leader in the local branch of the NAACP, made it through the primary but lost in the general election. Over the next several years, other black candidates ran for office; many of these candidates were associated with the Richmond NAACP, which had been established during the war years by newcomers. However, it was not until 1961 that a black candidate, George Carroll, won a council seat. In 1964 Carroll went on to become Richmond's first black mayor, a political development that must have dispelled any lingering hopes that migrants would return to the South.[33]

In Richmond, as in Berkeley, progressive Democrats found new power in building coalitions with migrant voters. In 1946 George Miller Jr., a Democrat, won a seat in the state assembly with the support of white liberals, migrants, and organized labor. Two years later, Miller won a state senate race with the backing of the same coalition. Miller's victory, like Carroll's, would not have been possible in prewar Richmond.[34]

Civil Rights

The World War II migration brought a new sense of urgency to East Bay civil rights struggles. Although employment and housing discrimination had been long-standing problems, the influx of newcomers placed strains on existing resources and led to a higher level of racial tension. With the backing of a new migrant constituency, East Bay black leaders established new organizations and pushed existing civil rights groups to adopt more militant tactics. Like political activism, civil rights struggles muted cultural differences between migrants and those established residents who were engaged in antidiscrimination battles.

Migrants who came west with high expectations wanted more than the crumbs handed out by paternalistic whites. They wanted full membership in the East Bay's political, economic, and cultural life. The NAACP and electoral politics provided the organizational framework through which to contest racial discrimination and antimigrant social and economic policies. Possessing a history of NAACP membership in the South, or at least the knowledge that because of the violent racial climate of their hometowns they had been denied the opportunity to join, all of the women in my sample joined this organization.

Along with migrant men, women enlarged the membership of existing East Bay NAACP chapters, founded a Richmond branch, and gave local and state leaders the numerical clout to press for fair employment and housing. For example, C. L. Dellums, a charismatic business agent for the Brotherhood of Sleeping Car Porters, was elected vice president of the Northern California NAACP in 1937. A militant activist by prewar standards, he helped organize "Don't Buy Where You Can't Work" campaigns, pressured the federal government to administer depression-era employment programs more equitably, and lobbied the City of Oakland to build and integrate low-income housing. As migrants arrived in the East Bay, Dellums acquired the necessary support to expand his agenda, and he pushed local NAACP branches to address newcomer's concerns: discrimination in defense industries, unions, housing, and public accommodations. Finally, Dellums mobilized black voters to institutionalize wartime gains by voting for state fair housing and employment legislation.[35]

By responding to migrants' needs, Dellums and other more militant East Bay leaders ushered in a new era of civil rights activism. This shift in focus was supported by migrants but was not always embraced by established residents. One incident that illuminates the conflicting agendas of migrants and established residents occurred in Richmond during the war years. Marguerite Williams, a longtime East Bay resident, attended the all-black Linden Street YWCA when she lived in Oakland. In 1946 Marguerite moved to Richmond. There the YWCA was all-white and located far from black neighborhoods, so she called the organization to suggest that they establish a branch for young black women in her section of town. When the Richmond NAACP learned about her request, its representatives tried to convince her that she was undermining their attempts to integrate public facilities. Marguerite reflected bitterly that "when we went to the 'Y' at Oakland, we never thought about we were being discriminated against. . . . That's why I say that a lot of NAACP policies . . . in a way they're detrimental."[36]

Migrant women, along with men, embraced this new militancy. During the 1940s, the Alameda County branch, which included the cities of Berkeley, Oakland, and Alameda, began a seven-year struggle to integrate the workforce of the Key System, a transportation line that ran buses and trains in the East Bay and across the bridge into San Francisco. After threatening a boycott and appealing to the Public Utilities Commission, the NAACP forced the system to hire black drivers in 1951.[37] During the same period, the Alameda County branch fought restrictive housing covenants, police brutality, discriminatory admissions policies at Heald's and Armstrong business schools, and the lack of minority access to low-cost housing. It also launched a study of minority treatment in county textbooks, brought suits against several local eating establishments that refused service to black patrons, and participated in legal battles against the Boilermakers' Jim Crow auxiliaries.[38]

The Alameda County branch continued this spirit of activism into the 1950s, successfully pressing General Motors to open its Chevrolet plant to black workers and forcing the Oakland fire department to integrate its firehouses. These and numerous other victories increased the popularity of the branch, swelling its membership to an unmanageable size. By the mid-1950s, local leadership created separate Oakland and Berkeley branches to accommodate the new militancy and increased numbers.[39]

The Berkeley branch, which attracted a charter membership of about four hundred people—almost half of whom were women—immediately became involved in the Codornices Village conflict. Constructed to house defense workers during the war, by 1954 the village had become a predominantly African American development. Migrant tenants, shut out of the local housing market by high costs and discriminatory real estate and lending practices, had few other alternatives. The federal government had offered to transfer the project, free of charge, to the City of Berkeley. However, the city rejected the plan, and the Public Housing Administration slated the village for demolition. This, the NAACP argued, was exactly what the city wanted: eviction and displacement of "undesirable" residents, who would hopefully leave town altogether.

Responding to pressure from migrant tenants, the Berkeley NAACP at first urged the city to reconsider its decision. When this failed, the branch fought to extend the life of the project until its residents could be humanely relocated. It then pressured the city, realty board, and various community organizations to cooperate in relocating village families. Although the project closed in 1955—a victory for the city's conservative white residents—its eight thousand displaced black tenants now viewed the NAACP as an ally in their struggle for stability and permanence.[40]

The Oakland branch similarly addressed newcomer's needs. As war industries closed, migrants were the first fired. Responding to the growing unemployment problem, the Oakland branch helped organize the East Bay Employment Committee, which adopted the slogan "Spend Your Money Where You Can Work." On a local and state level, the Oakland and other East Bay branches mobilized support for fair housing and employment legislation. In 1959, their efforts paid off: the state established a Fair Employment Practices Commission and a Commission on Discrimination in Housing. Later, in 1963, the state legislature passed the Fair Housing Act, which prohibited property owners and realtors from discriminating against buyers and renters on the basis of race, color, or creed. In November 1964, conservative voters defeated the Fair Housing Act, but it was reinstated in 1966 by the state supreme court.[41]

Of all the East Bay NAACP branches, the migrant-founded Richmond organization had the most militant membership and the most controversial history. Established during the war, the Richmond branch developed strong ties to the Boilermaker's Local A-36, the union's Jim Crow auxiliary for black shipyard workers. It also worked closely with, and drew some of its leadership from, the Communist Party. With this base in the labor movement and East Bay left, the Richmond NAACP grew rapidly throughout the 1940s and achieved some notable civil rights victories.

By 1945 the Richmond branch was engaged in a legal battle with the Boilermakers over their Jim Crow auxiliary system and was vocally accusing the Richmond Housing Authority of overcharging and illegally evicting black tenants, some of whom were NAACP members. The same year, white parents began to lobby the Richmond School Board to segregate city schools following a violent altercation between a black student and white youths who had been racially taunting him. The Richmond NAACP successfully blocked the school segregation proposal.[42]

Two years later, Richmond NAACP members organized a picket of Lucky Stores to protest the chain's failure to hire black clerks. Lucky Store management had earlier agreed to hire one black clerk for each market located in predominantly black sections of town. But after a black patron was assaulted by a white clerk for allegedly stealing some bacon, the NAACP demanded that Lucky continue to hire clerks until their proportion matched the percentage of African American customers in each store. Lucky refused, and NAACP members organized a Richmond-wide picket and boycott. The protest ended when Lucky received an injunction from the superior court of Contra Costa County. As a consequence, several demonstrators were arrested, charged with contempt, fined twenty dollars each, and sentenced to two days in jail. This episode only fueled the organization's popularity, however. By 1948, the Richmond NAACP was being commended by the West Coast Regional Office for exceeding its membership "quota of 600, by some 58."[43]

During the following year—1949—the Richmond branch successfully lobbied for a citywide fair employment practices ordinance. Richmond thus became the first city in California to adopt such legislation. But despite this impressive victory, particularly for such a new organization, the branch began to attract criticism for its Communist Party connections. As early as 1947, Cleophus Brown, a founding member of the branch and its president, was called before the Tenney Committee on Un-American Activities. Other Richmond members were also accused of having Party affiliations, prompting the local press to sensationalize and exploit the so-called Red infiltration of the NAACP. Worried that these reports would destroy the organization's public credibility and base of support, the regional director pressed local branches, including Richmond, to purge their leadership of Communist influence. By the early 1950s, Richmond "came clean," expelling the progressive leadership that had built the organization and steered it through the turbulent war and postwar years. In 1954, a memo from Richmond's NAACP secretary to the West Coast regional director triumphantly announced that former president Cleophus Brown had not only lost his office but had also been denied regular membership in the organization.[44]

Although men dominated the NAACP leadership, some migrant women enjoyed considerable influence within the organization. Olive Blue, for example, served as two-term secretary of the Richmond branch, while managing a full-time job, membership in the Richmond Democratic Club and National Council of Negro Women (NCNW), and an extraordinary schedule of church activities as well. More commonly, migrant women filled the NAACP's rank and file, performing most of the organization's clerical work, registering voters, distributing literature, and walking picket lines. Assuming that the Berkeley branch was representative of others, women constituted half of the East Bay membership, contributing significantly to the organization's political clout during the war and postwar years.[45]

Unlike the NAACP, the National Council of Negro Women encouraged and fostered female leadership. Before the war, established East Bay chapters served as fund-raising organizations for separate black institutions like the Linden Street YWCA, the Fannie Wall Children's Home, and the Home for Aged and Infirm Colored People. But during the 1940s, migrant women's needs and increasing involvement redirected its focus to child care, affordable housing, and fair employment. To survive, existing chapters of the NCNW needed to accommodate newcomers, admitting them to leadership positions and placing their concerns at the center of their agendas. In Richmond, migrant women created a new chapter from scratch. Lovie McIntosh, also active in the NAACP and Richmond's Democratic Party politics, organized the Richmond NCNW in 1951 around her kitchen table.[46]

While migrant women helped refashion local civil rights organizations and electoral politics, they kept a watchful eye on the South, supporting and celebrating the efforts of civil rights workers to dismantle segregation. Some of them, including Lovie McIntosh, maintained that "if I had stayed, I would have been at the forefront of the civil rights movement."[47] A few, such as Marlene Brown, did their part on return visits to the South. In 1954, during a trip back to Texas, Marlene got on a bus with her sick and crying child and asked a white woman seated in the front to make room for her. "When she refused, I sat down in her lap, and she jumped up and called me 'nigger.' But I stayed right there, and they didn't throw me off. When things like that happen, white folks don't credit you with having good sense. They think you're crazy. So nobody said anything, even the bus driver."[48] Lacey Gray, from rural Louisiana, recalled how whites resisted desegregation well into the late 1960s. "I remember going back home after segregation and having white people try to keep the old rules. They would try to move us to the back of the bus, but we would refuse, and that was after Dr. King!" She went on to remark that "I was glad for the people back there. We didn't have too much [discrimination] out here. There was some, and they'd try to hide it, but it was really bad back there. When a girl was fourteen you had to say, 'Yes, Miss,' and now we go back there and they tell us, 'Yes, ma'am' and 'No, ma'am.' "[49]

Education

Many migrant women cut their political teeth in East Bay Parent-Teacher Associations. Their involvement in education, like their church activism, received the sanction of tradition. Indeed, most women came from families that had made great sacrifices to educate their children. When southern school boards refused to build and furnish schools for black children, parents built their own or sent their sons and daughters to board with friends and relatives who lived near schools. In some instances, entire families relocated to areas with better educational opportunities. Women who attended college remember how aunts, uncles, and grandparents helped pay tuition, taking a special interest and pride in the success of one of their own.

When the war began, migrant women—many of whom now had children of their own—viewed the West Coast as a better place to raise and educate their young. The Tillmans, for example, "came to California for economic reasons, but also for education. . . . Could only have educated our children [in the South] by sending them away. We felt California would be better in that respect." Ethel Tillman went on to describe how her family lived in defense housing during the war in order to save money to buy a home. When they began to look for permanent housing, they chose Berkeley "because we liked the educational climate there . . . wanted the children to be near the university."[50]

Arriving in the Bay Area with high hopes for their children's education, migrant women were disappointed by the lack of integration within schools. Although the area's segregation resulted from residential segregation rather than official school board policy, the outcome was the same: older, overcrowded, and understaffed schools for black children. During the war years, for example, almost four-fifths of Richmond's black population lived in war-worker housing projects located on the south side of the city. Although they comprised 64 percent of elementary school enrollment in Richmond, south-side children were served by only seven schools. In contrast, the remaining 35 percent who lived on the city's north side or in the El Cerrito area attended nine schools.[51]

Migrant parents who protested severe overcrowding in their neighborhood schools received little relief from the school board and federal government. Some temporary classrooms were eventually added to existing schools, and a new school was built to accommodate students from the Harbor Gate housing project. Yet as one observer noted, these improvements were "woefully inadequate to take care of the numbers of children that were standing on their doorstep. They not only had split sessions, but the split sessions had to be split. . . . Since the schools in the Negro areas were among the chief sufferers, the Negro pupil made up a large portion of this inadequately educated group."[52]

Because of persistent overcrowding, all south-side schools went on double session, and one—Stege Elementary—held four sessions per day as of January 1944. There, students attended school for a maximum of two-and-a-half hours each day.[53] Overcrowding also led to other problems: poor lighting, inadequate sanitation and playground facilities, and the need for additional janitorial services and teaching staff. When migrant parents requested improvements from the school board, they were told to take their complaints to the federal government. White parents, however, could depend on the school board to allocate local improvement funds for their schools and shepherd their complaints through federal bureaucracies.[54]

After the war, new school construction eased overcrowding but failed to address the segregation issue. Migrant parents, whose vigorous protests had forced the reluctant school board to ease overcrowding during the war, now turned their energy to confronting de facto school segregation. In 1955, migrant parents successfully blocked a plan to build a new school in North Richmond, correctly observing that it would be mostly black. Then, in 1959, parents from Parchester Village protested a plan that would have rerouted all Parchester Village children to a predominantly black school. Previously, Parchester's children had attended two schools, one white and one black, and black parents wanted to keep it that way. Mary Lee, a Parchester resident and active PTA member, remembers how "black children were unwanted at the [white] Bayview school. But we went to court and won." And indeed they did. In 1959, the school board backed down and continued to send Parchester children to both schools.[55]

Throughout the 1960s, migrant parents advocated plans to adjust school boundaries to reduce or eliminate de facto segregation, though they encountered vigorous opposition from white parents who wanted to preserve "neighborhood schools." Similar battles took place in Oakland and Berkeley, and these conflicts were eventually resolved in favor of desegregation. However, as East Bay schools were desegregated, white parents increasingly relocated to the suburban fringe or placed their children in private schools, thereby undermining efforts to achieve school integration.[56]

While they were actively involved in efforts to relieve school overcrowding and foster integration, migrant women also took an interest in the day-to-day quality of their children's education. Yet most established residents, including educators, ignored their activism, viewing migrant parents as "floaters" and "drifters" who "didn't know what education was." However, the former dean of girls at Richmond High School offered a less biased account of newcomer involvement: "The parents I talked with wanted their kids in school, they wanted them to have an education. They were people who often didn't have much education themselves, but they wanted their kids to have what they didn't have so that their lives would be easier. Those parents often came to school to see me. I didn't encourage them to do that, but it was permitted. Sometimes they came to my hotel room at night. Many of them came to see me that way. I used to stay late to meet them at school, too."[57]

Migrant women frequently observed that schools dampened their children's aspirations—a charge substantiated by independent researchers, who documented the widespread use of tracking, the scarcity of black teachers and school administrators, and the entrenched racial biases of white personnel.[58] Lee Henderson, from Guthrie, Oklahoma, became active in the Girl Scouts, Boy Scouts, and PTA once she arrived in Oakland. She recalled with anger how "teachers had made up their minds that black kids were not going to do well. My son's teacher told him, after he had done well in machine shop, that he should forget about being a machinist—that no one would hire a black machinist." Lee went on to relate how "I went in and told that man that my son could be the first." With pride in her voice, she then disclosed how her son became a chemist after graduating from a southern black college. His success, she maintains, stems from a family tradition of supporting education. "Mother and Grandmother always stressed education, and my father left Texas because he wanted us to get a good education."[59] Ethel Tillman similarly felt that her children were not receiving enough encouragement, but she blamed the public school curriculum. African American history, she maintained, was completely ignored in the Berkeley schools, so she and her husband taught it in their home.[60]

Migrant women also volunteered within schools and assumed leadership positions within the PTA. Lovie McIntosh joined the Stege PTA soon after she arrived from Arkansas, and she used her involvement with this organization to develop a network of friends and learn about Richmond politics. After several years of volunteer service with the PTA, Lovie was elected president. Willa Suddeth also became president of her local PTA. Meeting at a PTA convention in Los Angeles, Willa and Lovie became friends and went on to co-found the Richmond branch of the National Council of Negro Women. Willa, who moved to Parchester Village in 1955, then met Mary Lee and joined the protest against school segregation.[61]

Although Lovie and Willa were exceptionally active, the majority of women in my sample did join their local PTA. In addition, several headed Scout troops. Mary Lee, for example, moved to Parchester Village in 1951. When her children were young, she organized her paid labor to accommodate PTA, Scouting, and school activities.[62] Similarly, Oma June Scott took piecework into her Oakland home when she was raising her children, and she "also worked as a Scout leader and PTA volunteer . . . was den mother for both the Girl and Boy Scouts."[63] Henrietta Bolden, who raised her children on welfare after she and her husband divorced, "was active in the PTA when all of my kids were young." Living in public housing on a shoestring budget, Henrietta struggled to be a "good" mother. To her, this meant staying at home while her children were young and supervising their education. Today, her advice to young people is "to get a good education. My father was really committed to education, and as a result I knew how to read and do my ABCs before I even went to school."[64]

Activist Mothers

As a consequence of their work in schools, churches, and local politics, some unusually dedicated migrant women attained highly visible positions in their communities. They became, in the words of Nancy Naples, "activist mothers." All migrant women in my sample did some form of community work. Indeed, the majority performed more community and church service than their white suburban counterparts did. However, a few migrant women became community representatives, activists who were widely recognized as movers and shakers. Henrietta McAlister and Lovie McIntosh fit into this latter category. Lovie McIntosh, from Little Rock, Arkansas, arrived in Richmond during the wet and cold winter of 1942. Through church and school volunteer work, she began to meet other women. Eventually she became president of the Stege PTA, met Willa Suddeth, and founded the Richmond branch of the National Council of Negro Women. By that time she was also active in the NAACP, voter registration drives, and efforts to elect white liberal and black candidates to state and local office. Then, in the late 1940s, she and a cousin opened a variety store in North Richmond, further increasing her visibility in the community.[65]

Henrietta McAlister, from Laurel, Mississippi, moved to Richmond in 1945 as Bay Area defense industries were demobilizing. "I was so disappointed. Had images of California which were different. I thought Richmond would be more urbanized, more like San Francisco." By late 1947, Henrietta found a job with Universal Life Insurance, joined a church and the NAACP, and began registering voters for the Democratic Club. And like

Lovie, she soon started her own business—an employment agency for black domestic workers.[66]

In the 1960s, as part of the War on Poverty, white community organizers started the Richmond Community Development Demonstration Project. Like similar projects in cities across the nation, this one identified local activists and trained them to be community organizers.[67] Henrietta McAlister, Lovie McIntosh, and a third migrant woman were hired as community workers and research aids and began working with tenant's groups, welfare mothers, and churches to increase migrant representation in local community improvement efforts. They also started a work-study program for junior high school students and organized citizens to participate in Richmond's Demonstration Cities Program.[68] Lovie remembers how her involvement with the project began: "One day because of my community connections, [a white organizer] came knocking at my door and introduced himself. He was straight from New York. So I got involved in the first federally funded program in Richmond."[69]

Activist mothers were recruited in a similar fashion in cities throughout the United States. But what made Henrietta and Lovie unusual was that they went on to establish their own grassroots community organization. Lovie remembers that the demonstration project was temporary "and we knew it would fold. So that was when we got together and decided to do something that was rooted in the community—started and run by the people of Richmond." With only thirty-five dollars between them, the women secured an abandoned building from the Richmond Redevelopment Agency and started People Pledged for Community Progress (PPCP). Lovie recalled that the group rapidly became self-sustaining: "We could do what people said needed to be done for them instead of doing what the powers thought we needed. Got nonprofit status and did fund-raising within the community." Showing characteristic concern for her community, Lovie went on to reflect that "if we had to spend a lot of time talking and negotiating, that took us away from the community and we were not into that. So if money was available without too many strings attached, we got it. But if it was going to be a long, drawn-out process and take us away from our work, we wouldn't take it."[70]

In its twelve years of operation, PPCP sponsored several projects that benefited Richmond's migrant community. Henrietta recalled how their earliest project documented employment discrimination in downtown Richmond. The three women surveyed young black men between the ages of eighteen and twenty-five and found that many "had never been gainfully employed—were out of the job market completely." Then they documented the almost total absence of black employees in downtown businesses and organized a "committee of community people to support increased hiring of minorities." Lovie recalled how they "learned from [white organizers] how to document [racial discrimination] and translate statistics into lay language."[71]

Following that project, PPCP started a food co-op, a recycling program, a job training program, a credit union, a food stamp distribution service, and a "demonstration project showing low-income people how to make their homes nice, even though they didn't have money." They also built two parks, provided funds for housing rehabilitation, and started a housing counseling program to "help people manage their money and work out payment plans with their creditors so they wouldn't lose their homes." The success of PPCP was at least partly due to Henrietta's and Lovie's networking skills. As Lovie noted, "we always built connections outside of our community . . . built networks with white liberals and the Greater Richmond Interfaith Program, which started the same year as PPCP. So we were always connected to other people who wanted changes and shared our beliefs." Their inclusiveness also extended to their own community. In addition to building ties with black churches and the NAACP, they worked with the Black Panthers: "Thought they did good work. We felt they were intelligent young men—were so proud of them—with a well-thought-out program which they laid out to the city council. They were nice kids." Lovie summed up the importance of building broad coalitions: "It's never just people of one kind who make changes, but people of like minds. And you can always build those connections . . . even if you are in a minority."[72]

In Berkeley, Susie Gaines represented the same tradition of activist mothering. After she arrived in the East Bay from Arkansas in 1943, Susie settled in South Berkeley, raised a family, and became a well-respected church member. First she established and ran an innovative senior services program at her church. Later in life, she became more of an activist: for example, she and other church members, including the Tillmans, successfully lobbied the City of Berkeley to build a senior center in their neighborhood. Susie then became director of this center and served on the city's Commission on Aging. At the same time, she began organizing residents of South Berkeley to counter the economic decline of their neighborhood. Called the "E. F. Hutton of South Berkeley," Gaines motivated her neighbors to "heckle the hell out of the city until they hear our voices." As a consequence, they obtained better police protection, a new child care center, park improvements, zoning adjustments to limit South Berkeley's growth, and funding for redevelopment and beautification projects. Now in her eighties, Gaines serves as president of the Tyler-King-California Neighborhood Association, as a board member of the South Berkeley Neighborhood Development Corporation, and as a member of the Homeless Task Force.[73]

Migrant women like Susie Gaines relied on a southern tradition of self-help and protest to sustain their families, neighborhoods, and institutions. This tradition, which had been so essential to survival in the Jim Crow South, allowed them to withstand racially motivated efforts to dislodge them from their new communities. When women came west, few hoped for complete liberation from racial oppression. Yet few expected such a long road to freedom, a journey that is still incomplete. In the East Bay, women found better lives: access to the voting booth, schools, a broader range of jobs, medical care, and many modern conveniences that had been unobtainable luxuries back home. They also escaped Jim Crow's innumerable dangers and humiliations. However, most women did not anticipate the racial hostility that greeted them—a hostility that generated residential segregation and employment discrimination, destroyed affordable housing in black neighborhoods, erased and divided vital communities with freeways and "redevelopment" projects, and culminated in white flight and deindustrialization. While few women saw themselves as creating oppositional institutions, that is exactly what they did. The fact that their communities survived is a tribute their southern cultural heritage of self-help, activism, and coalition-building.

Conclusion . . . . .

Migration and community-building involve a complex, gender-specific division of labor. Most migration studies focus on male experience and emphasize labor force participation, occupational discrimination, unionization, the development of workplace culture, and the growth of male-dominated political institutions. Although it produces important insights, this emphasis limits our understanding of where and how social change takes place and how community is established and maintained. As this study reveals, women also worked for wages, substantially contributing to family income and the economic stability of their new communities. At the same time, they took primary responsibility for child care and household maintenance—labor that most certainly enhanced the productivity of other family members who worked for wages.

In addition to balancing the roles of wage earner and homemaker, migrant women performed several tasks that were central to the migration and community-building process. Most of the women in my sample participated equally in the decision to migrate. Male family members frequently moved first, finding jobs and housing before sending for relatives. In the meantime, women sold family possessions, decided what to pack, and arranged transportation for remaining family members. Once they arrived in the East Bay, migrant women performed most of the orientation tasks associated with resettlement: transforming substandard and crowded housing into comfortable living quarters; locating schools, markets, medical services, and churches; negotiating public transportation; building mutual aid relationships; and maintaining ties to those back home. Once settled, migrant women created hospitality networks, providing newcomers with food, shelter, and information about jobs, permanent housing, and cultural resources. Finally, migrant women established institutions that helped stabilize their communities in the racially hostile climate of the East Bay Area. Drawing on their southern cultural tradition of self-help and resistance to enforced dependency, migrant women created cohesive neighborhoods, founded churches, and organized other newcomers to demand access to better housing, jobs, schools, and social services.

As wage workers, migrant women filled the least desirable, most poorly paid positions in the labor market, exchanging domestic jobs for relatively low-wage manufacturing and service-sector occupations. Most left domestic service jobs in the South only to find that their occupational mobility in the Bay Area was limited by gender and racial discrimination. The majority enjoyed relatively high wages during the war, but only in relation to what they had earned in the South. Following the war, most filled jobs in garment and food processing industries or in the urban service sector—all of which were characterized by low wages, poor benefits, and a lack of job security. Some women, however, did find custodial and clerical jobs in the public sector. These women, all of whom stressed their good fortune, enjoyed long, stable careers. The role of government in providing postwar employment to black women should, in fact, be explored more fully. Indeed, the number of black women employed in this sector grew steadily between 1940 and 1980. By 1979, nearly one-third of all employed African American women worked for local, state, or federal government.[1]

The war also had an ambiguous impact on established gender roles. Working-class black women had a long history of labor force participation. Just before the war, for example, one out of every three black women worked for wages, compared to one out of five white women. Nevertheless, working-class African American women obtained respect and authority as wives, mothers, and public or community workers. The breadwinner role, and the status it conferred, belonged to male household heads. The war did little to disrupt this configuration. This is not to suggest that role conflicts never emerged between men and women; however, because black working-class women worked for wages before, during, and after the war, those tensions and conflicts were negotiated on an ongoing basis.[2] Moreover, the economic contribution of working-class women was essential to family survival. While the black middle class voiced concerns about women's increased labor force participation, chiding them for being too ambitious and domineering, the black working class relied on women's wages to fend off poverty and facilitate upward mobility.[3]

Perhaps too ambitiously, I wish to contribute to the growing and increasingly lively debate on the origins of urban poverty. In *The Promised Land*, Nicholas Lemann revived the "culture of poverty" thesis by arguing that sharecropping undermined family stability, the work ethic, and moral values. As African Americans migrated North during and after World War II, he asserts, they transplanted an "ethic of dependency" marked by substance abuse, teenage pregnancy, female-headed families, and predatory behavior. I respond to this thesis on several different levels. First, most of the women in my sample were not sharecroppers. These women and the migrants described in several wartime population surveys that I used to support my own findings came from families that owned or rented farms or worked for wages in southern industry. Indeed, their skill and educational levels were strikingly similar to those of white workers who migrated during the same period. This, however, is a small point of contention, one that simply takes Lemann to task for his overgeneralizations about migrant populations.[4]

Although few of the women in my sample were sharecroppers, most of their grandparents and great-grandparents had been. When asked what cultural values they obtained from their elders, migrant women listed a commitment to formal education, a determination to own land, a respect for family ties and elders, the moral necessity of caring for less fortunate friends and neighbors, and an obligation to support community-sustaining institutions. Whether sharecroppers, small independent farmers, or industrial workers, black southerners shared a common desire for self-sufficiency. Their determination to resist white control over their lives was the primary legacy of southern black culture. As Jacqueline Jones noted in "Southern Diaspora: Origins of the Northern 'Underclass,'" an "emphasis on the struggles of black families and communities to provide for themselves, and resist the debilitating dependency forced upon them by white men of property, diverges from the 'conventional wisdom' that informs the current underclass debate." The migrant women's stories told in the preceding pages support Jones's concluding observation that "embedded in the historical record of ordinary families, then, is a powerful refutation of the culture of poverty or culture of dependency thesis."[5]

Once migrants arrived in the East Bay Area, they confronted enormous obstacles: residential segregation, employment discrimination, overcrowded schools, and substandard housing. Nevertheless, they created stable, permanent communities. Following the war, manufacturing jobs and white residents left East Bay cities for the racially exclusive suburbs. Poorly planned redevelopment schemes further eroded the quality of life in the urban core. For example, transportation officials razed single-family homes and black-owned businesses to make room for freeways and public transit systems. Finally, neighborhoods that survived the wrecking ball were separated from vital services and resources and then targeted as sites for public housing projects.

White flight, the relocation of industrial jobs to the suburbs, and redevelopment occurred simultaneously, nourished by postwar racial stereotypes, hostility, and discrimination. More recently, deindustrialization, or the shift from an industrial to a service-based economy, has added insult to these older injuries. White and black workers have been displaced during the transition to a postindustrial economy. However, white workers, "unhampered by racial stereotypes, racial antagonism, or statistical discrimination[,] . . . fare better than blacks, especially black males, in the competition" for low-paying, part-time replacement jobs. Thus, economic marginalization of migrant communities is a long, racially selective process that began during the war years and continues through the present.[6]

Like William Julius Wilson, I argue that spatial isolation and chronic unemployment, not an "ethic of dependency," are at the heart of urban poverty. However, I question his contention that middle and working-class African Americans have abandoned inner cities, leaving behind a poorer underclass, "collectively different from those that lived in these neighborhoods in earlier years." As Jones noted in "Southern Diaspora," this argument reinforces the popular preoccupation with the "alleged pathological aspects of African-American history" and promotes the idea that "compared to black life in general, ghetto life is 'a thousand times more' apart from white society."[7]

While examining the economic marginalization of East Bay migrant communities, this study emphasizes individual and collective efforts to create community-sustaining institutions and relationships—efforts that cut across class lines to reveal a common, historically rooted desire for independence and self-determination. East Bay black communities face severe problems, but they also have considerable resources. They are not, as commonly portrayed in the media, dominated by a violent, predatory youth culture. Many of these communities' residents, both poor and working-class, continue to draw on southern cultural traditions to keep their families together, build community-sustaining institutions, and challenge racial stereotypes and restrictions. This study, which focuses on the experience and contributions of migrant women, challenges generalizations about inner-city communities—generalizations that obscure their agency and diversity and the historical processes that have led to urban poverty.

Notes . . . .

Introduction

1. Waller interview.

2. Wenkert, *Historical Digest of Negro-White Relations*, 1–20; Hubert Owen Brown, "Impact of War Worker Migration," 40, 117, 118; Nash, *American West Transformed*, 3–14, 66, 69; Sokol, "Richmond during World War II," 13–14; Marilynn S. Johnson, *Second Gold Rush*, 51–55; Charles S. Johnson, *Negro War Worker in San Francisco*, 4–6; France, "Some Aspects of the Migration of the Negro," 24; Moore, "Black Community in Richmond, California," 80–82; Cy W. Record, *Characteristics of Some Unemployed Negro Shipyard Workers*, 9.

3. See, for example, Gottlieb, *Making Their Own Way*; Grossman, *Land of Hope*; Marks, *Farewell We're Good and Gone*; Trotter, *Black Milwaukee*.

4. Marilynn S. Johnson's *Second Gold Rush* is one of the first published studies detailing the demographic, cultural, and political transformation of the San Francisco East Bay area during World War II. Although this is a more general study of wartime migration to the East Bay, emphasizing the experience of white migrants, it contains richly descriptive sections on black migrant labor, housing, and civil rights activism. Shirley Ann Moore's forthcoming history of African Americans in Richmond, California, which contains sections on wartime migration, will also contribute to our knowledge of this subject.

5. For an overview of women's experience during World War II see Chafe, *Paradox of Change*; Anderson, "Last Hired, First Fired"; Anderson, *Wartime Women*; Hartman, *Home Front and Beyond*; and Gluck, *Rosie the Riveter Revisited*.

6. Jones, "Southern Diaspora," 38.

7. Aggregate statistics from fifty oral interviews with former migrants conducted by the author; Shyrock "Wartime Shifts of the Civilian Population," found that the majority of migrants to the West Coast were from towns and cities. His findings are supported by Charles S. Johnson, *Negro War Worker in San Francisco*, 8, 80, and Wilson Record, "Willie Stokes at the Golden Gate," 176. Other studies point to the relatively high skill levels of migrants: Cy W. Record, *Characteristics of Some Unemployed Negro Shipyard Workers*, 33; U.S. Department of Labor, Bureau of Labor Statistics, "Labor Force in Durable Goods Manufacture," 718; and Charles S. Johnson, *Negro War Worker in San Francisco*, 8, 15, 16.

8. McAllister interview.

9. Oakley, "Interviewing Women"; Geiger, "What's So Feminist about Doing Women's Oral History?"; Finch, " 'It's Great to Have Someone to Talk To' "; Personal Narratives Group, *Interpreting Women's Lives*.

10. Wilson Record, "Willie Stokes at the Golden Gate," 187.

Chapter One

1. For a theoretical analysis of segregation see Cell, *Highest Stage of White Supremacy*. For a treatment of the various forms of segregation see Charles S. Johnson, *Backgrounds to Patterns of Negro Segregation*.

2. Charles S. Johnson, *Backgrounds to Patterns of Negro Segregation*, 5. The evolution of Jim Crow is traced in detail and with attention to regional variations in Wright, *Life behind a Veil*; Dittmer, *Black Georgia in the Progressive Era*; and McMillen, *Dark Journey*. The debate over where and when segregation was first instituted is covered in great detail by Cell, *Highest Stage of White Supremacy*; Holt, *Black over White*; Foner, *Short History of Reconstruction*; Rabinowitz, *Race Relations in the Urban South*; Woodward, *Strange Career of Jim Crow*; and Woodman, "Sequel to Slavery."

3. Murray, *Song in a Weary Throat*, 36.

4. Grant, *Black Protest*, 175; Charles S. Johnson, *Backgrounds to Patterns of Negro Segregation*, 5.

5. Waller interview.

6. Murray, *Song in a Weary Throat*, 34; Charles S. Johnson, *Backgrounds to Patterns of Negro Segregation*, 8–10.

7. Charles S. Johnson, *Backgrounds to Patterns of Negro Segregation*, 8–9, 26–55; Angelou, *I Know Why the Caged Bird Sings*, 160.

8. Charles S. Johnson, *Backgrounds to Patterns of Negro Segregation*, 14–21; McAlister interview.

9. Charles S. Johnson, *Backgrounds to Patterns of Negro Segregation*, 14–21.

10. Ibid.

11. Henry interview; Potter interview.

12. Gray interview.

13. Charles S. Johnson, *Backgrounds to Patterns of Negro Segregation*, 99–103.

14. Ibid., 83–99.

15. Gottlieb, *Making Their Own Way*, 31–32; Charles S. Johnson, *Backgrounds to Patterns of Negro Segregation*, 85.

16. Jones, *Labor of Love, Labor of Sorrow*, 197, 206, 208.

17. Waller interview.

18. U.S. Department of Commerce, Bureau of the Census, *Fifteenth Census of the United States* (1930), Population, vol. 6, table 13, *Families Classified by Sex, Age, Color, and Nativity of Head*.

19. McMillen, *Dark Journey*, 119–23; Gottlieb, *Making Their Own Way*, 15–16.

20. Gray interview.

21. Wolters, *Negroes and the Great Depression*, 7–8; Gottlieb, *Making Their Own Way*, 13–15.

22. Daniel M. Johnson and Rex R. Campbell, *Black Migration in America*, 98–99; Wolters, *Negroes and the Great Depression*, 21–34.

23. Murray, *Song in a Weary Throat*, 31, 34; Charles S. Johnson, *Backgrounds to Patterns of Negro Segregation*, 117–55.

24. Lawson, *Black Ballots*, 11.

25. Suddeth interview; McMillen, *Dark Journey*, 314–17.

26. For a discussion of black radicalism in the pre–World War II South, see Rosengarten, *All God's Dangers*; Painter, *Narrative of Hosea Hudson*; Kelley, *Hammer and Hoe*; and Dunbar, *Against the Grain*.

27. For a discussion of women's roles in the black community see Giddings, *When and Where I Enter*; Harley, "For the Good of Family and Race"; Jones, *Labor of Love, Labor of Sorrow*.

28. McMillen, *Dark Journey*, 3–14, 39–56.

29. U.S. Department of Commerce, Bureau of the Census, *Fifteenth Census of the United States* (1930), *Population*, 2:1270; McMillen, *Dark Journey*, 72–108.

30. U.S. Department of Commerce, Bureau of the Census, *Fifteenth Census of the United States* (1930), *Population*, 2:1265; ibid., 4:175, 188, 214, 276.

31. McMillen, *Dark Journey*, 111–12, 113, 140, 153.

32. Ibid., 153–66; U.S. Department of Commerce, Bureau of the Census, *Fifteenth Census of the United States* (1930), *Population*, 2:1273; ibid., 4:873–74; ibid., *Sixteenth Census of the United States, 1940: Population and Housing, Families, General Characteristics*, 197.

33. U.S. Department of Commerce, Bureau of the Census, *Fifteenth Census of the United States* (1930), *Population*, 6:702.

34. McMillen, *Dark Journey*, 166–94; U.S. Department of Commerce, Bureau of the Census, *Fifteenth Census of the United States* (1930), *Population*, 4:873–74.

35. McMillen, *Dark Journey*, 197–223, 224–53.

36. Ibid., 155, 257–81, 297–302.

37. U.S. Department of Commerce, Bureau of the Census, *Fifteenth Census of the United States* (1930), *Population*, 2:965.

38. U.S. Department of Commerce, Bureau of the Census, *Fifteenth Census of the United States* (1930), *Population*, 4:626–27; Blassingame, *Black New Orleans*, 64, 235.

39. U.S. Department of Commerce, Bureau of the Census, *Fifteenth Census of the United States* (1930), *Population*, 4:626–27; ibid., 2:20.

40. Blassingame, *Black New Orleans*, 129–30; U.S. Department of Commerce, Bureau of the Census, *Fifteenth Census of the United States* (1930), *Population*, 4:626–27; ibid., *Sixteenth Census of the United States, 1940: Population and Housing, Families, General Characteristics*, 197; ibid., *Fifteenth Census of the United States* (1930), *Population*, 6:534; ibid., 2:967.

41. Thomson and Meador, *Shreveport*, 20, 112.

42. Ibid., 112.

43. U.S. Department of Commerce, Bureau of the Census, *Fifteenth Census of the United States* (1930), *Agriculture*, 4:175, 277.

44. Beeth and Wintz, *Black Dixie*, 88, 158, 182, 196; U.S. Department of Commerce, Bureau of the Census, *Fifteenth Census of the United States* (1930), *Population*, 2:946.

45. U.S. Department of Commerce, Bureau of the Census, *Fifteenth Census of the United States* (1930), *Population*, 2:941; ibid., *Fifteenth Census of the United States* (1930), *Agriculture*, 4:175, 215, 277, 188.

46. U.S. Department of Commerce, Bureau of the Census, *Fifteenth Census of the United States* (1930), *Population*, 4:1582–84; ibid., *Sixteenth Census of the United States, 1940: Population and Housing, Families, General Characteristics*, 198.

47. Beeth and Wintz, *Black Dixie*, 176.

48. Ibid., 88–90, 187–88.

49. Ibid., 91–92.

50. Ibid., 178–79.

51. Bullard, *Invisible Houston*, 15–27; Beeth and Wintz, *Black Dixie*, 92–94.

52. Bullard, *Invisible Houston*, 119, 22; Beeth and Wintz, *Black Dixie*, 96, 104, 119, 122, 129–33, 158–60.

53. Franklin, *Journey toward Hope*, 44–46, 50–51, 108–16.

54. Ibid., 61–62; U.S. Department of Commerce, Bureau of the Census, *Fifteenth Census of the United States* (1930), *Population*, 2:546.

55. U.S. Department of Commerce, Bureau of the Census, *Fifteenth Census of the United States* (1930), *Agriculture*, 4:175, 215, 188, 277; Franklin, *Journey toward Hope*, 86–99.

56. U.S. Department of Commerce, Bureau of the Census, *Fifteenth Census of the United States* (1930), *Population*, 4:1336–37; ibid., *Sixteenth Census of the United States, 1940: Population and Housing, Families, General Characteristics*, 197; Franklin, *Journey toward Hope*, 92.

57. Franklin, *Journey toward Hope*, 33, 133–39, 146–48, 151.

58. Ibid., 52–54.

59. Tucher, *Arkansas*, 44–48; Whayne and Gatewood, *Arkansas Delta*, 110–12.

60. Whayne and Gatewood, *Arkansas Delta*, 113. See also Cortner, *Mob Intent on Death*.

61. U.S. Department of Commerce, Bureau of the Census, *Fifteenth Census of the United States* (1930), *Population*, 4:160–61; Whayne and Gatewood, *Arkansas Delta*, 120; Tucher, *Arkansas*, 52, 81; U.S. Department of Commerce, Bureau of the Census, *Fifteenth Census of the United States* (1930), *Agriculture*, 4:175, 215.

62. U.S. Department of Commerce, Bureau of the Census, *Fifteenth Census of the United States* (1930), *Population*, 4:160–61; ibid., *Sixteenth Census of the United States, 1940: Population and Housing, Families, General Characteristics*, 196; ibid., *Fifteenth Census of the United States* (1930), *Population*, 2:211.

63. Whayne and Gatewood, *Arkansas Delta*, 116–19.

64. Ibid.; U.S. Department of Commerce, Bureau of the Census, *Fifteenth Census of the United States* (1930), *Population*, 2:172.

65. Charles S. Johnson, *Negro War Worker in San Francisco*, 4.

66. U.S. Department of Commerce, Bureau of the Census, *Fifteenth Census of the United States* (1930), *Population*, 2:183, 967, 1281, 557, 973.

67. McAllister interview; Jones, "Southern Diaspora"; Cohen, *At Freedom's Edge*; Grossman, *Land of Hope*; Painter, *Exodusters*; Trotter, *Great Migration in Historical Perspective*.

68. Shyrock, "Wartime Shifts of the Civilian Population," found that the majority of wartime migrants to the West Coast were from towns and cities. Only 13 to 19 percent were former farm residents. Other studies point to the relatively high skill levels of black migrants: Cy W. Record, *Characteristics of Some Unemployed Negro Shipyard Workers*; U.S. Department of Labor, Bureau of Labor Statistics, "Labor Force in Durable Goods Manufacture"; and Charles S. Johnson, *Negro War Worker in San Francisco*. Johnson's study also indicates that white and black migrants shared similar educational levels; Hall interview.

69. U.S. Department of Commerce, Bureau of the Census, *Sixteenth Census of the United States, 1940: Population, Families, Types of Families*, table 18: White and Negro Families by Detailed Marital Status and Sex of Head, for the United States, Urban and Rural, 1930.

70. Charles S. Johnson, *Negro War Worker in San Francisco*; Cy W. Record, *Characteristics of Some Unemployed Negro Shipyard Workers*; Shyrock, "Wartime Shifts in the Civilian Population"; U.S. Department of Labor, Bureau of Labor Statistics, "Labor Force in Durable Goods Manufacture."

71. Susan Mann, in "Slavery, Sharecropping, and Social Inequality," states that "the notion of patriarchy should be reconceptualized to include a number of patriarchies" that vary by degree of domination according to "class, race, ethnicity, and sexual orientation." I am in no way suggesting a complete absence of male domination in working-class families, but I am positing that relative to middle-class and poor fam-

ilies, working-class couples shared authority more equally. See Mann's article for a discussion of sexual inequality between poor men and women, and see Giddings, *When and Where I Enter*, for a discussion of middle-class roles.

72. Phillips interview.

73. Tillman interview.

74. Simonsen, *You May Plow Here*, 159.

75. Ibid., 31; and Moss interview.

76. Moss interview; Tillman interview; and Hall interview. The prevalence of nuclear families in my sample supports other findings which suggest that the extended family structure is related primarily to economic status rather than cultural preference. In their article "Determinants of Extended Household Structure," Ronald Angel and Marta Tienda analyze their own data in relation to existing studies and conclude that "the extension mechanism may help alleviate poverty, or at least provide households with greater flexibility in allocating market and domestic roles among members" (p. 1381). Thus, low levels of extension among working-class families may be explained by their relative economic stability.

77. Phillips interview; Bolden interview.

78. See Dickson, "Toward a Broader Angle of Vision"; Rouse, *Lugenia Burns Hope*, 89–90; and Linda Gordon, "Black and White Visions of Welfare Activism," 578, for a discussion of elitism among middle-class club women.

79. Steele interview.

80. Hall interview.

81. Suddeth interview.

82. The best work on the importance of these networks to the financial health and cultural stability of black families is Stack's *All Our Kin*.

83. Suddeth interview.

84. Chauvin and Duvernay interview.

85. Tillman interview.

86. Moss interview.

87. Waller interview; Chauvin and Duvernay interview.

88. Moss interview; and Simonsen, *You May Plow Here*, 157.

89. McIntosh interview.

90. Waller interview; Ethel Phillips interview; and aggregate statistics compiled from fifty oral interviews.

91. Montgomery, *Under Their Own Vine and Fig Tree*, 261–306.

92. Charles S. Johnson, in *Negro War Worker in San Francisco*, 87, found similar patterns of religious affiliation among the migrants whom he interviewed; Phillips interview.

93. Gray interview.

94. Moss interview.

95. Steele interview.

96. Hall interview. This form of leadership is also discussed in Payne, "Ella Baker and Models of Social Change," and Sacks, *Caring by the Hour*.

97. Blue interview.

98. Giddings, *When and Where I Enter*, 101.

99. Aggregate statistics; Charles S. Johnson, in *Negro War Worker in San Francisco*, 7–8,

reported that migrants' education levels nearly equaled those of the nonmigrant black population and were higher for migrant women than for migrant men. His statistics were based on a larger sample than mine and are thus probably more reliable. In his sample, 74 percent of all migrant women completed eight years of school; 65 percent had some high school; 35 percent completed high school; and 9 percent had college or professional training.

100. Suddeth interview; McAllister interview.

101. McAlister interview.

102. Lemann, Promised Land; Lemann, "Origins of the Underclass;" Jones, "Southern Diaspora."

Chapter Two

1. Angelou, I Know Why the Caged Bird Sings, 151−52.

2. Nash, American West Transformed, 26, 66, 67; Marilynn S. Johnson, Second Gold Rush, 32.

3. Hubert Owen Brown, "Impact of War Worker Migration," 109, 110; U.S. Congress, House, Committee on Naval Affairs, Subcommittee of the Committee on Naval Affairs, Investigation of Congested Areas, 78th Cong., 1st sess., 1943, vol. 1, pt. 3, p. 855; Marilynn S. Johnson, Second Gold Rush, 33.

4. Richmond Chamber of Commerce, History of Richmond, 117, 121, 128; Hubert Owen Brown, "Impact of War Worker Migration," 40, 117.

5. Nash, American West Transformed, 29.

6. Wollenberg, Golden Gate Metropolis, 245, 248; Nash, American West Transformed, 69; France, "Some Aspects of the Migration of the Negro," 24.

7. Hausler, "Blacks in Oakland," 111.

8. Ibid., 112; Nash, American West Transformed, 69; Marilynn S. Johnson, Second Gold Rush, 35, 53.

9. Daniel, "Going among Strangers," 886−911; Nelson, "Organized Labor and the Struggle for Black Equality," 960; Thomson and Meador, Shreveport, 120.

10. Nelson, "Organized Labor and the Struggle for Black Equality," 981−82, 952; Cy W. Record, Characteristics of Some Unemployed Negro Shipyard Workers, 31.

11. It is difficult to determine exactly how many migrants actually returned to the South following World War II. Many of the women I interviewed stated that large numbers of people returned home after war industries closed in 1945−46. However, few of my interviewees knew people who went back. About 10 percent of the women in my sample planned to return to the South following the war but changed their minds. Tarea Hall Pittman, a black community activist and California native, worked with Traveler's Aid of Contra Costa County during the war years. After the war, she helped unemployed migrants find the resources to return home. Her master's thesis, "Operation of State and County Resident Requirements under the California Indigent Aid Law in Contra Costa County," discusses some of the difficulties migrants encountered after war industries closed but does not provide information on how many migrants actually returned to the South. In "Willie Stokes at the Golden Gate," Wilson

Record suggests that as many as 85 percent of all black migrants remained (p. 187). Similarly, Ira De A. Reid, in "Special Problems of Negro Migration during the War," expressed his belief that most in-migrants were in the East Bay to stay (p. 289).

12. Aggregate statistics; Charles S. Johnson, *Negro War Worker in San Francisco*, 5, 6.

13. Gray interview.

14. Waller interview.

15. Aggregate statistics; Charles S. Johnson, *Negro War Worker in San Francisco*, 15, 16, 80. In *Black Migration in America*, E. Marvin Goodwin argues that nonmigrants were more likely to be business owners and professionals than migrants (p. 126).

16. Charles S. Johnson, *Negro War Worker in San Francisco*, 5.

17. Dennis, *African American Exodus and White Migration*, 293; Levine, *Black Culture and Black Consciousness*, 261–67, 160, 30–80, 81–135; Smith, *Where I'm Bound*.

18. Hall interview.

19. Blue interview.

20. Shyrock, "Wartime Shifts of the Civilian Population," 280–81; Reid "Special Problems of Negro Migration during the War," 288; Cy W. Record, *Characteristics of Some Unemployed Negro Shipyard Workers*, 27.

21. Hubert Owen Brown, "Impact of War Worker Migration," 116–19, 174–77; Nash, *American West Transformed*, 89; letter from Mr. A. L. Nickerson, director of the Bureau of Placement, War Manpower Commission, to George M. Johnson, assistant executive secretary, Fair Employment Practice Committee, June 30, 1943, Reel 103, Kaiser file, in Fair Employment Practice Committee, *Selected Documents from the Records of the Committee on Fair Employment Practice*; Marilynn S. Johnson, *Second Gold Rush*, 52.

22. Marilynn S. Johnson, *Second Gold Rush*, 52–53; Gray interview.

23. Hall interview.

24. Waller interview.

25. Tillman interview.

26. Eaton interview, *In Search of the American Dream*, 52.

27. Phillips interview.

28. Charles S. Johnson, *Negro War Worker in San Francisco*, 7, 12.

29. Tillman interview.

30. Peoples interview.

31. McIntosh interview.

32. Potter interview.

33. Charles S. Johnson, *Negro War Worker in San Francisco*, 5.

34. Ibid.; Marilynn S. Johnson, *Second Gold Rush*, 46–47.

35. Patton interview; Henry interview.

36. Chauvin interview.

37. Phillips interview.

38. Lewis interview.

39. James interview; Peoples interview.

40. Tillman interview.

41. Fair Employment Practice Committee, *Selected Documents from the Records of the Committee on Fair Employment Practice*, Reel 112, Boilermakers Union Misc. Complaints file.

42. Blue interview; James interview; Tillman interview.

43. Waller interview.

44. Charles S. Johnson, *To Stem This Tide*, 38.

45. Gracon interview.

46. Waller interview.

47. Lee interview; Gray interview; Smith interview.

48. Jennings interview.

49. Richmond Chamber of Commerce, *History of Richmond*, 119.

50. Cherry interview; Waller interview.

51. Henry interview.

52. Chauvin interview; McIntosh interview; Smith interview.

53. Gracon interview.

Chapter Three

1. *Oakland Observer*, March 11, 1944.

2. U.S. Congress, House, Committee on Naval Affairs, *Investigation of Congested Areas*, 867.

3. Ibid., 754.

4. Archibald, *Wartime Shipyard*, 56; Marilynn S. Johnson, *Second Gold Rush*, 143–84.

5. Oakland Institute on Human Relations, *Seminar Report on What Tensions Exist*; Marilynn S. Johnson, *Second Gold Rush*, 169.

6. Archibald, *Wartime Shipyard*, 69–78; *Oakland Observer*, March 1, 1944.

7. See, for example, U.S. Congress, House, Committee on Naval Affairs, *Investigation of Congested Areas*. Investigators were clearly distressed at the prospect of white and black tenants being housed together in war projects. One investigator, attempting to justify segregation in Oakland's projects, drew on the separate but equal doctrine: "Now, if you put all the whites in one project and all the Negro in another, you don't have discrimination." He went on to explain that "Surely, you don't mix the whites and blacks—especially when they, the whites, come from southern areas" (p. 1013).

8. Broussard, *Black San Francisco*, 76–85; Crouchett et al., *Visions toward Tomorrow*, 32.

9. Crouchett et al., *Visions toward Tomorrow*, 26, 32, 39–41.

10. Ibid., 9–18, 23–41.

11. Daniels, *Pioneer Urbanites*, 174.

12. Benedict interview.

13. Cravanas interview. Robert E. Colbert observed similar attitudes among existing black residents of Portland and Seattle: see "Attitude of Older Negro Residents," 695–703. His survey revealed that established black residents felt that newcomers had ruined peaceful relations between whites and blacks. Seattle and Portland, he noted, had small prewar black populations that traded good behavior for liberal civil rights. However, existing residents, by their own admission, experienced employment and housing discrimination and unequal access to public accommodations.

14. Harry and Marguerite Williams interview, *Reflections of a Longtime Black Family in Richmond*, 40, 41, 103, 104.

15. Cravanas interview; Broussard, *Black San Francisco*, 59–60, 61–74, 134–42;

Daniels, *Pioneer Urbanites*, 44–58, 162–75; Marilynn S. Johnson, *Second Gold Rush*, 53. Statistics on population growth verify how quickly migrants became the majority. In Oakland, for example, the black population grew from 8,462 in 1940 to 47,562 in 1950. Even if the established black population increased by 50 percent over this ten-year period, migrants and their offspring would still have constituted 74 percent of the total black population in that city. In Richmond, using the same calculation, migrants and their offspring constituted 97 percent of the total population in 1950.

16. Ibid.; St. Clair interview.

17. Ibid.; Cravanas interview; and Judith Dunning, ed., *Reflections of a Longtime Black Family in Richmond*.

18. Crouchett et al., *Visions toward Tomorrow*, 53–61.

19. Daniels, *Pioneer Urbanites*, xiv–xv; Marilynn S. Johnson, *Second Gold Rush*, 139.

20. Gray interview.

21. Ibid.

22. Ibid.

23. France, "Some Aspects of the Migration of the Negro," 32–33; Oakland Council of Social Agencies, *Our Community*; Barbara Lou Sawyer, "Negroes in West Oakland" (mimeographed ms.), 1952, Black Social Conditions file, Oakland History Room, Oakland Public Library.

24. St. Clair interview; U.S. Congress, House, Committee on Naval Affairs, *Investigation of Congested Areas*, 798; Kerns, *Social and Economic Conditions Affecting the Local Negro Population*.

25. France, "Some Aspects of the Migration of the Negro," 48–49.

26. Ibid., 47.

27. Wenkert, *Historical Digest of Negro-White Relations*, 10–22; and Hubert Owen Brown, "Impact of War Worker Migration," 41.

28. Henderson interview; and Peoples interview.

29. Hall interview; Phillips interview.

30. June Williams interview.

31. Lee interview.

32. Johnson interview.

33. Charles S. Johnson, *Negro War Worker in San Francisco*, 26–27.

34. June Williams interview; Lee interview; Henry interview; Tillman interview.

35. Peoples interview; aggregate statistics. Church and other organizational affiliations are discussed in greater detail in Chapter 5.

36. Waller interview.

37. Lee interview; Blue interview.

38. Hubert Owen Brown, "Impact of War Worker Migration," 128, 130, 180; Marilynn S. Johnson, *Second Gold Rush*, 97–107.

39. U.S. Congress, House, Committee on Naval Affairs, *Investigation of Congested Areas*, 799; Lois Markus, "Problems of the Negroes in Oakland" (mimeographed ms.), 1945, Black Social Conditions file, Oakland History Room, Oakland Public Library.

40. Oakland Council of Social Services, *Our Community*; France, "Some Aspects of the Migration of the Negro," 43–45.

41. France, "Some Aspects of the Migration of the Negro," 48–53.

42. Wenkert, *Historical Digest of Negro-White Relations*, 10–23; and Hubert Owen Brown, "Impact of War Worker Migration," 179.

43. France, "Some Aspects of the Migration of the Negro," 54.

44. Hubert Owen Brown, "Impact of War Worker Migration," 133–34; Marilynn S. Johnson, *Second Gold Rush*, 106–9.

45. Gray interview; Eaton interview, *In Search of the American Dream*; Charles S. Johnson, *Negro War Worker in San Francisco*, 25.

46. Kramer, "Story of the Richmond Shipyards" (typescript), 1945, Henry Kaiser Papers, Record No. 83/42c–327, Bancroft Library, University of California, Berkeley; Phillips interview.

47. Tillman interview.

48. Ibid. In 1942 Kaiser started its Permanente Health Plan, providing health care to all shipyard employees for a weekly fee of fifty cents per worker. By August 1944, 92.2 percent of all Kaiser employees belonged to the plan. See Kramer, "Story of the Richmond Shipyards."

49. James interview.

50. McIntosh interview.

51. Tillman interview.

52. Duvernay and Chauvin interview.

53. U.S. Department of Commerce, Bureau of the Census, *Seventeenth Census of the United States* (1950), *Census of Housing*, vol. 1, pt. 2: California, table 17; ibid., *Eighteenth Census of the United States* (1960), *Census of Housing*, vol. 1, pt. 2: California, tables 12, 38; Citizens Committee, *Housing Discrimination in Berkeley*, 26.

54. Nichols and Babbie, *Oakland in Transition*, 167–68; Reid, "Special Problems of Negro Migration during World War II," 289; Wenkert, *Historical Digest of Negro-White Relations*, 34.

55. Wenkert, *Historical Digest of Negro-White Relations*, 21–22; "No Place to Live, Negroes Fear," *San Francisco Chronicle*, August 18, 1953; "Where Can Displaced Tenants Find Homes?," *San Francisco Chronicle*, August 21, 1953.

56. Wenkert, *Historical Digest of Negro-White Relations*, 41–44.

57. Ibid., 21, 22, 43.

58. France, "Some Aspects of the Migration of the Negro," 50–51; Nathan and Scott, *Experiment and Change in Berkeley*, 79.

59. St. Clair interview.

60. Nathan and Scott, *Experiment and Change in Berkeley*, 92–93; St. Clair interview.

61. Nichols and Babbie, *Oakland in Transition*, 65–68, 169; Hausler, "Blacks in Oakland," 122–28, 134–39.

62. Hausler, "Blacks in Oakland," 130. The Rumford Fair Housing Act passed the California state legislature in 1963 but was nullified by white voters a year later through State Proposition 14. In 1966 the state supreme court ruled Proposition 14 unconstitutional and thereby reinstated the Fair Housing Act of 1963. Although this act prohibited housing discrimination on the basis of race, the practice continued and still continues throughout parts of the East Bay.

63. Aggregate statistics; Far West Surveys, *Negro Consumer*, 2:20; Nichols and Babbie, *Oakland in Transition*, 47–57.

64. Gracon interview.

Chapter Four

1. U.S. Department of Labor, Bureau of Labor Statistics, "Labor Force in Durable Goods Manufacture," 712.

2. U.S. Department of Labor, Bureau of Labor Statistics, "Postwar Status of Negro Workers in the San Francisco Area," 614–16.

3. Anderson, "Last Hired, First Fired," 84.

4. Cy W. Record, Characteristics of Some Unemployed Negro Shipyard Workers, 11–12; U.S. Department of Labor, Bureau of Labor Statistics, "Labor Force in Durable Goods Manufacture," 713–14; Hubert Owen Brown, "Impact of War Worker Migration," 174–75.

5. U.S. Department of Labor, Women's Bureau, Women Workers in Ten Production Areas.

6. U.S. Department of Labor, Bureau of Labor Statistics, "Postwar Status of Negro Workers in the San Francisco Area," 614.

7. Nichols and Babbie, Oakland in Transition, 108–9.

8. California State Employment Service, Economic Status of Negroes in the San Francisco Bay Area, 8.

9. U.S. Department of Labor, Postwar Status of Negro Workers in the San Francisco Area, 616; California State Employment Service, Economic Status of Negroes in the San Francisco Bay Area, 1–11.

10. Cy W. Record, Characteristics of Some Unemployed Negro Shipyard Workers, 30.

11. U.S. Department of Labor, Bureau of Labor Statistics, "Labor Force in Durable Goods Manufacture," 718, 714.

12. Fair Employment Practice Committee, Selected Documents from the Records of the Committee on Fair Employment Practice, Reel 106, Steamfitters file, and Reel 108, Armour file; Cy W. Record, Characteristics of Some Unemployed Negro Shipyard Workers, 33.

13. Nichols and Babbie, Oakland in Transition, 104–11, 124, 162–63, 184–85.

14. California State Employment Service, Economic Status of Negroes in the San Francisco Bay Area, 1–3, 8.

15. Nichols and Babbie, Oakland in Transition, 162–63, 167–69.

16. Crouchett et al., Visions toward Tomorrow, 47; Marilynn S. Johnson, Second Gold Rush, 71.

17. Marilynn S. Johnson, Second Gold Rush, 48.

18. Harley, "For the Good of Family and Race," 348.

19. Ibid., 349.

20. Bolden interview.

21. Blue interview.

22. Chauvin interview.

23. Smith interview.

24. Marilynn S. Johnson, Second Gold Rush, 126–27.

25. Tillman interview.

26. Henderson interview.

27. Cherry interview.

28. Scott interview.

29. Waller interview.

30. Johnson interview.

31. Lewis interview.

32. Henry interview.

33. Patton interview.

34. Wenkert, *Historical Digest of Negro-White Relations*, 20; McAllister interview; Fair Employment Practice Committee, *Selected Documents from the Records of the Committee on Fair Employment Practice*, Reel 111, Richmond Prefabrication Plant file, 12-BR-108; Reel 111, Richmond Shipyard #1 file, 12-BR-81; Reel 110, Machinists Local 824 file; Reel 108, Complaints against Boilermakers file.

35. Archibald, *Wartime Shipyard*, 79; Richmond Shipbuilding Corporation, Shipyard No. 2, *Handbook for Workers*, 90; Walling interview.

36. McAllister interview.

37. Archibald, *Wartime Shipyard*, 88–89; Fair Employment Practice Committee, *Selected Documents from the Records of the Committee on Fair Employment Practice*, Reel 109, California Manufacturing Company file.

38. Fair Employment Practice Committee, *Selected Documents from the Records of the Committee on Fair Employment Practice*, Reel 110, Moore Shipyard file.

39. Marilynn S. Johnson, *Second Gold Rush*, 37–38, 72–73; Broussard, *Black San Francisco*, 194–96.

40. Peoples interview; Lee interview.

41. Wenkert, *Historical Digest of Negro-White Relations*, 76.

42. McIntosh interview.

43. Wenkert, *Historical Digest of Negro-White Relations*, 77.

44. California State Employment Service, *Economic Status of Negroes in the San Francisco Bay Area*, 1–3.

45. Nichols and Babbie, *Oakland in Transition*, 124.

46. Descriptive aggregate statistics.

47. Steele interview.

48. Gray interview.

49. Lee interview.

50. Smith interview.

51. Peoples interview.

52. Blue interview.

53. June Williams interview.

54. Gracon interview.

55. Bolden interview.

56. Duvernay interview.

57. Cherry interview.

58. Suddeth interview.

59. Moss interview.

60. Steele interview.

61. Johnson interview; Hall interview.

62. Lewis interview.

Chapter Five

1. Douglas Daniels, *Pioneer Urbanites*, 128.
2. Marilynn S. Johnson, *Second Gold Rush*, 92–93, 19.

3. Douglas Daniels, *Pioneer Urbanites*, 171–72, 150.

4. Ibid., 165–66, 173; Henry interview.

5. Descriptive aggregate data; see also Collins, "Meaning of Motherhood in Black Culture," 174.

6. Hall interview.

7. Smith interview; Tillman interview.

8. Duvernay and Chauvin interview.

9. Paule Marshall quoted in Brown, "Mothers of the Mind," 4–5.

10. hooks, *Yearning*, 46; Waller interview.

11. Suddeth interview; Cherry interview.

12. Moss interview; Phillips interview.

13. Tillman interview; Duvernay and Chauvin interview.

14. Scott interview.

15. Johnson interview.

16. Duvernay and Chauvin interview; Tillman interview.

17. Genovese, *Roll, Jordan, Roll*, 535–37.

18. Descriptive aggregate data; see also Deutsch, *No Separate Refuge*. In this social history, Deutsch describes how Hispanic women similarly derived status from their gardens and the exchange of produce.

19. Logan, *Motherwit*, 6.

20. Gray interview; Lee interview.

21. James interview; McAllister interview; Tillman interview.

22. Ferris, *Afro-American Folk Art and Crafts*, 86–93.

23. Ibid., 103–4; Suddeth interview.

24. Ferris, *Afro-American Folk Art and Crafts*, 100; Phillips interview.

25. Bolden interview; Scott interview.

26. Kirkland and Mathews, *Herbal and Magical Medicine*, 69–78.

27. Piersen, *Black Legacy*, 108–14.

28. Kirkland and Mathews, *Herbal and Magical Medicine*, 75.

29. Tillman interview.

30. Gray interview; Lee interview.

31. Steele interview.

32. Ibid; Blue interview.

33. For a very interesting discussion of home-based caregiving and its relationship to the paid health-care system, see Glazer, "Home as Workshop," 479–99.

34. Steele interview.

35. Lewis interview; Blue interview.

36. Steele interview .

37. McIntosh interview; Tillman interview.

38. Brown interview; Scott interview; Lee interview.

39. Blue interview.

40. Gray interview.

41. Waller interview.

42. Blue interview; Waller interview. See also Stack, *All Our Kin*, 62–89, for a discussion of "child-keeping" within a contemporary urban black community.

43. Aggregate statistics. See also Naples, "Activist Mothering," for a similar discussion of women's community-based caregiving activities.

44. Tillman interview; Gracon interview; Scott interview; Lee interview.

45. Hippler, "Family Structure and Social Structure," 246–47.

46. Angelou, *I Know Why the Caged Bird Sings*, 4.

47. Bethel, *Promiseland*, 239.

48. Scott interview.

49. Smith interview.

50. Gray interview.

51. Bolden interview.

52. Gracon interview.

53. McAlister interview; Suddeth interview.

54. McAlister interview; Blue interview.

55. McIntosh interview.

Chapter Six

1. Naples, " 'Just What Needed to be Done,' " 491. See also Collins, *Black Feminist Thought*, for a discussion of how lived experience constitutes meaning and authority within African American communities.

2. Descriptive aggregate data. See also Naples, "Activist Mothering."

3. Payne, "Ella Baker and Models of Social Change," 885–86. See also Sacks, *Caring by the Hour*.

4. Suddeth interview; Cherry interview; McAlister interview.

5. Montgomery, *Under Their Own Vine and Fig Tree*, 267–75, 291, 293–95.

6. Scott and Black, "Deep Structures of African American Family Life," 22. For a discussion of women's work in the church see Montgomery, *Under Their Own Vine and Fig Tree*, 95–96, 114–15, 139, 320–22.

7. Funeral Program for Precious Handy, Deaths file, Northern California Center for Afro-American History and Life.

8. Funeral Program for Elizabeth Ward, Deaths file, Northern California Center for Afro-American History and Life.

9. Montgomery, *Under Their Own Vine and Fig Tree*, 115; *San Francisco Examiner*, November 24, 1971.

10. Hall interview.

11. Johnson interview.

12. Blue interview.

13. Taylor Memorial United Methodist Church, *History of the Church, Founders and Ministers 1921–1988*, Church file, Northern California Center for Afro-American History and Life.

14. Progressive Baptist Church, *Twenty Years of Progress 1935–1955*, Church file, Northern California Center for Afro-American History and Life.

15. Downs Memorial Methodist Church, *A Brief History of Downs*, Church file, Northern California Center for Afro-American History and Life.

16. Cooper A.M.E. Zion Church, *Souvenir Program* 1898–1948, Church file, Northern California Center for Afro-American History and Life.

17. Peoples interview.

18. Hausler, "Blacks in Oakland," 154.

19. Pettitt, "Berkeley in the Good Old Days," 42.

20. Marilynn S. Johnson, *Second Gold Rush*, 193–94.

21. Ibid., 194–95; Branches in the West Coast Region, September 1946, in file titled "O. A. Reports, Regional Secretary (Noah W. Griffin)," carton 25, NAACP West Coast Region Records.

22. McAlister interview.

23. McIntosh interview.

24. Gray interview.

25. Potter interview.

26. Suddeth interview.

27. Waller interview.

28. Monthly Report for March 1946, West Coast Regional Office, NAACP, in file titled "O. A. Reports, Regional Secretary (Noah W. Griffin)," carton 25, NAACP West Coast Region Records.

29. Far West Surveys, *The Negro Consumer in the San Francisco Bay Area*, volume 2, page 12.

30. Evelio Grillo, "D. G. Gibson: A Black Who Led the People and Built the Democratic Party in the East Bay," in Nathan and Scott, *Experiment and Change in Berkeley*, 7.

31. Bishop Roy C. Nichols, "A Few Thoughts," in Nathan and Scott, *Experiment and Change in Berkeley*, 21.

32. Hausler, "Blacks in Oakland," 172–82.

33. Wenkert, *Historical Digest of Negro-White Relations*, 67–68.

34. Ibid.

35. Crouchett et al., *Visions toward Tomorrow*, 37, 39, 55; Albert Broussard, *Black San Francisco*, 125.

36. Judith Dunning, ed., *Reflections of a Longtime Black Family in Richmond: The Oral History of Harry and Marguerite Williams* (Berkeley: University of California Regional Oral History Office), 170.

37. NAACP Annual Report, West Coast Region, 1952, in file titled "O. A. Reports, Regional Director (Franklin H. Williams)," carton 25, NAACP West Coast Region Records.

38. Monthly Report for February 1946 and Monthly Report for April 1946, both in file titled "O. A. Reports, Regional Secretary (Noah W. Griffin)," carton 25, NAACP West Coast Region Records.

39. 1951 Annual Report, West Coast Regional NAACP; NAACP Annual Report, West Coast Region 1952; and West Coast Region NAACP 1953 Annual Report, all in file titled "O.A. Reports, Regional Director (Franklin H. Williams)," carton 25, NAACP West Coast Region Records.

40. Report on the Relocation Problem of Families Residing in Codornices Village, August 10, 1954, and Open Letter to the City Councils of Berkeley and Albany, both in file titled "Berkeley," carton 14, NAACP West Coast Region Records.

41. Memorandum to Gloster B. Current, Director of Branches, from Franklin H. Williams, Secretary Council, May 23, 1955, in file titled "O.A. Reports, Regional Director (Franklin H. Williams)," carton 25, NAACP West Coast Region Records; Dolores Nason McBroome, *Parallel Communities: African Americans in California's East Bay, 1850–1963*, 139–47, 151–52.

42. Annual Report of the West Coast Regional Office NAACP, 1945, in file titled "O. A. Reports, Regional Secretary (Noah W. Griffin)," carton 25, NAACP West Coast Region Records; Reports to the Board of Directors of the NAACP West Coast Regional Office, April 20 to May 20, 1945, in file titled "O. A. Reports, Regional Secretary (Noah W. Griffin)," carton 25, NAACP West Coast Region Records.

43. To Defend the Legal Right to Picket in Protest of Anti-Negro Discrimination in Employment, in file titled "Richmond Correspondence, Branch Undated 1944–45," carton 16, NAACP West Coast Region Records; NAACP West Coast Regional Office Monthly Report for January 1949, in file titled "O. A. Reports, Regional Secretary (Noah W. Griffin)," carton 25, NAACP West Coast Region Records.

44. NAACP Report of West Coast Regional Secretary, 1950, in file titled "O. A. Reports, Regional Secretary (Noah W. Griffin)," carton 25; letter to Franklin Williams from Hazel Hall, Secretary, October 22, 1954, in file titled "O.A. Correspondence, Branch 1952–59," carton 16; NAACP West Coast Regional Office Monthly Report for January 1949, in file titled "O. A. Reports, Regional Secretary (Noah W. Griffin)," carton 25; and NAACP West Coast Regional Office Report for November 1946, in file titled "O. A. Reports, Regional Secretary (Noah W. Griffin)," carton 25, all in NAACP West Coast Region Records.

45. Blue interview.

46. McIntosh interview; Crouchett et al., *Visions toward Tomorrow*, 55.

47. McIntosh interview.

48. Brown interview.

49. Gray interview.

50. Tillman interview.

51. Wenkert, *Historical Digest of Negro-White Relations*, 51–52.

52. Barbour, *Exploratory Study*, 38.

53. Hubert Owen Brown, "Impact of War Worker Migration," 213–14.

54. Ibid., 222–26.

55. Wenkert, *Historical Digest of Negro-White Relations*, 53; Lee interview.

56. Hausler, "Blacks in Oakland," 189; Margaret S. Gordon, "From Liberal Control to Radical Challenge," 276.

57. Hubert Owen Brown, "Impact of War Worker Migration," 228–30.

58. Ibid., 306–21; Berkeley Board of Education, *Interracial Problems*.

59. Henderson interview.

60. Tillman interview.

61. McIntosh interview; Suddeth interview.

62. Lee interview.

63. Scott interview.

64. Bolden interview.

65. McIntosh interview.

66. McAlister interview.

67. Naples, " 'Just What Needed to be Done.' "

68. Contra Costa Council of Human Services, *New Careerist Casebook*, nos. 1, 2, and 3.

69. McIntosh interview.

70. Ibid.

71. Ibid.

72. Ibid.; McAlister interview.

73. *Berkeley Voice*, July 6, 1991.

Conclusion

1. Amot and Matthaei, *Race, Gender, and Work*, 179.

2. Giddings, *When and Where I Enter*, 232.

3. Ibid., 243–58.

4. Lemann, *Promised Land*. See also Katz, *"Underclass" Debate*, for the most recent synthesis of research on the origins of urban poverty.

5. Jones, "Southern Diaspora," 38.

6. Katz, *"Underclass" Debate*, 454.

7. Wilson, *Truly Disadvantaged*, 41, and *Declining Significance of Race*; Jones, "Southern Diaspora," 29.

Bibliography . . . . .

Manuscript Collections

Albrier, Frances. Papers. Bancroft Library, University of California, Berkeley.

Dellums, C. L. Papers. Bancroft Library, University of California, Berkeley.

East Bay Churches. Records. Northern California Center for Afro-American History and Life, Oakland.

Kaiser, Henry. Papers and Pictorial Collection. Bancroft Library, University of California, Berkeley.

Lange, Dorothea. Photograph Collection. Oakland Museum, Oakland.

National Association for the Advancement of Colored People, West Coast Region. Records, 1946–70. Bancroft Library, University of California, Berkeley.

Oakland History Collection. Oakland History Room, Oakland Public Library.

Pittman, Tarea Hall. Papers. Bancroft Library, University of California, Berkeley.

Interviews

Established Residents Interviewed by the Author

Note: These interviews are in the author's possession unless otherwise noted.

Acty, Ruth. Telephone interview, March 3, 1991.

Benedict, Emmaline. Oakland, Calif., March 19, 1991.

Cravanas, Virginia. Oakland, Calif., February 4, 1991.

Crawford, Matt. Berkeley, Calif., 1987. Tape donated to the Berkeley Historical Society.

Lasartemay, Eugene. Berkeley, Calif., 1987. Tape donated to the Northern California Center for Afro-American History and Life, Oakland.

St. Clair, Katherine. Berkeley, Calif., April 26, 1991.

Migrants Interviewed by the Author

Note: These interviews are in the author's possession unless otherwise noted.

Blue, Olive. Richmond, Calif., May 7, 1991.

Bolden, Henrietta. Oakland, Calif., March 14, 1991.

Brown, Marlene. Oakland, Calif., March 20, 1991.

Chauvin, Carmelia. Hayward, Calif., February 28, 1991.

Cherry, Ruth. Oakland, Calif., March 8, 1991.

Duvernay, Cornelia. Hayward, Calif., February 28, 1991.

Gracon, Ruth. Oakland, Calif., March 16, 1991.

Gray, Lacey. Richmond, Calif., May 21, 1991.

Hall, Louisa. Oakland, Calif., April 26, 1991.

Henderson, Lee. Emeryville, Calif., May 8, 1991.

Henry, Willa. Oakland, Calif., September 26, 1990.

James, Cornelia. Richmond, Calif., May 21, 1991.

Jennings, Blanche. Berkeley, Calif., April 26, 1991.

Johnson, Best. Richmond, Calif., May 21, 1991.

Lee, Mary. Richmond, Calif., February 20, 1991.

Lewis, Marlene. Oakland, Calif., February 22, 1991.

McAlister, Henrietta. Richmond, Calif., January 17, 1991.

McAllister, Faith. Emeryville, Calif., May 2, 1991.

McIntosh, Lovie. Richmond, Calif., March 6, 1991.

Moss, Lucille. Oakland, Calif., April 23, 1991.

Patton, Frankie. Emeryville, Calif., May 5, 1991.

Peoples, Estelle. Emeryville, Calif., April 30, 1991.

Phillips, Ethel. Oakland, Calif., March 20, 1991.

Potter, Gracie. Oakland, Calif., March 19, 1991.

Scott, Oma June. Oakland, Calif., February 6, 1991.

Smith, Opal. Richmond, Calif., April 30, 1991.

Steele, Louise. Richmond, Calif., June 3, 1991.

Suddeth, Willa. Richmond, Calif., March 6, 1991.

Tillman, Ethel. Berkeley, Calif., September 21, 1990.

Waller, Theresa. Oakland, Calif., March 4, 1991.

Williams, June. Oakland, Calif., March 12, 1991.

Other Regional Residents

Note: The following interviews are all held in the Regional Oral History Office, Bancroft Library, University of California, Berkeley.

Albrier, Frances. Determined Advocate for Racial Equality. Interview by Malca Chall, 1979.

Cathey, Margaret Louise. A Wartime Journey: From Ottumwa, Iowa, to the Richmond Shipyards, 1942. Interview by Judith Dunning, 1985.

Clausen, Marguerite. Memories of a Lifelong Richmond Resident, 1912–1987. Interview by Judith Dunning, 1985.

Dellums, C. L. International President of Sleeping Car Porters and Civil Rights Leader. Interview by Joyce Henderson, 1973.

Eaton, Eddie. In Search of the American Dream: From Houston, Texas, to Richmond, California, in 1943. Interview by Judith Dunning, 1986.

Nystrom, Stanley. A Family's Roots in Richmond: Recollections of a Lifetime Resident. Interview by Judith Dunning, 1985.

Pittman, Tarea Hall. NAACP Official and Civil Rights Worker. Interview by Joyce Henderson, 1974.

Rumford, William Byron. Legislator for Fair Employment, Fair Housing, and Public Health. Interview by Joyce Henderson, Amelia Fry, and Edward France, 1973.

Walling, Effie. Interview by Nancy Ledeboer, May 1979. Women Workers in World War II: Oral History Transcripts of Tape-Recorded Interviews Conducted by Students in History 103D.

Williams, Harry and Marguerite. Reflections of a Longtime Black Family in Richmond. Interview by Judith Dunning, 1985.

Surveys and Reports

Barbour, W. Miller. *An Exploratory Study of the Socio-Economic Problems Affecting the Negro White Relationship.* Richmond: United Community Defense Services Inc. and the National Urban League, 1952.

Berkeley Board of Education. *Interracial Problems and Their Effect on Education in the Public Schools of Berkeley.* Berkeley: Berkeley Board of Education, 1959.

Berkeley Study Committee on Equal Employment Opportunities. *Employment Opportunities for Members of Minority Groups.* Berkeley: BSCEEO, 1958.

California State Employment Service. *The Economic Status of Negroes in the San Francisco Bay Area.* San Francisco: California State Employment Service, 1963.

Casstevens, Thomas W. *Politics, Housing and Race Relations: The Defeat of Berkeley's Fair Housing Ordinance.* Berkeley: Institute of Governmental Studies, 1965.

Citizens Committee. *Housing Discrimination in Berkeley: A Report by the Citizens Committee to the Community Welfare Commission.* Berkeley: City of Berkeley, 1962.

Contra Costa Council of Human Services. *New Careerist Casebook.* Richmond: Richmond Community Development Demonstration Project, 1967.

Dizard, Jan E. *Patterns of Unemployment in Berkeley, California.* Berkeley: University of California Survey Research Center, 1968.

Fair Employment Practice Committee. *Selected Documents from the Records of the Committee on Fair Employment Practice: Region 12, Field Records.* Glen Rock, N.J.: Microfilming Corporation of America, 1971.

Far West Surveys. *The Negro Consumer in the San Francisco Bay Area.* 2 vols. San Francisco: The Firm, 1958–60.

Hunter, Floyd. *Housing Discrimination in Oakland, California: A Study Prepared for the Oakland Mayor's Committee on Full Opportunity and the Council of Social Planning.* Berkeley: Floyd Hunter Company, 1963.

Johnson, Charles. *The Negro War Worker in San Francisco.* San Francisco: YWCA and the Race Relations Program of the American Missionary Association, 1944.

Kerns, Harvey J. *Study of Social and Economic Conditions Affecting the Local Negro Population.* Oakland: Council of Social Agencies and the Community Chest, 1942.

Nichols, William III, and Earl Babbie. *Oakland in Transition: A Summary of the 701 Household Survey.* Berkeley: University of California Survey Research Center, 1969.

Oakland Council of Social Agencies. *Our Community: A Factual Presentation of Social Conditions.* Oakland: Oakland Community Chest, 1945.

Oakland Institute on Human Relations. *Seminar Report on What Tensions Exist between Groups in the Local Community.* Oakland: n.p., 1946.

Record, Cy W. *Characteristics of Some Unemployed Negro Shipyard Workers in Richmond, California.* Berkeley: Institute of Governmental Studies, 1947.

Record, Wilson. *Minority Groups and Intergroup Relations in the San Francisco Bay Area.* Berkeley: Institute of Governmental Studies, 1966.

Richmond Shipbuilding Corporation. *Shipyard No. 2. Handbook for Workers.* Richmond: Richmond Shipbuilding Corporation, 1942.

U.S. Congress. House. Committee on Naval Affairs, Subcommittee of the Committee on Naval Affairs. *Investigation of Congested Areas.* 78th Cong., 1st sess., 1943, vol. 1, pt. 3.

U.S. Department of Commerce. Bureau of the Census. *Fifteenth Census of the United States* (1930), Population, vol. 2: *Composition and Characteristics of the Population*; vol. 4: *Occupations by State*; vol. 6: *Families*.

——. *Fifteenth Census of the United States* (1930), Agriculture, vol. 4: *General Report, Statistics by Subject*.

——. *Sixteenth Census of the United States* (1940), 2 vols.: *Population, Families, Types of Families; Population and Housing, Families, General Characteristics*.

——. *Seventeenth Census of the United States* (1950), Census of Housing, vol. 1: *General Characteristics of the Population*, pt. 2: California.

——. *Eighteenth Census of the United States* (1960), Census of Housing, vol. 1: *General Characteristics of the Population*, pt. 2: California.

U.S. Department of Labor. Bureau of Labor Statistics. "The Labor Force in Durable Goods Manufacture in the San Francisco Bay Area, 1943." *Monthly Labor Review*, October 1945.

——. "Postwar Status of Negro Workers in the San Francisco Area." *Monthly Labor Review*, June 1950.

U.S. Department of Labor. Women's Bureau. *Women Workers in Ten Production Areas and Their Postwar Employment Plans*. U.S. Women's Bureau Bulletin #209.

U.S. Federal Works Agency. Works Progress Administration. "Recent Migration to Oakland, California and Environs." February 3, 1942. Copy in the Oakland History Room, Oakland Public Library.

Wenkert, Robert. *A Historical Digest of Negro-White Relations in Richmond, California*. Berkeley: University of California Survey Research Center, 1967.

Dissertations, Theses, and Unpublished Manuscripts

Alancraig, Helen Smith. "Codornices Village: A Study of Non-Segregated Public Housing." M.A. thesis, University of California, Berkeley, 1953.

Brown, Hubert Owen. "The Impact of War Worker Migration on the Public School System of Richmond, California from 1940–1945." Ph.D. diss., Stanford University, 1973.

de Graaf, Lawrence B. "Negro Migration to Los Angeles, 1930–1950." Ph.D. diss., University of California, Los Angeles, 1962.

France, Edward E. "Some Aspects of the Migration of the Negro to the San Francisco Bay Area since 1940." Ph.D. diss., University of California, Berkeley, 1962.

Hamachi, Roy. "Postwar Housing in Richmond, California." M.A. thesis, University of California, Berkeley, n.d.

Hausler, Donald. "Blacks in Oakland: 1852–1987." Typescript, 1987.

Hippler, Arthur E. "Family Structure and Social Structure: Matrifocality in Hunter's Point." Ph.D. diss., University of California, Berkeley, 1968.

Kramer, Alyce M. "Story of the Richmond Shipyards." Typescript, 1945.

Lemke, Gretchen. "Afro-Americans in Berkeley: 1859–1987." 1987. Typescript copy at the Northern California Center for Afro-American History and Life.

Lichtman, Sheila Tropp. "Women at Work, 1941–1945: Wartime Employment in the San Francisco Bay Area." Ph.D. diss., University of California, Davis, 1981.

Moore, Shirley Ann. "The Black Community in Richmond, California, 1910–1987." 1987. Typescript copy at the Northern California Center for Afro-American History and Life.

——. "The Black Community in Richmond, California, 1910–1987." Ph.D. diss., University of California, Berkeley, 1989.

Pittman, Tarea Hall. "Operation of State and County Resident Requirements under the California Indigent Aid Law in Contra Costa County." M.A. thesis, University of California, Berkeley, 1946.

Sokol, William. "From Workingman's Town to All American City: The Socio-Political Economy of Richmond, California during World War II." June 1971. Typescript copy in Richmond Public Library.

——. "Richmond during World War II: Kaiser Comes to Town." University of California, Berkeley, 1971. Typescript copy in Richmond Collection, Richmond Public Library.

Stripp, Fred. "The Relationship of the San Francisco Bay Area Negro-American Worker with Labor Unions Affiliated with the American Federation of Labor and the Congress of Industrial Organizations." Th.D. thesis, Pacific School of Religion, 1948. Copy in the Graduate Theological Union Library, University of California, Berkeley.

Books and Articles

Amot, Teresa L., and Julie A. Matthaei. *Race, Gender, and Work: A Multicultural Economic History of Women in the United States.* Boston: Southend Press, 1991.

Anderson, Karen. "Last Hired, First Fired: Black Women Workers during World War II." *Journal of American History* 69 (June 1982).

——. *Wartime Women: Sex Roles, Family Relations and the Status of Women during World War II.* Westport, Conn.: Greenwood Press, 1981.

Angel, Ronald, and Marta Tienda. "Determinants of Extended Household Structure: Cultural Pattern or Economic Need?" *American Journal of Sociology* 87 (1982).

Angelou, Maya. *I Know Why the Caged Bird Sings.* New York: Bantam, 1969.

Archibald, Katherine. *Wartime Shipyard: A Study in Social Disunity.* Berkeley: University of California Press, 1947.

Beeth, Howard, and Cary D. Wintz, eds. *Black Dixie: Afro-Texan History and Culture in Houston.* College Station: Texas A&M University Press, 1992.

Bethel, Elizabeth Rauh. *Promiseland: A Century of Life in a Negro Community.* Philadelphia: Temple University Press, 1981.

Blassingame, John. *Black New Orleans, 1860–1880.* Chicago: University of Chicago Press, 1973.

Borchert, James. *Alley Life in Washington: Family, Community, Religion and Folklife in the City, 1850–1970.* Urbana: University of Illinois Press, 1980.

Broussard, Albert S. *Black San Francisco: The Struggle for Racial Equality in the West, 1900–1954.* Lawrence: University Press of Kansas, 1993.

Brown, Elsa Barkley. "Mothers of the Mind." *Sage* 6 (Summer 1989).

Bullard, Robert D. *Invisible Houston: The Black Experience in Boom and Bust.* College Station: Texas A&M University Press, 1987.

Camp, William Martin. *Skip to My Lou*. Garden City, N.Y.: Doubleday, 1945.

Campbell, Bruce. "Bay Area Migrants." *San Francisco Chronicle*, March 19–22, 1944.

Cell, John. *The Highest Stage of White Supremacy: Origins of Segregation in South Africa and the American South*. New York: Cambridge University Press, 1982.

Chafe, William. *The Paradox of Change: American Women in the Twentieth Century*. New York: Oxford University Press, 1991.

Cohen, William. *At Freedom's Edge: Black Mobility and the Southern Quest for Racial Control*. Baton Rouge: Louisiana State University Press, 1991.

Colbert, Robert E. "The Attitude of Older Negro Residents toward Recent Negro Migrants in the Pacific Northwest." *Journal of Negro Education* 15 (Fall 1946).

Collins, Patricia Hill. *Black Feminist Thought: Knowledge, Consciousness, and the Politics of Empowerment*. Boston: Unwin Hyman, 1990.

———. "The Meaning of Motherhood in Black Culture." In *The Black Family: Essays and Studies*, edited by R. Staples (Belmont: Wadsworth, 1991).

Cortner, Richard C. *A Mob Intent on Death: The NAACP and the Arkansas Riot Cases*. Middleton, Conn.: Wesleyan University Press, 1988.

Crouchett, Lawrence, Lonnie Bunch III, and Martha Kendall Winnaker, eds. *Visions toward Tomorrow: The History of the East Bay Afro-American Community 1852–1977*. Oakland: Northern California Center for Afro-American History and Life, 1989.

Dance, Daryl. *Long Gone: The Mecklenburg Six and the Theme of Escape in Black Folklore*. Knoxville: University of Tennessee Press, 1987.

Daniel, Pete. "Going among Strangers: Southern Reactions to World War II." *Journal of American History* 77 (December 1990): 886–911.

Daniels, Douglas Henry. *Pioneer Urbanites: A Social and Cultural History of Black San Francisco*. Berkeley: University of California Press, 1990.

Dennis, Sam Joseph. *African American Exodus and White Migration, 1950–1970: A Comparative Analysis of Population Movements and Their Relations to Labor and Race Relations*. New York: Garland, 1989.

Deutsch, Sarah. *No Separate Refuge: Culture, Class, and Gender on the Anglo-Hispanic Frontier, 1800–1940*. New York: Oxford University Press, 1987.

Dickson, Lynda F. "Toward a Broader Angle of Vision in Uncovering Women's History: Black Women's Clubs Revisited." *Frontiers* 9, no. 2 (1987): 62–73.

Dittmer, John. *Black Georgia in the Progressive Era 1900–1920*. Urbana: University of Illinois Press, 1977.

Dunbar, Anthony. *Against the Grain: Southern Radicals and Prophets 1929–1959*. Charlottesville: University of Virginia Press, 1981.

Ferris, William, ed. *Afro-American Folk Art and Crafts*. Boston: G. K. Hall, 1990.

Finch, Janet. " 'It's Great to Have Someone to Talk To': The Ethics and Politics of Interviewing Women." In *Social Researching: Politics, Problems and Practice*, edited by Colin Bell and Helen Roberts (London: Routledge and Kegan Paul, 1984).

Foner, Eric. *A Short History of Reconstruction*. New York: Harper and Row, 1990.

Franklin, Jimmie Lewis. *Journey toward Hope: A History of Blacks in Oklahoma*. Norman: University of Oklahoma Press, 1982.

Geiger, Susan. "What's So Feminist about Doing Women's Oral History?" *Journal of Women's History* 2 (Spring 1990).

Genovese, Eugene. *Roll, Jordan, Roll: The World the Slaves Made*. New York: Pantheon, 1974.

Giddings, Paula. *When and Where I Enter: The Impact of Black Women on Race and Sex in America*. New York: William Morrow, 1984.

Glazer, Nona. "The Home as Workshop: Women as Amateur Nurses and Medical Care Providers." *Gender and Society* 4 (December 1990).

Gluck, Sherna. *Rosie the Riveter Revisited: Women, the War, and Social Change*. Boston: Twayne, 1987.

Goodwin, E. Marvin. *Black Migration in America from 1915 to 1960*. Lewiston, N.Y.: Edwin Mellen Press, 1990.

Gordon, Linda. "Black and White Visions of Welfare: Women's Welfare Activism, 1890–1945." *Journal of American History* 78 (September 1991).

Gordon, Margaret S. "From Liberal Control to Radical Challenge." In *Experiment and Change in Berkeley: Essays on City Politics 1950–1975*, edited by Harriet Nathan and Stanley Scott (Berkeley: Institute of Governmental Studies, 1978), 271–316.

Gottlieb, Peter. *Making Their Own Way: Southern Black's Migration to Pittsburgh, 1916–1930*. Urbana: University of Illinois Press, 1987.

Grant, Joanne, ed. *Black Protest*. New York: Fawcett, 1968.

Graves, John William. *Town and Country, Race Relations in an Urban-Rural Context: Arkansas, 1865–1905*. Fayetteville: University of Arkansas Press, 1990.

Gregory, James. *American Exodus: The Dust Bowl Migration and Okie Culture in California*. New York: Oxford University Press, 1989.

Grossman, James R. *Land of Hope: Chicago, Black Southerners and the Great Migration*. Chicago: University of Chicago Press, 1989.

Harley, Sharon. "For the Good of Family and Race: Gender, Work, and Domestic Roles in the Black Community, 1890–1930." *Signs* 15 (Winter 1990).

Hartman, Susan. *The Home Front and Beyond: American Women in the 1940s*. Boston: Twayne, 1982.

Hildebrand, Lee. "North Richmond Blues." *East Bay Express*, February 9, 1979.

———. "Westside Story." *East Bay Express*, September 28, 1979.

Holt, Thomas. *Black over White*. Urbana: University of Illinois Press, 1977.

hooks, bell. *Yearning: Race, Gender and Cultural Politics*. Boston: South End Press, 1990.

Johnson, Charles S. *Backgrounds to Patterns of Negro Segregation*. New York: Thomas Y. Crowell, 1943.

———. *The Negro War Worker in San Francisco*. San Francisco: YWCA, 1944.

———. *To Stem This Tide*. New York: AMS Press, 1943.

Johnson, Daniel M., and Rex R. Campbell. *Black Migration in America*. Durham: Duke University Press, 1981.

Johnson, Marilynn. *The Second Gold Rush: Oakland and the East Bay in World War II*. Berkeley: University of California Press, 1993.

Jones, Jacqueline. *Labor of Love, Labor of Sorrow: Black Women, Work, and Family, from Slavery to the Present*. New York: Basic Books, 1985.

———. "Southern Diaspora: Origins of the Urban 'Underclass.'" In *The Underclass Debate: Views from History*, edited by Michael Katz (Princeton: Princeton University Press, 1993), 27–54.

Katz, Michael, ed. *The "Underclass" Debate: Views from History*. Princeton: Princeton University Press, 1993.

Kelley, Robin. *Hammer and Hoe: Alabama Communists during the Great Depression*. Chapel Hill: University of North Carolina Press, 1990.

Kesselman, Amy. *Fleeting Opportunities: Women Shipyard Workers in Portland and Vancouver during World War II and Reconversion*. Albany: State University of New York Press, 1990.

Kirkland, James, and Holly F. Mathews, eds. *Herbal and Magical Medicine: Traditional Healing Today*. Durham: Duke University Press, 1992.

Lawson, Steven P. *Black Ballots: Voting Rights in the South, 1944–1969*. New York: Columbia University Press, 1976.

Lemann, Nicholas. "The Origins of the Underclass," pts. 1 and 2, *Atlantic Monthly*, June 1986 and July 1986.

——. *The Promised Land: The Great Black Migration and How It Changed America*. New York: Knopf, 1991.

Levine, Lawrence. *Black Culture and Black Consciousness*. New York: Oxford University Press, 1977.

Logan, Onnie Lee. *Motherwit: An Alabama Midwife's Story as Told to Katherine Clark*. New York: Penguin, 1989.

McBroome, Dolores Nason. *Parallel Communities: African Americans in California's East Bay, 1850–1963*. New York: Garland, 1993.

McMillen, Neil R. *Dark Journey: Black Mississippians in the Age of Jim Crow, 1890–1930*. Urbana: University of Illinois Press, 1989.

McWilliams, Carey. "Jim Crow Goes West." *Negro Digest* 3 (August 1945).

Mann, Susan. "Slavery, Sharecropping, and Social Inequality." *Signs* 14 (Summer 1989).

Marks, Carole. *Farewell We're Good and Gone: The Great Black Migration*. Bloomington: Indiana University Press, 1989.

Mitford, Jessica. *A Fine Old Conflict*. New York: Knopf, 1977.

Montgomery, William E. *Under Their Own Vine and Fig Tree: The African American Church in the South 1865–1900*. Baton Rouge: Louisiana State University Press, 1993.

Murray, Pauli. *Song in a Weary Throat*. New York: Harper and Row, 1987.

Naples, Nancy. "Activist Mothering: Cross-Generational Continuity in the Community Work of Women from Low-Income Neighborhoods." *Gender and Society* 6 (September 1992).

——. " 'Just What Needed to Be Done': The Political Practice of Women Community Workers in Low-Income Neighborhoods." *Gender and Society* 5 (December 1991).

Nash, Gerald D. *The American West Transformed: The Impact of the Second World War*. Bloomington: Indiana University Press, 1985.

——. *World War II and the West: Reshaping the Economy*. Lincoln: University of Nebraska Press, 1990.

Nathan, Harriet, and Stanley Scott, eds. *Experiment and Change in Berkeley: Essays on City Politics 1950–1975*. Berkeley: Institute of Governmental Studies, 1978.

Nelson, Bruce. "Organized Labor and the Struggle for Black Equality in Mobile during World War II." *Journal of American History* 80 (December 1993).

——. *Workers on the Waterfront: Seamen, Longshoremen, and Unionism in the 1930s*. Urbana: University of Illinois Press, 1990.

Oakley, Ann. "Interviewing Women: A Contradiction in Terms." In *Doing Feminist Research*, edited by Helen Roberts (London: Routledge and Kegan Paul, 1981).

Painter, Nell Irvin. *Exodusters: Black Migration to Kansas after Reconstruction*. Lawrence: University Press of Kansas, 1976.

——. *Narrative of Hosea Hudson*. Cambridge: Harvard University Press, 1979.

Payne, Charles. "Ella Baker and Models of Social Change." *Signs* 14 (Summer 1989).

Personal Narratives Group. *Interpreting Women's Lives: Feminist Theory and Personal Narratives*. Bloomington: Indiana University Press, 1989.

Pettitt, George A. "Berkeley in the Good Old Days." In *Experiment and Change in Berkeley: Essays on City Politics 1950–1975*, edited by Harriet Nathan and Stanley Scott (Berkeley: Institute of Governmental Studies, 1978), 41–69.

Piersen, William. *Black Legacy: America's Hidden Heritage*. Amherst: University of Massachusetts Press, 1993.

Rabinowitz, Howard N. *Race Relations in the Urban South 1865–1890*. New York: Oxford University Press, 1978.

Raudebaugh, Charles. "Richmond, a Town with a Purple Heart, Looks to the Future." *San Francisco Chronicle*, March 18, 1946, p. 14.

Record, Wilson. "Willie Stokes at the Golden Gate." *Crisis* 56 (June 1949): 175–79, 187–88.

Reddick, L. D., ed. "Race Relations on the Pacific Coast." *Journal of Educational Sociology* 19 (November 1945).

Reid, Ira De A. "Special Problems of Negro Migration during the War." *Milbank Memorial Fund Quarterly* 25 (July 1947).

Richmond Chamber of Commerce. *A History of Richmond, California*. Richmond: Richmond Chamber of Commerce, 1944.

"Richmond Took a Beating." *Fortune* (February 1945): 262–70.

Rosengarten, Theodore. *All God's Dangers*. New York: Vintage, 1989.

Rouse, Jacqueline Anne. *Lugenia Burns Hope: Black Southern Reformer*. Athens: University of Georgia Press, 1989.

Sacks, Karen Brodkin. *Caring by the Hour: Women, Work, and Organizing at Duke Medical Center*. Urbana: University of Illinois Press, 1988.

Scott, Joseph W., and Albert Black. "Deep Structures of African American Family Life: Female and Male Kin Networks." *Western Journal of Black Studies* 13 (Spring 1989).

Shyrock, Henry S., Jr. "Wartime Shifts of the Civilian Population." *Milbank Memorial Fund Quarterly* 25 (July 1947).

Silverman, Milton. "The Second Gold Rush Hits the West." *San Francisco Chronicle*, April 25–May 20, 1943.

Simonsen, Thordis, ed. *You May Plow Here: The Narrative of Sara Brooks*. New York: Simon and Schuster, 1986.

Smith, Sidonie. *Where I'm Bound: Patterns of Slavery and Freedom in Black American Autobiography*. Westport, Conn.: Greenwood Press, 1974.

Stack, Carol B. *All Our Kin: Strategies for Survival in a Black Community*. New York: Harper and Row, 1974.

Thomson, Bailey, and Patricia L. Meador. *Shreveport: A Photographic Remembrance, 1873–1949*. Baton Rouge: Louisiana State University Press, 1987.

Trotter, Joe. *Black Milwaukee: The Making of an Industrial Proletariat, 1915–1945*. Urbana: University of Illinois Press, 1985.

——, ed. *The Great Migration in Historical Perspective: New Dimensions of Race, Class and Gender.* Bloomington: University of Indiana Press, 1991.

Tucher, David. *Arkansas: A People and Their Reputations.* Memphis: Memphis State University Press, 1985.

Whayne, Jeannie, and Willard B. Gatewood, eds. *The Arkansas Delta: Land of Paradox.* Fayetteville: University of Arkansas Press, 1993.

Wilson, William Julius. *The Truly Disadvantaged: The Inner City, the Underclass and Public Policy.* Chicago: University of Chicago Press, 1987.

——. *The Declining Significance of Race: Blacks and Changing American Institutions.* Chicago: University of Chicago Press, 1980.

Wollenberg, Charles. *Marineship at War: Shipbuilding and Social Change in Wartime Sausalito.* Berkeley: Western Heritage Press, 1990.

——. *Golden Gate Metropolis.* Berkeley: Institute of Governmental Studies, 1985.

Wolters, Raymond. *Negroes and the Great Depression.* Westport, Conn.: Greenwood Press, 1970.

Woodman, Harold D. "Sequel to Slavery: The New History Views the South." *Journal of Southern History* 43, no. 4 (November 1977): 523–54.

Woodward, C. Vann. *Strange Career of Jim Crow.* 3d rev. ed. New York: Oxford University Press, 1974.

Wright, George C. *Life behind a Veil: Blacks in Louisville, Kentucky 1865–1930.* Baton Rouge: Louisiana State University Press, 1985.

Civil rights activism: prewar East Bay, 166; and employment discrimination, 166–68, 175–76; role of NAACP in, 166–69; postwar, 166–77; and housing discrimination, 167–68; and Jim Crow auxiliaries, 168; and school segregation, 168, 170–74

Class, 46–47, 75, 130–31, 133–34, 153

Cobb, Ned, 19

Codornices Village, 87, 92, 167

Collins, Melvin L., 25

Communist Party: and Sharecroppers' Union, 19; and Unemployed Councils, 19; and East Bay Shipyard Workers' Committee Against Discrimination, 123; ties to Richmond NAACP, 168–69

Community organizing: women's role in, 174–77

Cooking: as cultural preservation, 136–39; as reciprocal exchange, 136–39; food substitutes, 138

Cooper A.M.E. Zion Church, 161

Cravanas, Virginia, 74–76

Crawford, Matt, 162

Cultural continuity, 134–35, 151–52; women and, 136, 151–52; and cooking, 136–39; and gardening, 139–40; and quilting, 140–41; and folk healing, 141–44; and caregiving, 144–47; and return visits to the South, 147–51

"Culture of poverty," 3–4, 46–47, 180–81

Daniels, Douglas, 74, 133–34

Defense industry: in the South, 51–52, 56; wartime employment in, 107–8, 114–24; discrimination in, 108, 110–11, 113, 121–22

Dellums, C. L., 76–77, 162, 166

Del Monte, 127

Disfranchisement: in the South, 18, 163–64; in Mississippi, 21; in

Louisiana, 23; in Texas, 25–26; in Oklahoma, 28; in Arkansas, 31

Domestic service: in the South, 1, 16, 45–46; in Mississippi, 22; in Louisiana, 24; in Texas, 27; in Arkansas, 31; in the East Bay, 107, 110

Downs Memorial Church, 161

Dungee, Roscoe, 30

Duvernay, Cornelia, 40–41, 60–61, 90, 128, 137–39

East Bay: wartime population growth, 50–51, 66, 70, 76; growth and racial tensions, 52, 76; prewar demographics, 69; prewar race relations, 72–75; housing discrimination, 78–81, 86–87, 91–94, 167–68; employment discrimination, 109–11, 113

East Bay Employment Committee, 168

East Bay Shipyard Workers' Committee Against Discrimination, 123

East Bay Women's Welfare Club, 73

Easter Hill Village, 92

Eaton, Myrtle, 57, 88

Employment: women's prewar occupations, 16, 22, 24, 29, 31, 46, 49, 53–54, 107; during wartime, 107–8, 114–24; postwar, 107–10, 112, 124–30; with the federal government, 109

Employment discrimination: in southern trades and industry, 15–16, 22, 24, 26–27, 29; prewar East Bay, 71, 75; in defense industry, 108, 110–11, 113, 121–22; postwar, 109, 111–12, 120, 124–25; and wartime protest, 121–23; and postwar protest, 128–30

Established residents: attitudes toward white migrants, 70–71; attitudes toward black migrants, 70–71, 74–77, 133–35, 166–67

Fair Employment Practices Act, 164, 168